IMAGES
of America

CRANE

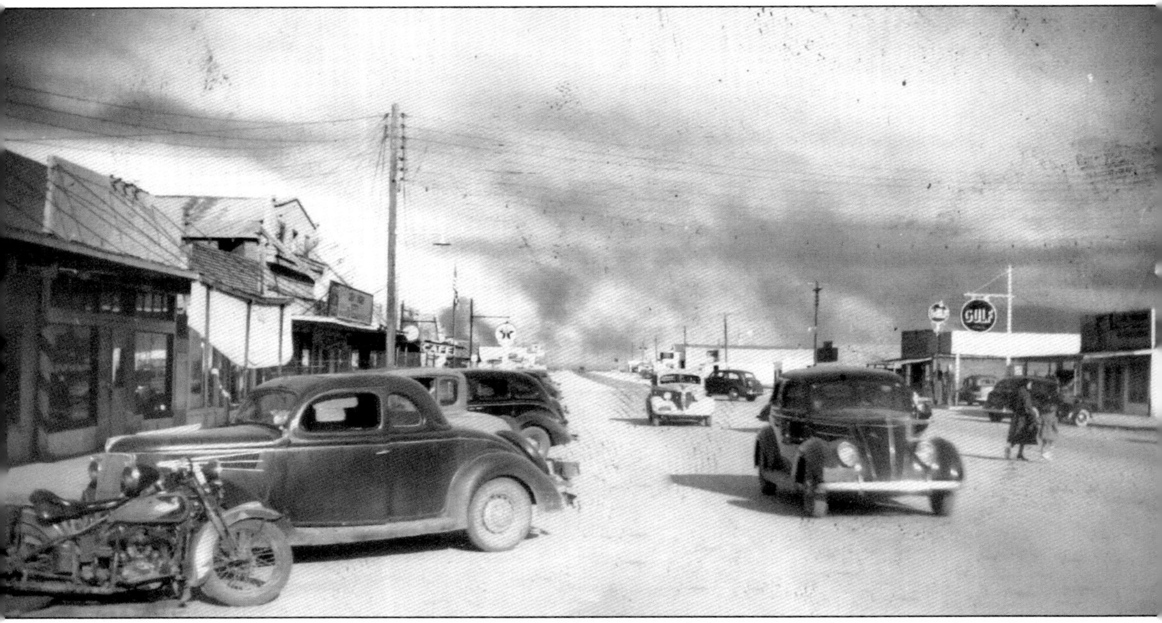

This late-1930s or early-1940s photograph, taken around the time Hitler was wreaking destruction on Europe, shows early Crane, Texas, with a massive dust storm looming on the horizon. Crane County was formed in 1887 and organized in 1927 with the city of Crane being the county seat and the only town in the county. Crane is considered a boomtown, as its primary reason for existence is the prevalence of oil in the region. Although the town only goes back to the 1920s, when oil was first discovered in the area, a few ranchers inhabited the region before oil. Previous to them, indigenous peoples roamed the barren landscape, which later included the Native American tribes of the Comanche, Lipan Apache, and Kiowa. (Courtesy of the Crane County Chamber of Commerce.)

On the Cover: This decades-old image offers a view of Crane's downtown. The Crane High School marching band, under the expert direction of J.R. Dickson, plays to a gathering of Crane's citizenry prior to a much-anticipated football game scheduled for later that evening. The man on the donkey is Tiny Earp, a much-loved Crane luminary who was an integral part of the Crane community. (Courtesy of Angela Cooper.)

IMAGES
of America

CRANE

Audrey Fain and Bradley D. Pettit on behalf of
the Crane County Historical Commission

ARCADIA
PUBLISHING

ISBN 978-0-7385-9582-5

Published by Arcadia Publishing
Charleston, South Carolina

Printed in the United States of America

Library of Congress Control Number: 2012949016

For all general information, please contact Arcadia Publishing:
Telephone 843-853-2070
Fax 843-853-0044
E-mail sales@arcadiapublishing.com
For customer service and orders:
Toll-Free 1-888-313-2665

Visit us on the Internet at www.arcadiapublishing.com

Both authors would like to dedicate this work to God, without whom nothing is possible.

Contents

ACKNOWLEDGMENTS

We would like to acknowledge the past and present citizens of Crane County. To the Crane County Historical Commission (CHC), whose encouragement and assistance throughout this process has been invaluable, we would like to extend our heartfelt thanks; unless otherwise noted, all images appear in this book thanks to the generosity of the CHC.

To our families, whose love, understanding, and support allowed us the much-needed time to complete our research, we would like to say *muchas gracias*! We could not have finished this project without the support and guidance of our loved ones.

We have been collaborating on this project for several months, and throughout this process, we have learned so much about the rich history of Crane County. Many people have helped us along the way, thus allowing us to realize that, although our names appear on the cover of this book, this volume would not have been possible without the help and kindness of so many.

We would like to thank our editors at Arcadia Publishing, Laura Bruns and Lauren Hummell, for their expert guidance (when requested) and prodding (when needed).

We would like to thank Bill Dawson, Betty Damron, and Genny Townsend for all of their help and support. Additionally, there are many other people who have contributed to the formation of this book through their research, writing, photography, and sheer enthusiasm for local history. We thank you all, knowing we owe so much to you for your guidance and assistance.

Audrey Fain would like to recognize and thank the Szaloy family, Spud Curfew, and Gordon Hooper for their eager assistance with this project. Bradley D. Pettit would like to recognize his beautiful wife, Jessica Pettit, and his two handsome sons, Nicolas Craig Pettit and Cash Nelson Pettit.

We would like to thank the many people who contacted us over the past few months to offer insight and memories into the various stages of Crane history. We cannot thank you all enough, and it is our sincere hope that the citizens of Crane, both now and in the future, enjoy this book!

INTRODUCTION

To the ignorant eye, the mesquite-infested terrain of Crane County seems devoid of redeeming qualities. To be sure, there are significant problems with the land in terms of comfortable habitability. With no lakes for more than 100 miles, an absence of lush greenery, and a blistering heat that often rides in on the gusty West Texas wind, one might wonder how anybody ever inhabited this dusty region prior to the advent of central air-conditioning. However, countless people have called this place home, and thousands still do to this day. It is these people who bring the story of the unique Texas county of Crane to life.

Named for William Carey Crane, an author and one-time president of Baylor University, the story of Crane has two separate periods: pre-oil and post-oil. Prior to the division of Tom Green County into six new counties on February 26, 1887, only Native Americans, antelope, and buffalo roamed the 796 square miles east of the Pecos River. However, even after the creation of Crane County, it would not be for another several decades before people began to come to the area in any significant numbers.

When George M. Church and Bert Fields discovered oil in 1926 after drilling a well, people began migrating to Crane County during its first oil boom. Soon, Crane County was ranked among the highest oil-producing regions in the United States, producing more than one billion barrels of oil. The oil fields of Crane County, located within the Permian Basin, thrive to this day. As of the 2010 census, the county's population was 4,375. Since then, however, this number has significantly grown, and substantially so since the previous census in 2000 due to an oil boom that has driven up the population. Because of the robust oil economy in Crane County, people have migrated to the area in recent years from all over the United States as well as the globe.

In August 1927, Crane County was officially organized, and the city of Crane became the county seat and only town in the county, remaining so to this day. The first courthouse was completed in Crane in 1928, and the small hamlet of Crane was incorporated on July 25, 1933. As the town began to see significant development, one realtor, O.C. Kinnison, took advantage of this opportunity by drawing up the town map. Wanting his family's names to survive in posterity, he came up with the notion of naming the city streets after his children. Even today, when one drives down the streets of Crane, the dated names on city street signs are evidence of this curious fact.

In 1927, there were an estimated 6,000 people living in Crane County. The town of Crane at that time had a population of approximately 4,500 people. Since the region is virtually all land, water had to be trucked in to the county. Water, being an especially precious resource in the area, could be purchased anywhere from $1 a barrel to $2.25 a barrel.

Crane County contains several historical landmarks that are of interest to Permian Basin history buffs. These sites include Horsehead Crossing, a stop on the Goodnight-Loving Trail, Castle Gap, the Pecos River, and the Juan Cordona Salt Lake.

In 1583, Spanish explorers traversed the Pecos at a ford known as Horsehead Crossing. In 1858, the crossing became an important stop on the Butterfield Overland Mail route. Famous adventurers

Charles Goodnight and Oliver Loving trekked through the crossing in 1866. The crossing, which is believed to have gotten its name due to the large number of horse skulls marking its banks, was one of the few fordable points on the Pecos River at that time. Before damming and extreme drought in the region drained the Pecos to a shadow of its former glory, the river was a difficult one to traverse. Back in the days when the river ran wild, citizens of the county caught gargantuan catfish there, and many citizens would spend the entire day enjoying the mighty Pecos and all the entertainment and recreation it afforded. Today, the Pecos River slowly crawls through Crane County, resembling in no way the river it was in decades past.

Castle Gap, a mountain with castle-like boulders, offered shelter to prehistoric people. Likewise, Forty-niners sought protection there while migrating to California. Legend states that Mexican emperor Maximilian once buried vast golden treasures there. Because of this legend and other buried treasure stories that persist, many treasure hunters have—and continue to—search for hidden fortunes that might be concealed in Castle Gap.

Juan Cordona Salt Lake is another historical attraction in Crane County. The salt lake once provided salt to Native Americans and other settlers. Needing salt to cure their meat, Native Americans and other settlers would use all the they could dredge up from the lake to scratch out a living in the area.

Historically, ranching and farming have been somewhat important in Crane County. However, oil continues to be king in the region. While many ranchers have had success raising cattle and other livestock in Crane County, oil is by far the largest segment of the economy. From its discovery until the present, oil has been the lifeblood of the region. In fact, by the beginning of 1991, almost 1,552,324,000 barrels of oil had been produced in the county since oil was first discovered there in 1926. Since then, many more millions of barrels of oil have been produced in the county.

The people of Crane County are the salt of the earth. Many notable men and women once called the region home, including All-Time Best Western Author Elmer Kelton, notable oilman Clayton Williams Sr., and one of the only completely deaf people to ever play in the National Football League, Kenny Walker. However, it is thanks to the sweat and tears of the most common of Crane County's past and present citizens that the region is what it is today.

The Crane Historical Commission as well as many present and former Crane citizens graciously provided images to illustrate the rich history of Crane County. Bradley D. Pettit, teacher and Crane native, along with Audrey Fain, Crane resident and creative writing major, volunteered to navigate this journey. Come along! Take a trip back to the early days of Crane County.

One

Crane's Early Years

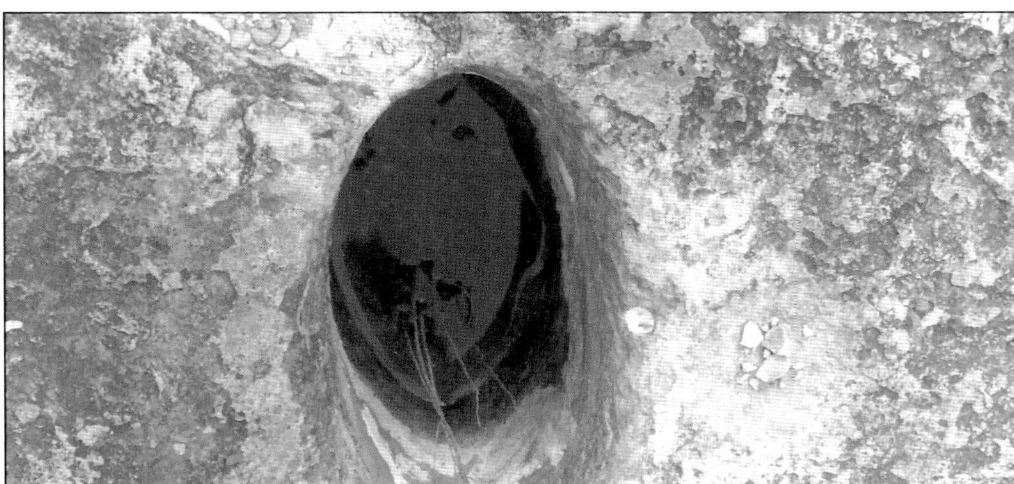

Before the ranchers, who preceded the influx of oilfield workers, Native Americans dwelled in the land that would later become known as Crane County. Shown here is a Native American "grinding rock" located on Handlin Ranch. Grinding rocks bear witness to ancient history, when Native Americans would use large rocks for grinding acorns, nuts, or corn. The depth of this grinding rock is evidence of long-term use over the course of successive generations. (Courtesy of Bill Dawson.)

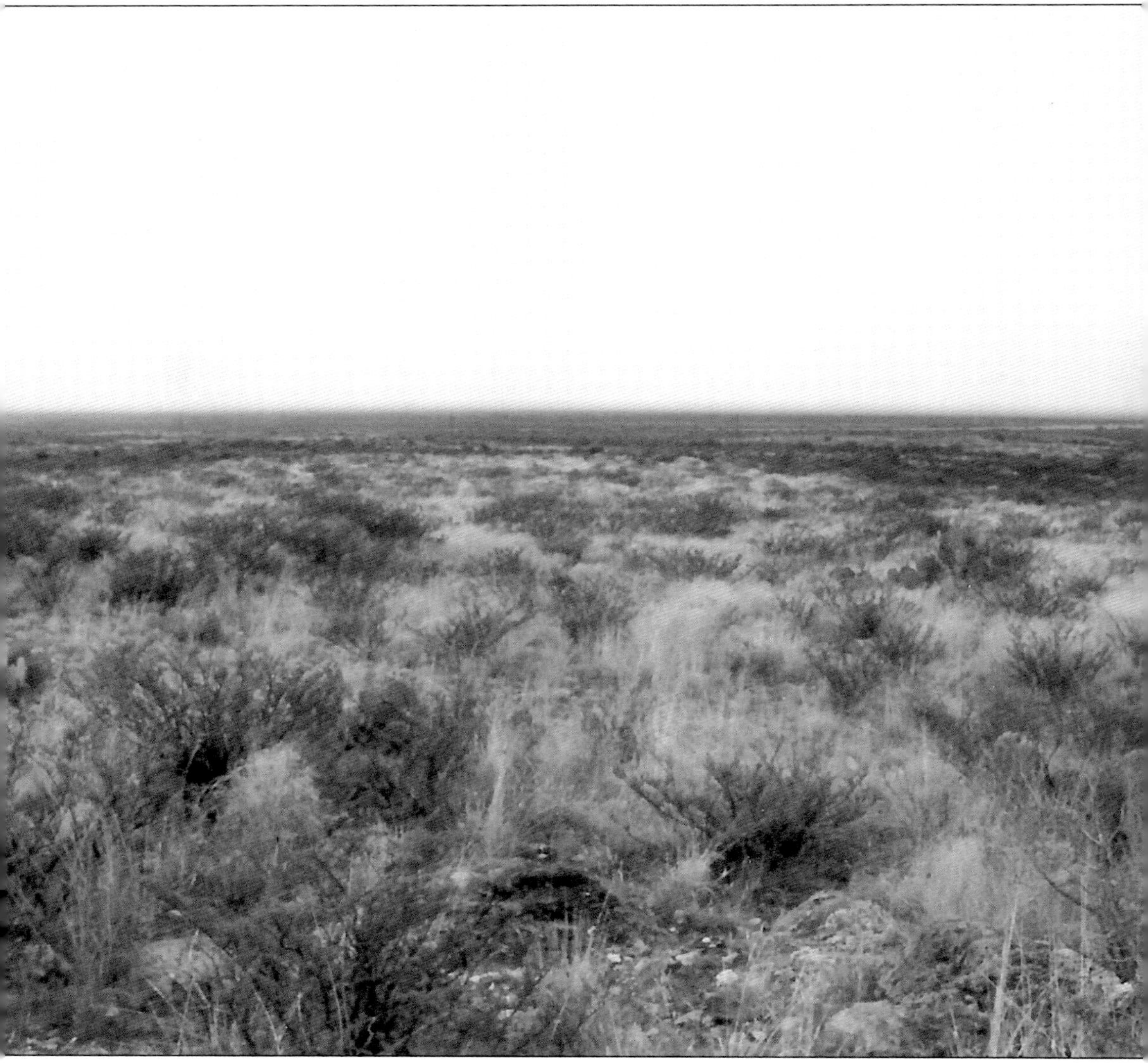

Shown here is an old Native American campground on Handlin Ranch. Burned soil is still visible where ancient campfires cooked food and warmed the area's indigenous peoples. To this day, one can find arrowheads and other artifacts left behind by those who once gathered around these campfires in earlier times. Because of the particularly rugged environment in which these natives carved out their existence, many of them were particularly tough and fierce. (Courtesy of Bill Dawson.)

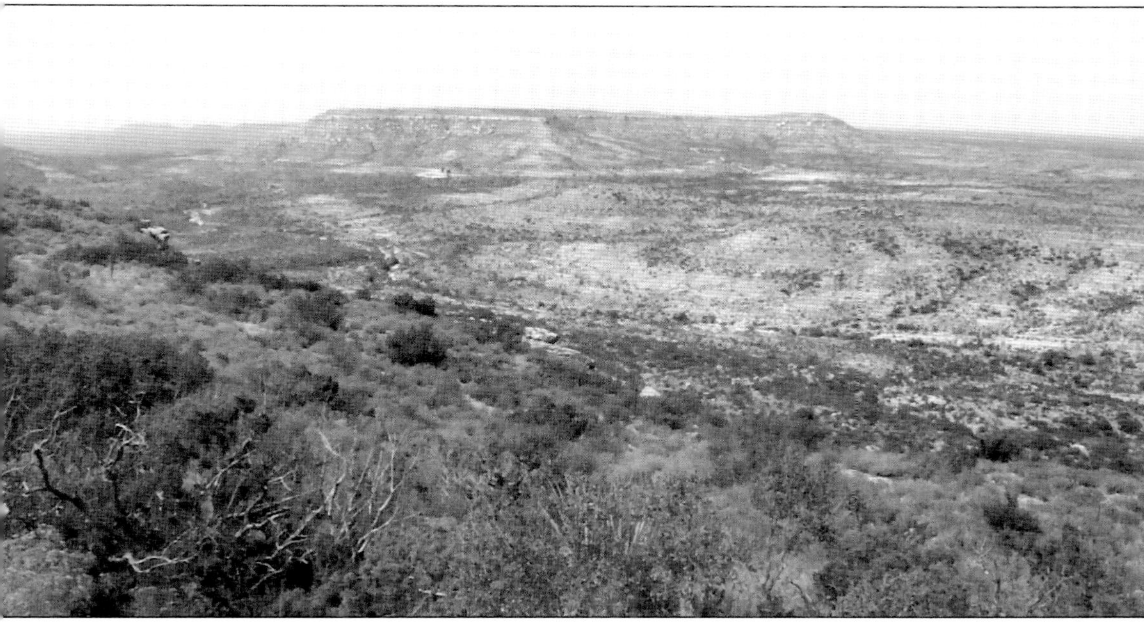

Castle Gap, as viewed from the west, is a natural landmark in Crane County. Castle Gap is a pass through the Castle Mountains that has large boulders resembling the parapets of a castle, hence its name. The gap, which is one mile long and lies 421 feet below the summits of Castle Mountain to the north and King Mountain to the south, opens westward towards Horsehead Crossing on the Pecos River. Treasure hunters still move through the area in search of the Butterfield stage treasure, which is believed to have been hidden there in 1860. Another treasure that draws in many fortune seekers is believed to have been deposited in or near Castle Gap. This treasure is that of Mexican emperor Maximilian, who might have stashed a considerable amount of treasure there in 1867. Maximilian was the only monarch of the Second Mexican Empire. (Courtesy of Bill Dawson.)

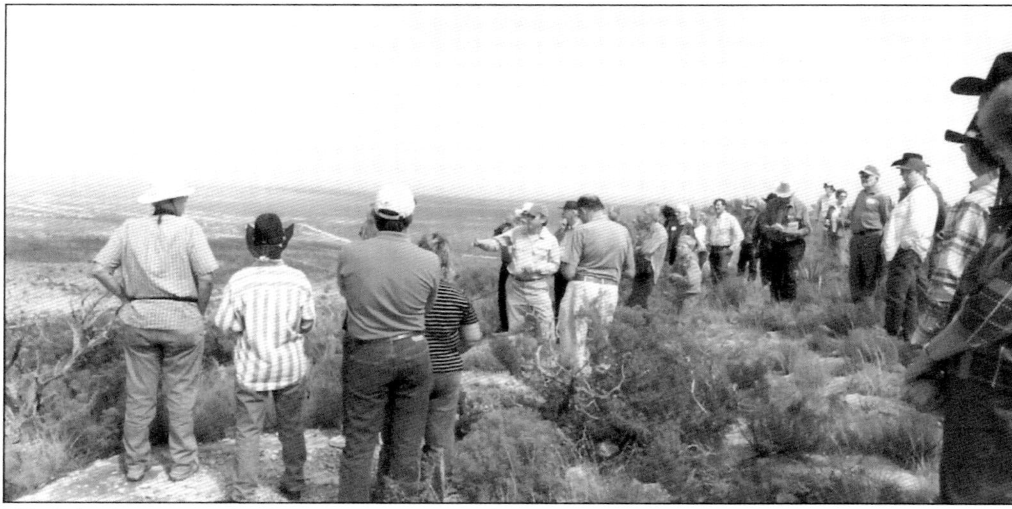

While leading a tour for the Permian Historical Society (PHS), Arlen White shows PHS members various natural landmarks and points of historical interest in Crane County. The PHS focuses on the story of petroleum, but it also focuses on "regional developments and events, including Native Americans and their cultures, Spanish and Mexican explorations, frontier forts and buffalo hunters, ranching and farming, and stage stops and railroads." (Courtesy of Bill Dawson.)

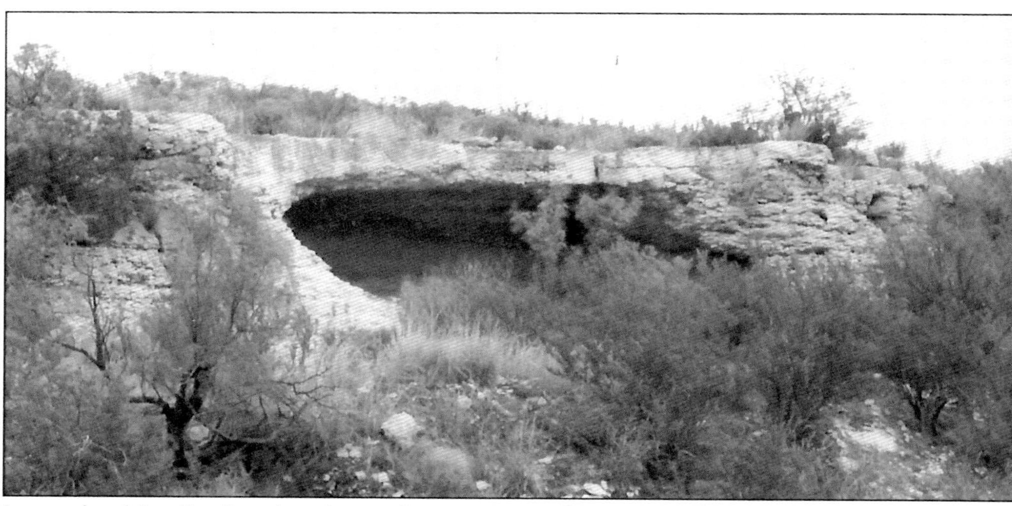

Located on Handlin Ranch is this washout near a site known as Indian Spring. Washouts like this made excellent natural shelters for the area's earliest settlers, providing a place to escape the relentless heat and even the occasional—albeit very rare—rain shower. (Courtesy of Bill Dawson.)

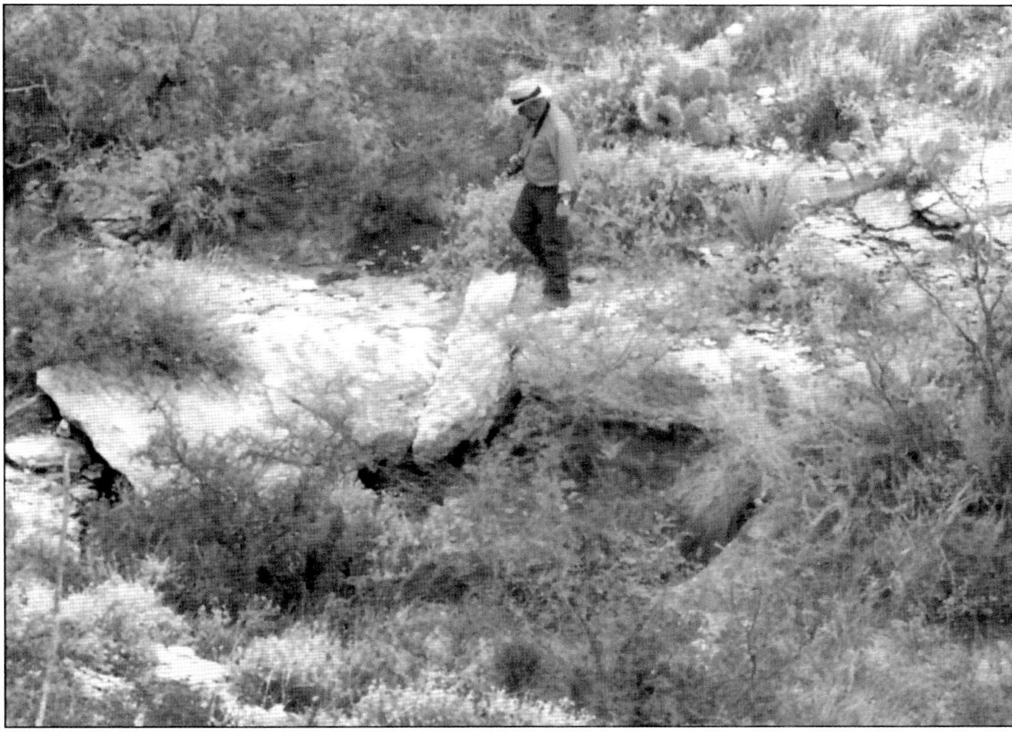

A member of the Permian Historical Society walks above a spring that was once used by Native Americans and other early settlers in the area. Water in the desert has always been viewed as a particularly precious resource. Crane County is part of the larger Permian Basin, which comprises a large portion of the western part of Texas and the southeastern part of New Mexico. Throughout the Permian Basin, water sources are few and far between. (Courtesy of Bill Dawson.)

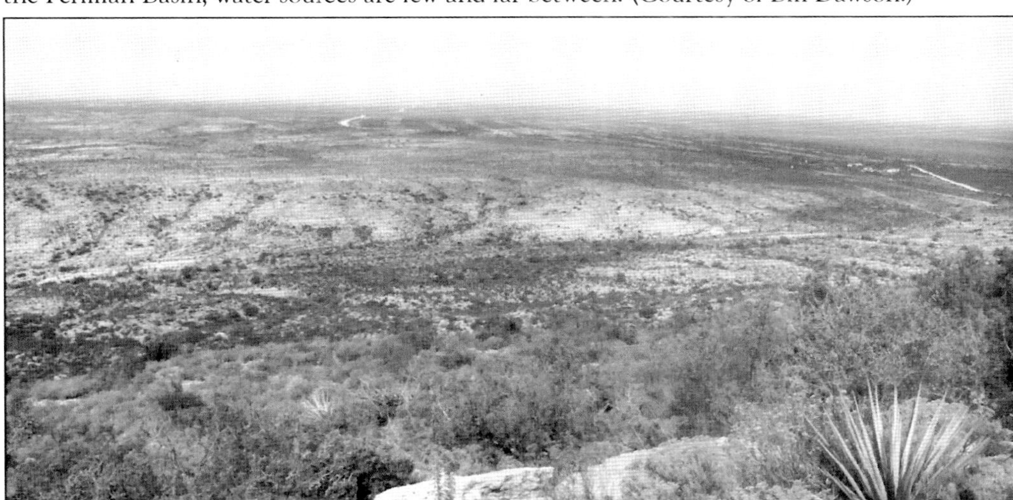

High ground is important for a variety of practical and metaphorical reasons; however, it can be quite difficult to locate any of it in Crane County, as much of the landscape is flat as a board. Shown here is an elevated view looking northwest from a radar site on Handlin Ranch. This type of view is the exception rather than the rule in Crane County. (Courtesy of Bill Dawson.)

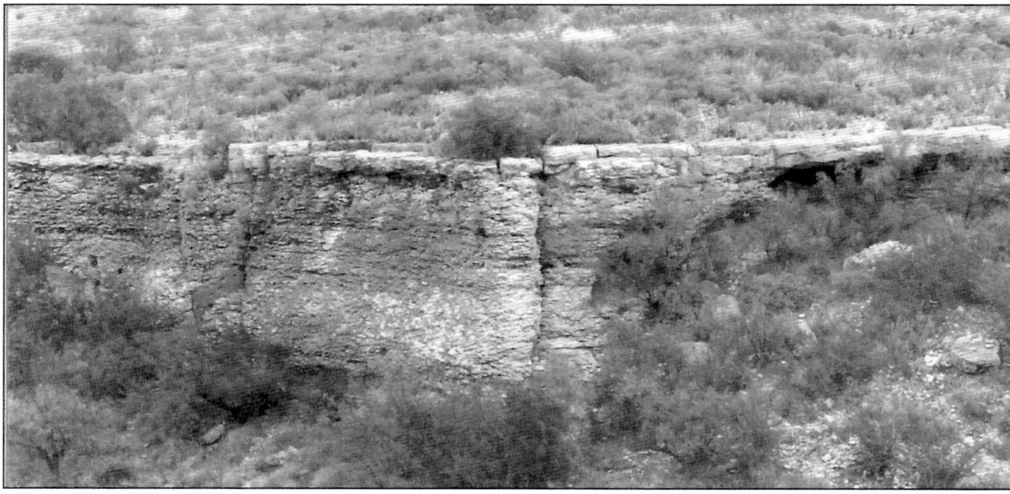

Faults in the rock formation, like this one, provided an excellent place for early settlers or Native Americans to create a lean-to against the steep rock face. A lean-to is a term used to describe a roof that has a single slope. Its primary function is to provide shelter from the elements, thus creating a semi-safe place for one to retire for the night. (Courtesy of Bill Dawson.)

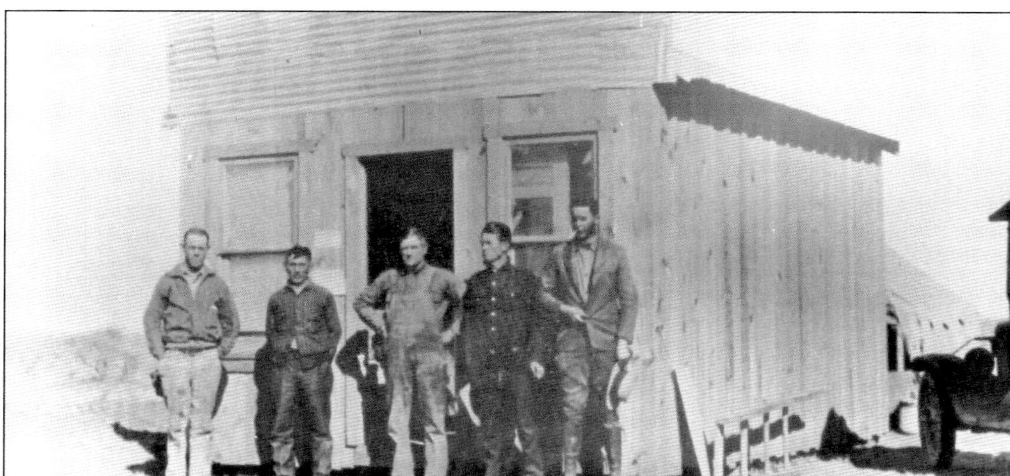

After the days of the Native Americans, the age of the rancher and oilman began. Members of the Seward family comprised some of the early population of settlers migrating to the area. Pictured from left to right are Marvin Seward, Dave Seward, unidentified, George Seward, and Alvin Seward. The entrepreneurial Seward family posed in front of the first "modern" grocery store in Crane County, which they built, owned, and operated. This 1927 photograph was taken when other stores in the area were operating from tents or tailgates. (Courtesy of Ray Yancey.)

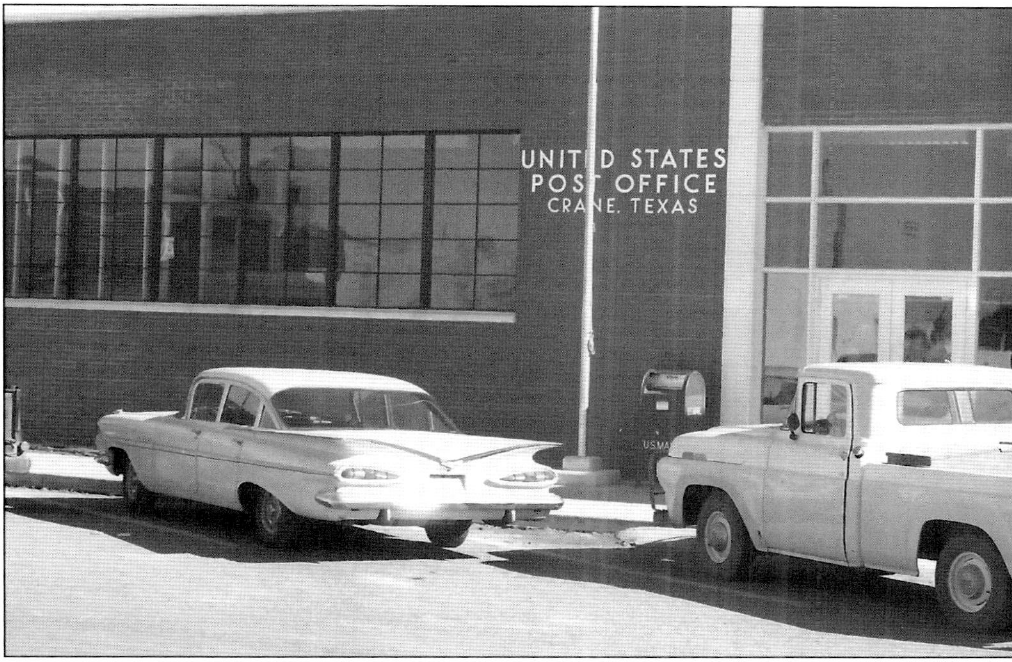

Before Crane was officially a town, the ranchers in the area had a place to send and receive their mail. In fact, the post office officially dates back to 1908, although it was not until after the discovery of oil in 1926 that enough people migrated to the area to sufficiently populate a town. For example, only 15 people lived in Crane County in 1890. By the turn of the 20th century, the population had increased to a paltry 51 people.

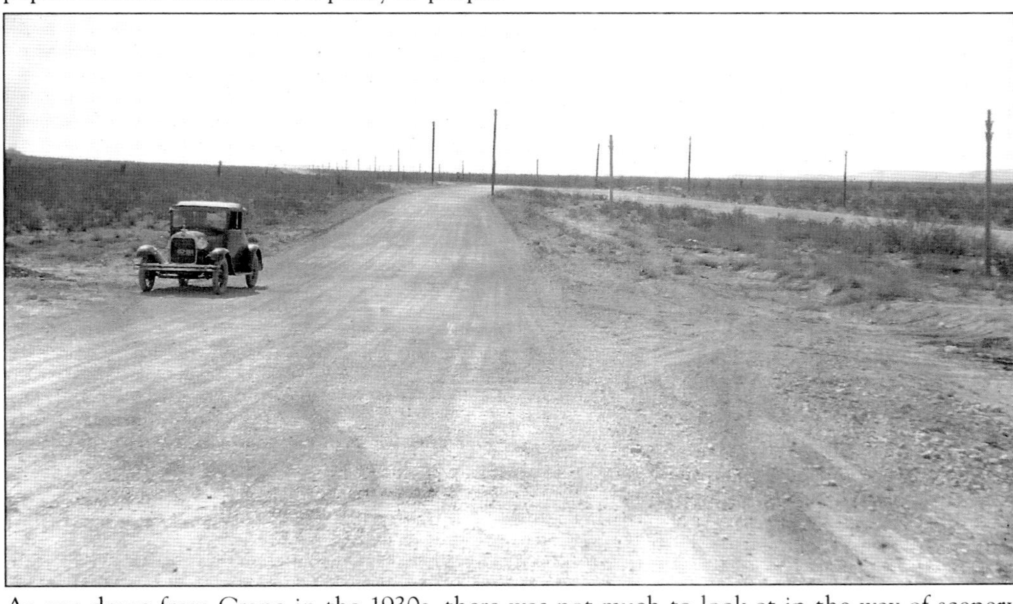

As one drove from Crane in the 1930s, there was not much to look at in the way of scenery. Shown here is one of Crane's early citizens heading out of town on the way to Odessa. One can only imagine how long a "quick shopping trip" might have taken back then, when the phrase "speed limit" was not even needed due to the limitations of the period's automobiles.

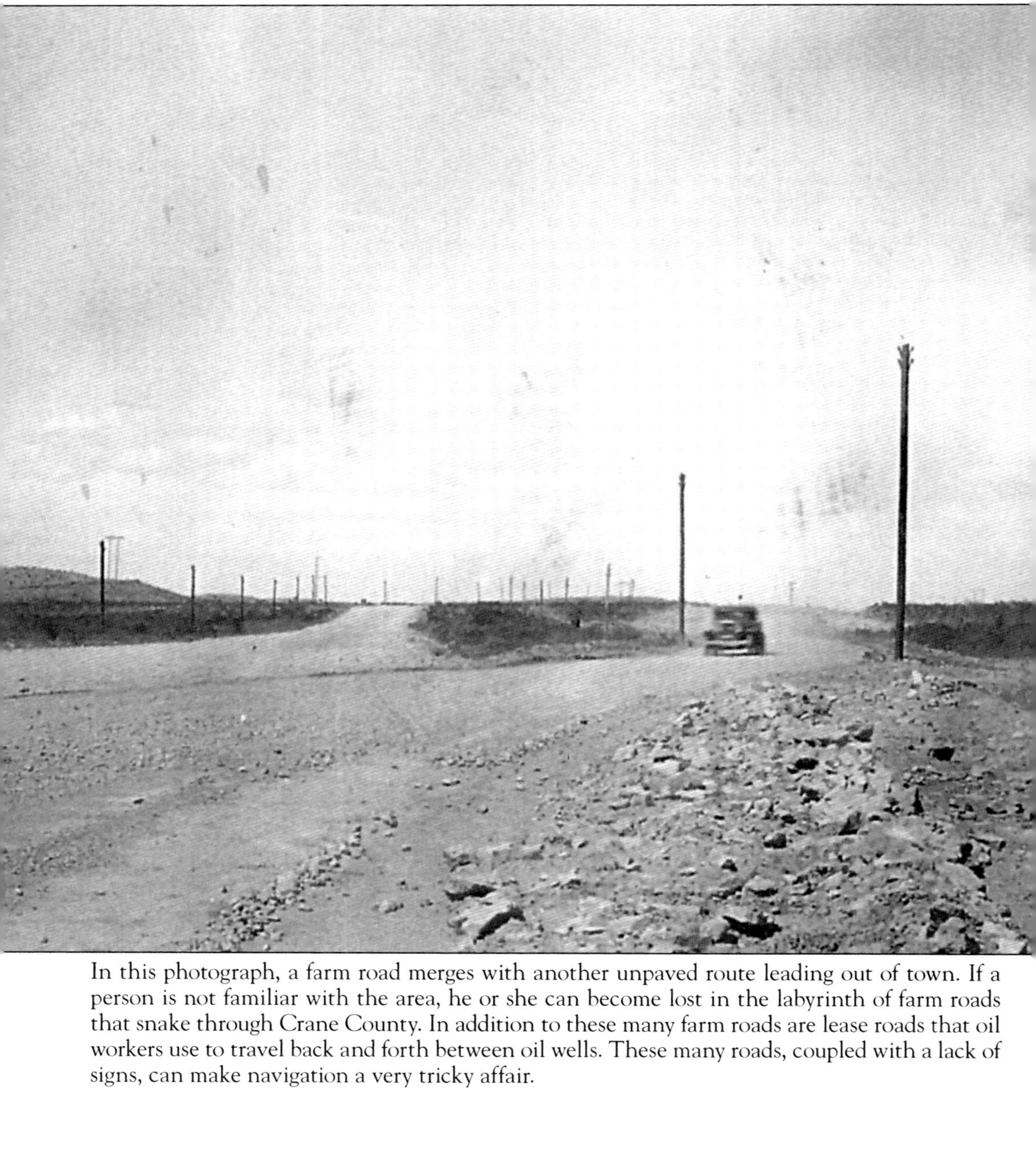

In this photograph, a farm road merges with another unpaved route leading out of town. If a person is not familiar with the area, he or she can become lost in the labyrinth of farm roads that snake through Crane County. In addition to these many farm roads are lease roads that oil workers use to travel back and forth between oil wells. These many roads, coupled with a lack of signs, can make navigation a very tricky affair.

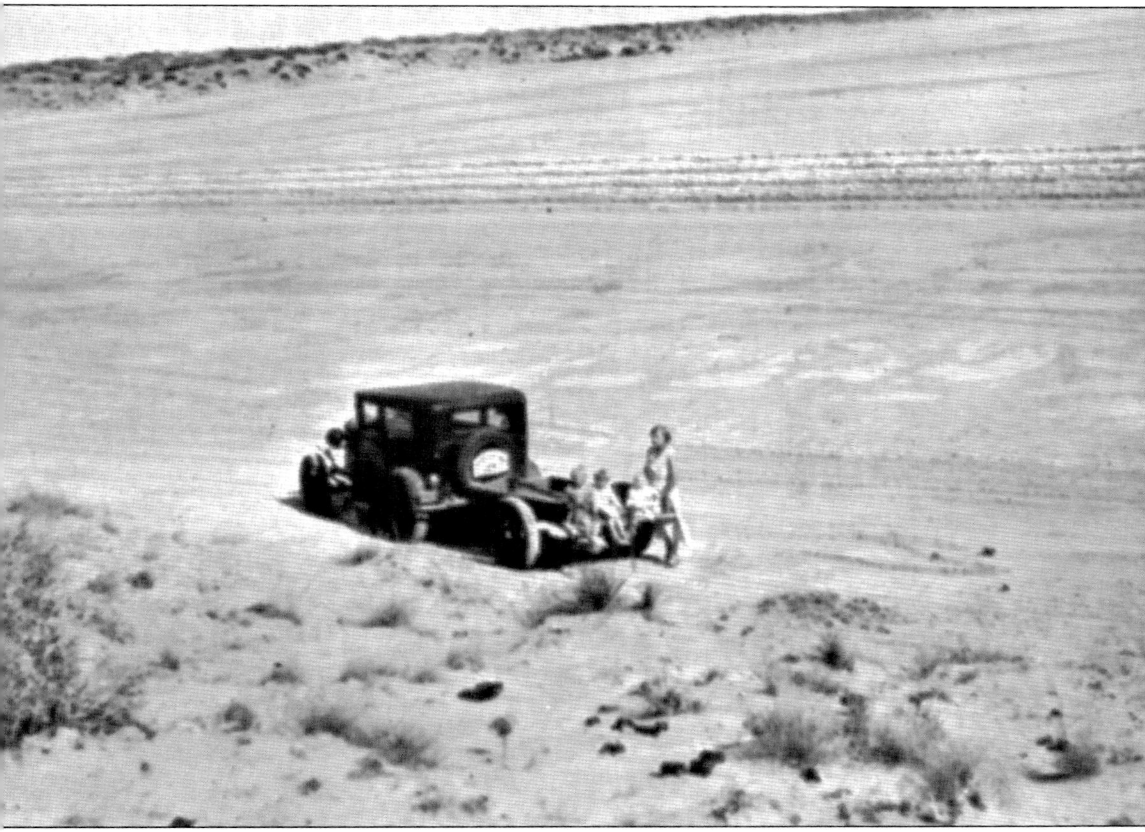

Max Omo and his family are pictured enjoying a day out at Juan Cordona Salt Lake, a natural mineral deposit that has been used for more than 300 years. Juan Cordona Salt Lake has a rich history. In 1683, Apaches were encountered there by explorers, and up until 1884, the deposit, which lies four miles north of the Pecos River in southern Crane County, provided salt to Native American traders from the La Junta region of the Rio Grande. Omo, a salt cutter, held an exclusive lease for more than a decade allowing him ownership of all the salt he could dredge up there.

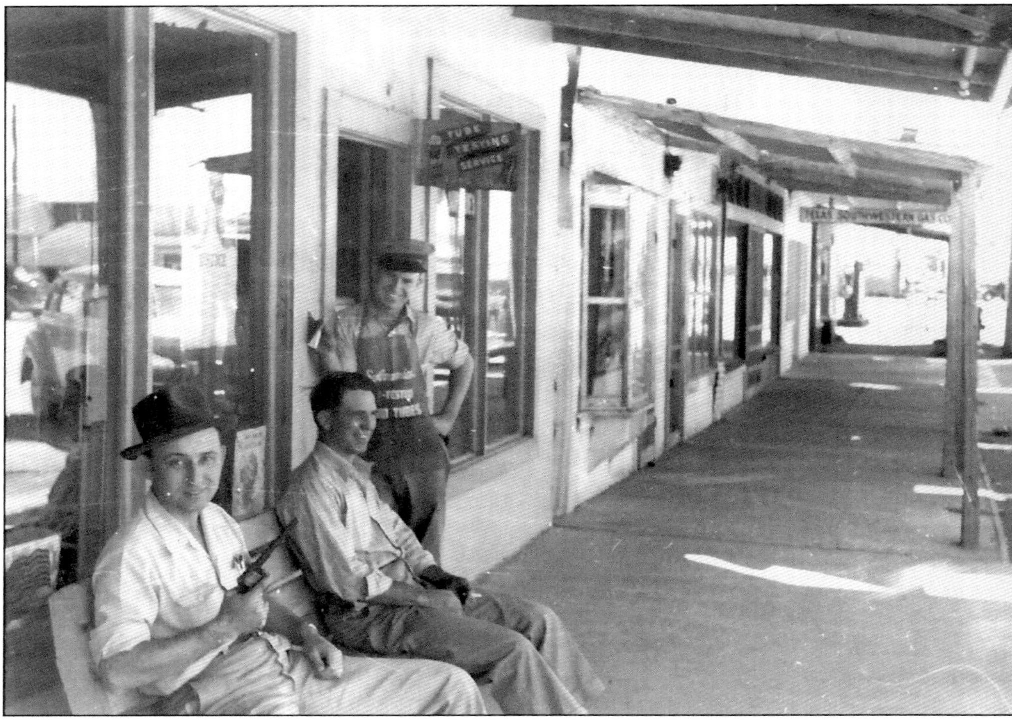

Many people look back to the late 1940s and early 1950s as a simpler time. In this photograph, two young men laugh at another man who holds a small-caliber pistol while posing for the camera. While Crane County citizens are allowed to own firearms (and some who possess Texas concealed handgun licenses are even allowed to carry them), gone are the days when one can jokingly brandish a pistol on a city sidewalk.

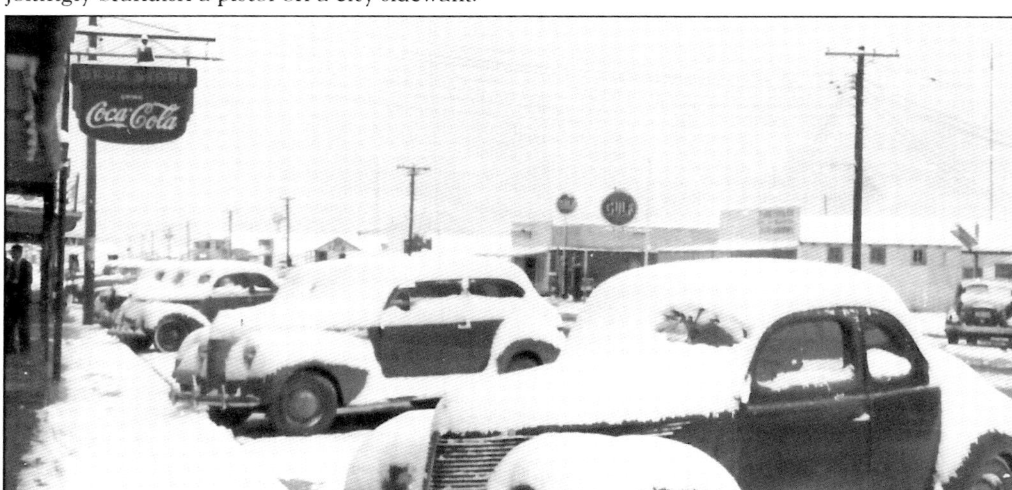

Crane County earns a meager average rainfall of 12.97 inches annually, which is less than half of what average US cities receive. While rain is uncommon, snow is especially so. This photograph, taken in Crane's yesteryear, shows the aftermath of a very rare snowstorm. Cold days are certainly more rare than warm ones in Crane, with the lowest recorded temperature being -6 degrees Fahrenheit. Conversely, the hottest day on record was 115 degrees Fahrenheit.

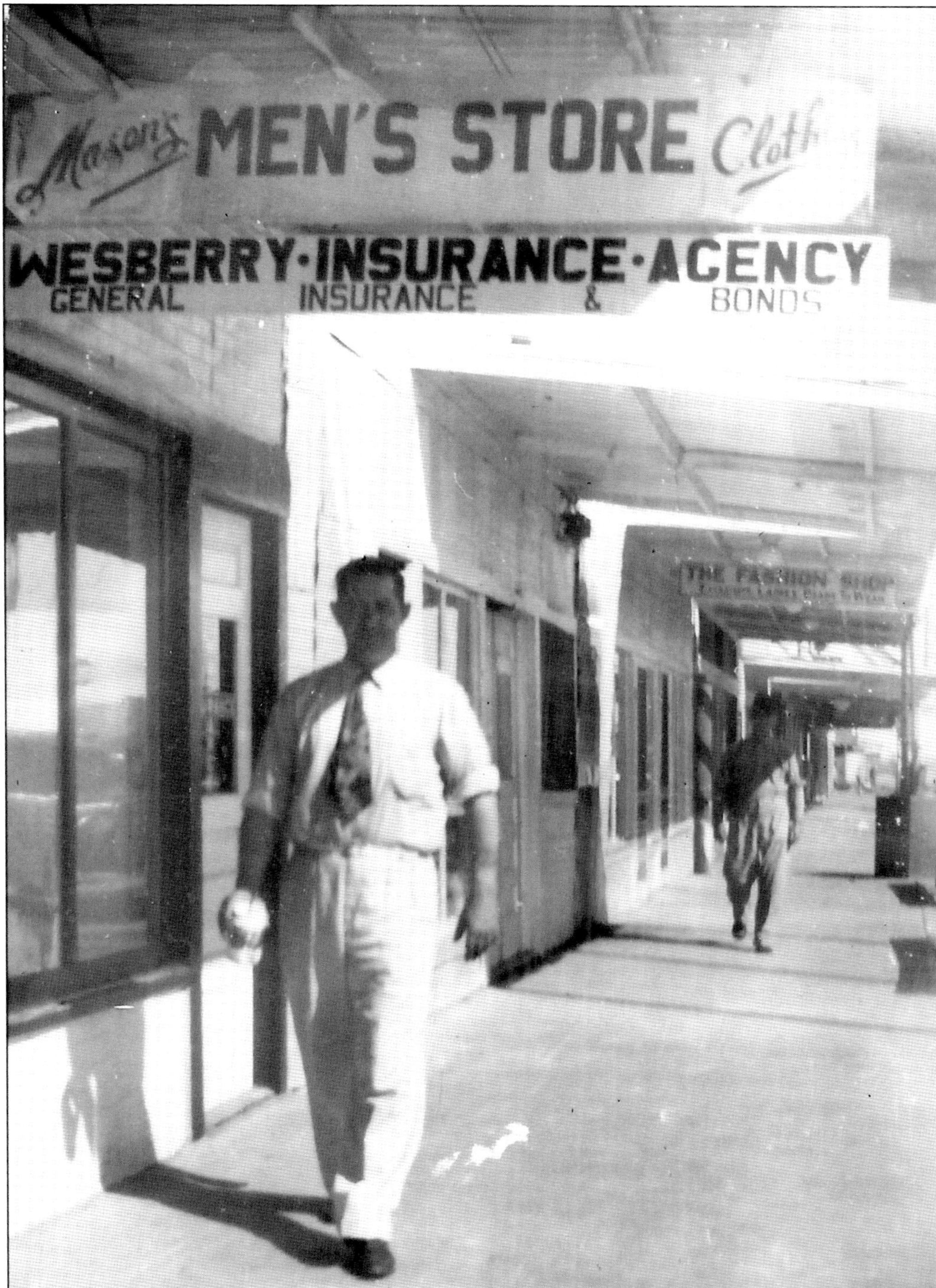

Downtown Crane has changed much since the town's formative years. The businesses behind the strolling men have all vanished and been replaced with newer architecture and different companies.

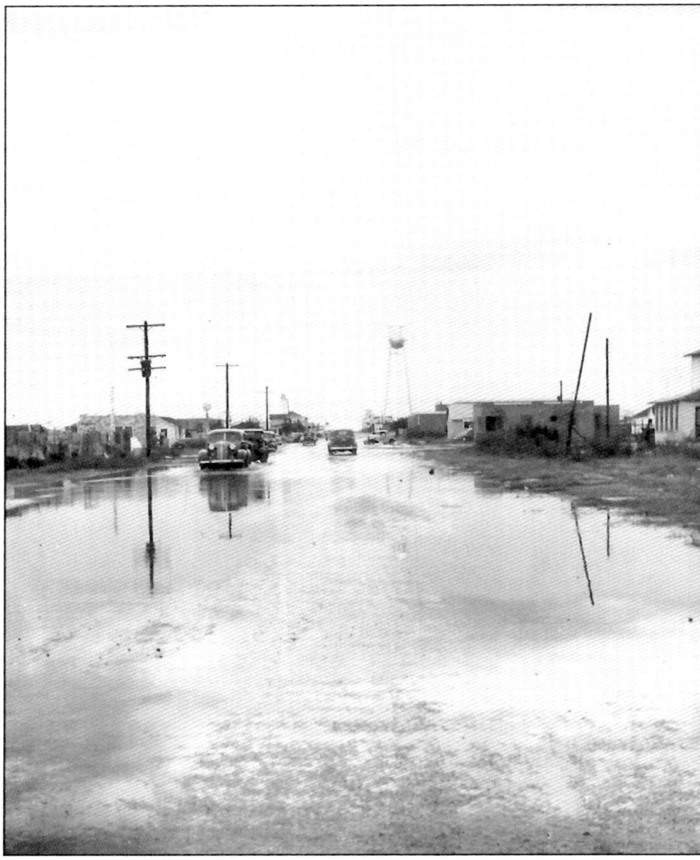

Although rain is rare, when thunderstorms swept the town back in the early days, many of the unpaved roads would flood, making any travel a difficult and muddy affair. Crane's saturated streets are shown here following a massive flood in 1958. Although the parched earth can usually absorb water fairly quickly, the flat nature of the land causes flood water to collect in massive pools.

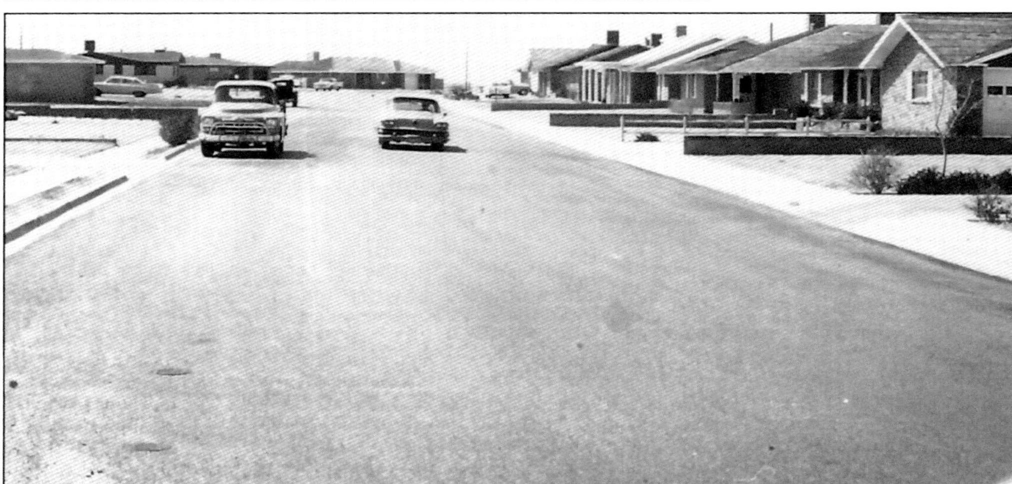

The faces of city neighborhoods were shiny and new when this undated photograph captured Gulf Camp. The neighborhood gets its name from Gulf Oil, which was a major global oil company from the 1900s to 1980s. Oil camps were common during the early days of Permian Basin oil, and these communities functioned as virtual cities, where citizens were employed and—to a certain extent—taken care of by a particular oil company.

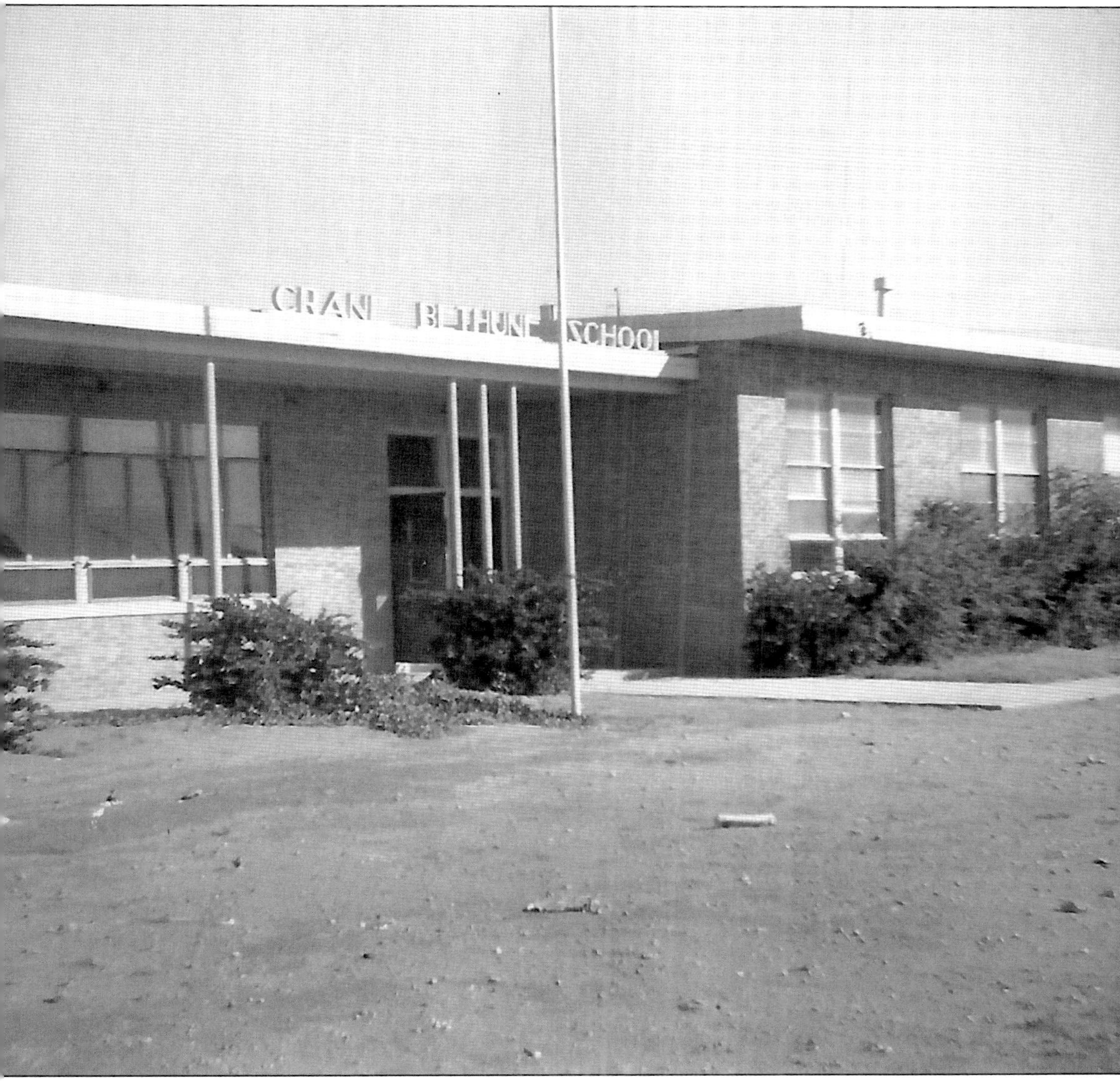

The Crane Bethune School was the "colored school" for Crane's African American citizens in the days prior to desegregation. Along with these "separate-but-equal" facilities was the "colored swimming pool," which disappeared after those trying times in American history. Presently, there is one school for each of the educational stages: Crane Elementary School, Crane Middle School, and Crane High School. Students of all races, religions, and creeds are educated together at these facilities. The Crane Bethune School is presently used to house and educate Crane High School vocational students taking cosmetology and auto mechanics classes.

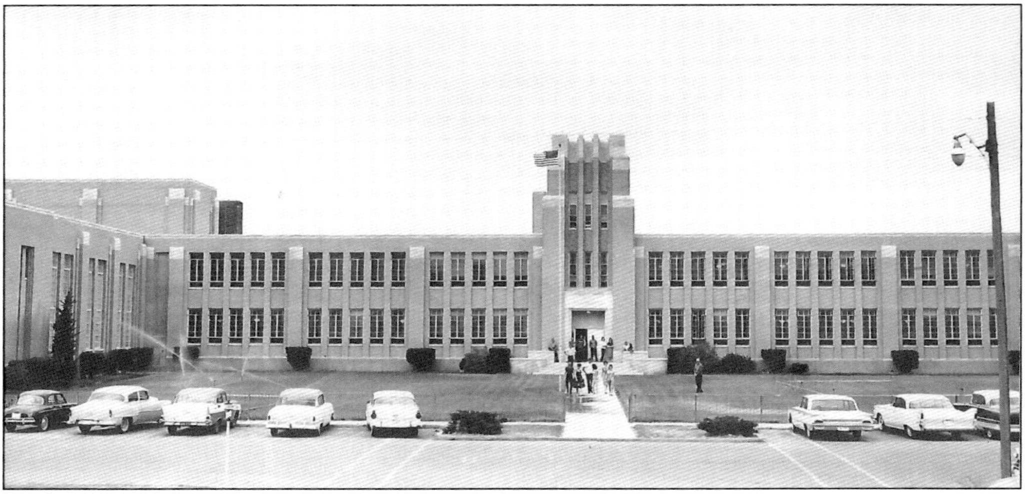

Crane High School has not changed much since this photograph was taken more than half a century ago. The average student body for grades nine through 12 is approximately 275, with the graduating class swelling or dwindling based on the state of the local economy. Likewise, the town's population swells and recedes according to the demand for oil. The population, according to the census in 2000, was only 3,191. Due to a recent oil boom, however, this number has consequently grown by several hundred.

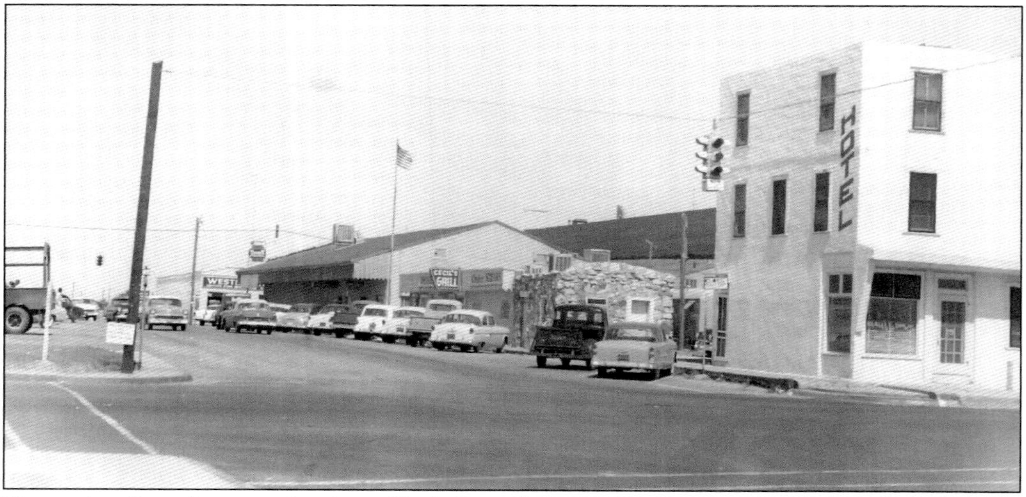

Pictured is Crane's one and only traffic light, still located in the same spot after many decades. The traffic light operates in the only major intersection in town.

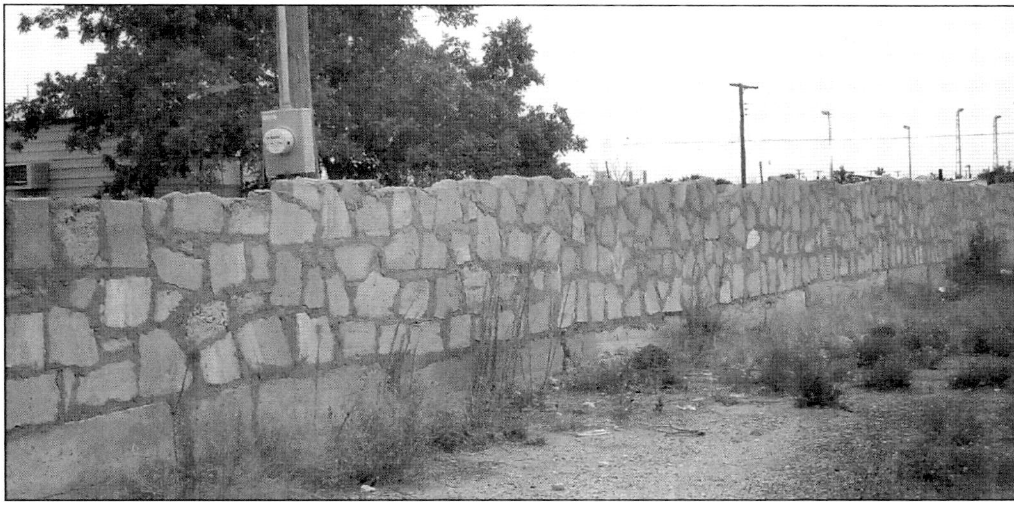

This dilapidated wall, located at the cross streets of West Third and South Gloria Streets, was once a major source of contention among Crane residents during the era of segregation. Essentially used as a line of demarcation to separate the African American citizens of Crane from the rest of the population, the wall became a hot topic again, years later, when Pulitzer Prize–winning author H.G. "Buzz" Bissinger described its dark history in his bestselling book *Friday Night Lights: A Town, a Team, and a Dream*. A plaque was later placed beside the wall to detail the history of this controversial structure.

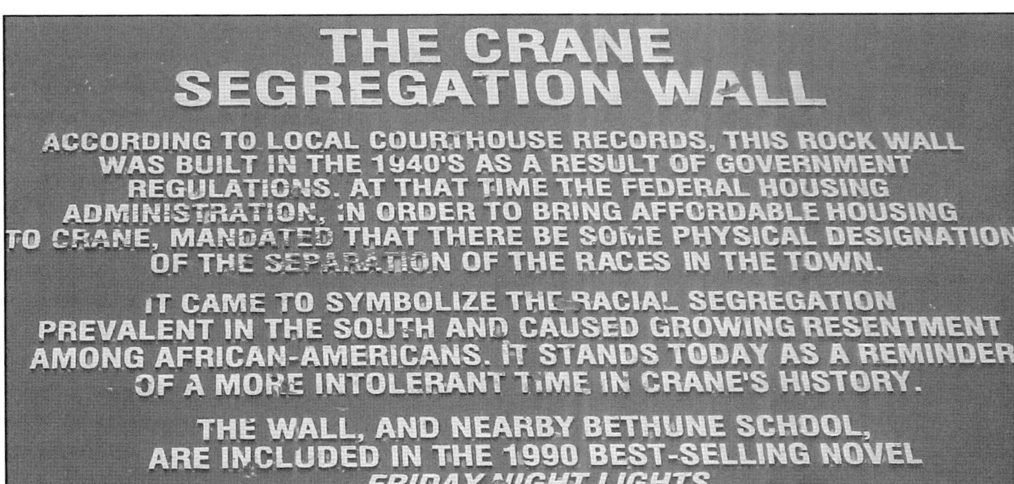

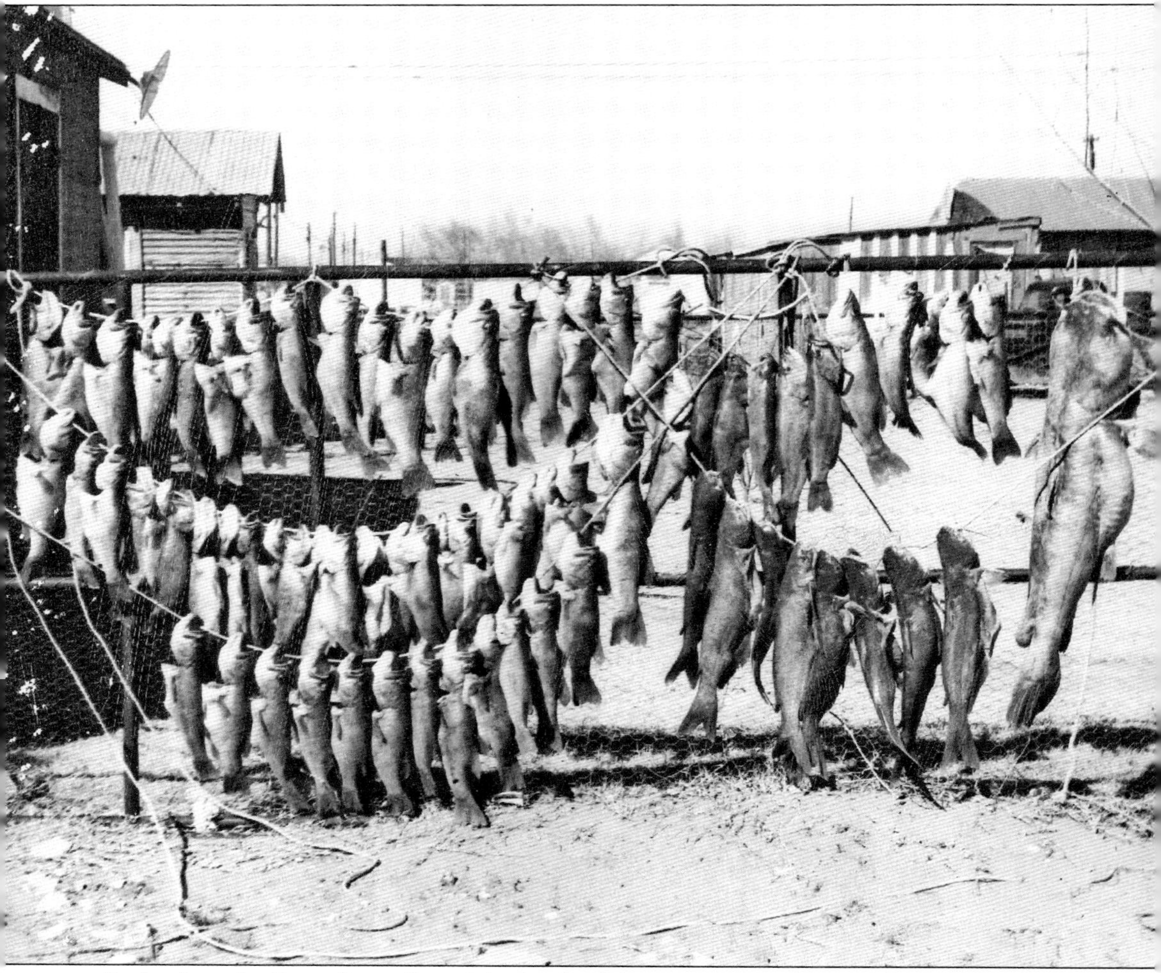

Back when the Pecos River flowed freely, the fishing was more than good, as evidenced in this undated photograph. According to the handwritten caption on the back, these fishermen caught "over 80 pounds of catfish in one day." At present, due to upriver damming and extreme drought, the Pecos River crawls through Crane County, a shadow of its former glory. In fact, the river was so wild at one time that there were only a few fordable locations on it. One of these locations in Crane County is known as Horsehead Crossing, which likely received its name due to the large number of horse skulls that are said to have marked its banks. As cattle drives declined and the railroads were finished, the crossing was totally abandoned by the 1880s.

Oscar Pearl, a Texas Highway employee, climbs a ladder to install new street signs in 1959. The new signs went up after Texas Highway 51 was renamed US Highway 385. Highway 385 begins in Texas and runs north through the heart of the United States.

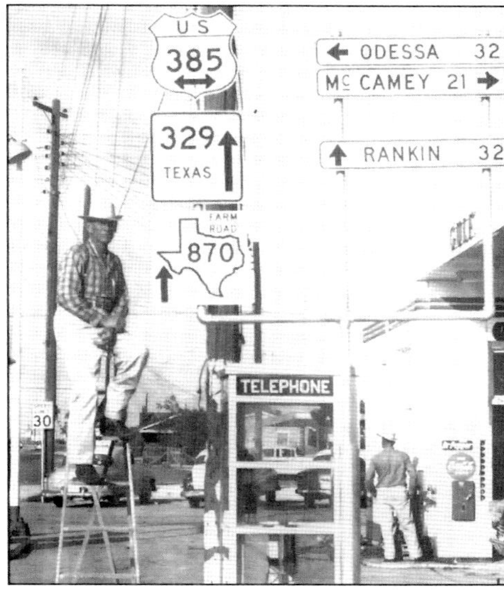

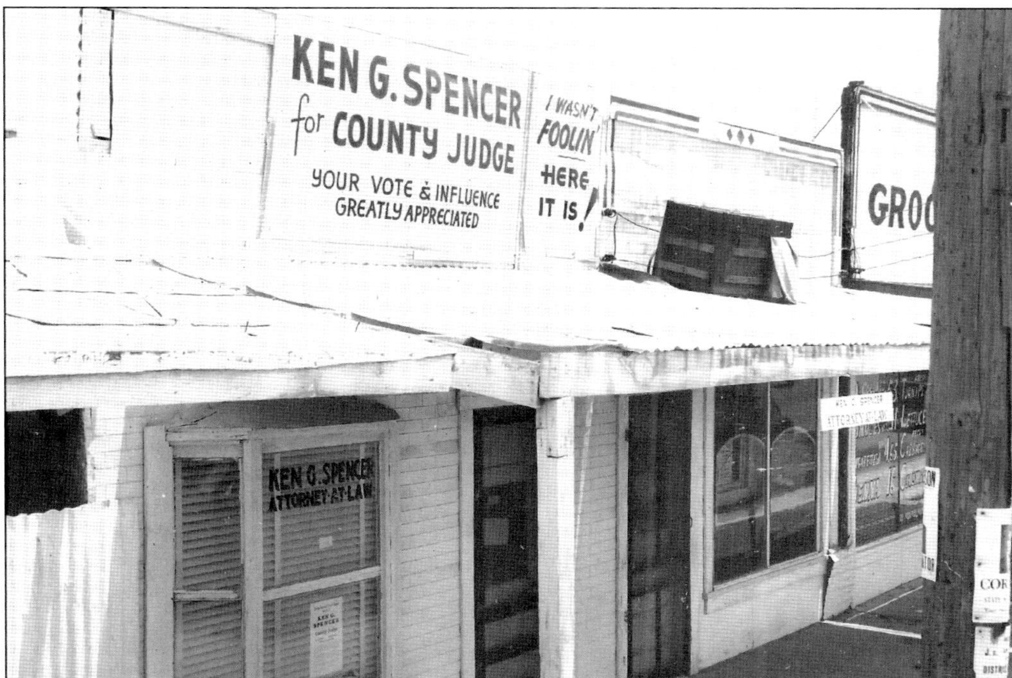

From Crane's earliest days, the office of the county judge has been a choice fruit of political power for the town's more ambitious residents. Shown here in the 1960s is Ken G. Spencer's law practice, which he utilized in his political campaign to become the next county judge. Spencer, who arrived in Crane looking for a place to practice law, was accused by some of the town's early citizens as "merely passing through." In order to show his dedication to Crane and willingness to stay in town, Spencer removed his luggage trunk from his car and placed it on the metal awning outside of his law firm. The trunk stayed there for many years—rusting and weathering in the desert climate—proving Spencer's word was his bond. In this photograph, the wooden trunk can be seen resting on the awning.

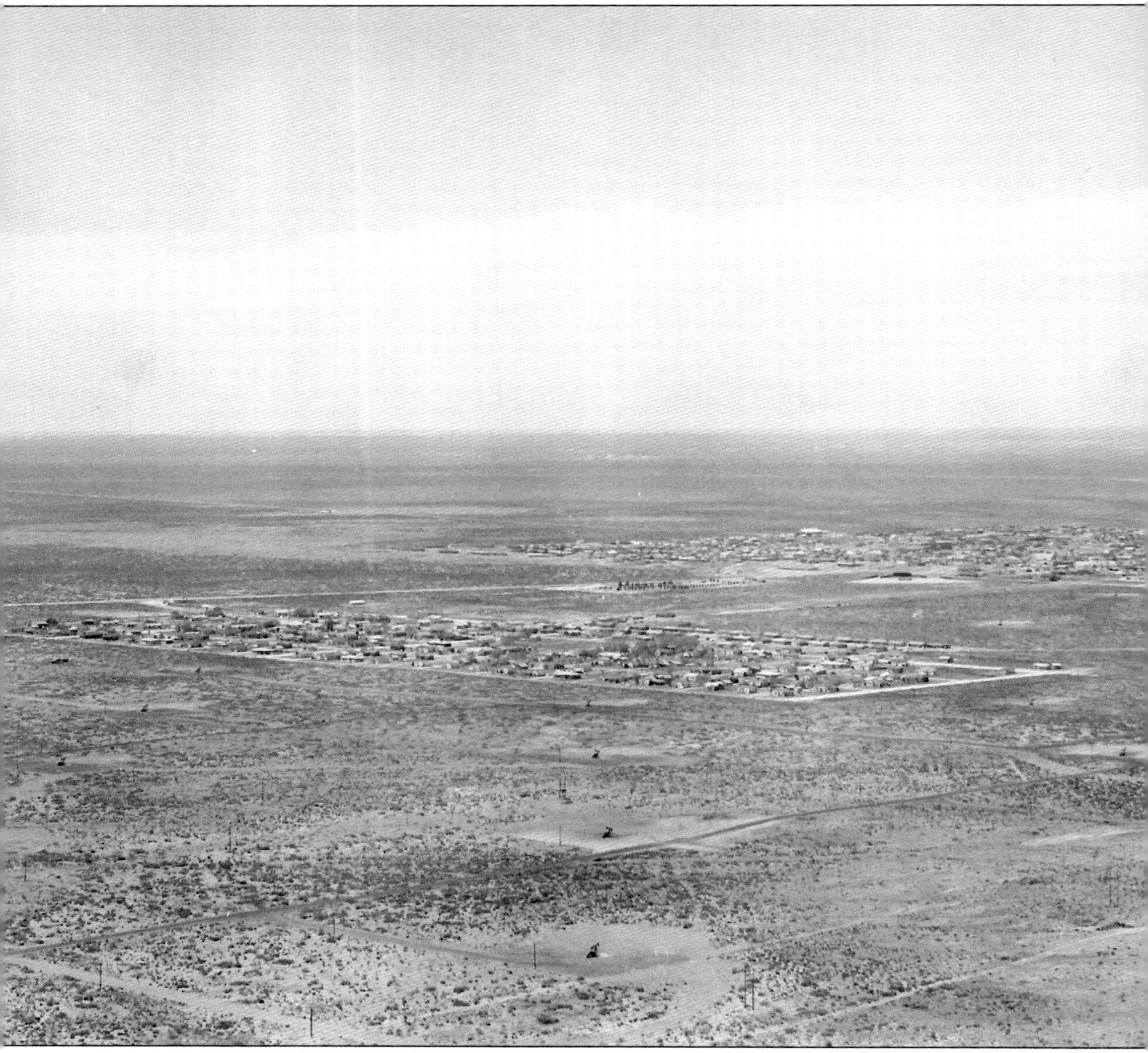

Pictured above is the city of Crane, along with a good portion of Crane County surrounding it, as it appeared from the air in 1975. Crane County is exceptionally flat and sparsely vegetated. The wood from the mesquite tree—the predominate greenery of the area—is used to make fence posts or for kindling to cook barbecue. Notice the orderly rows of pump jacks in the foreground. A pump jack is an above-ground drive for a reciprocating piston pump in an oil well. As it stands today, pump jacks have become a regular and sentimental part of the Permian Basin landscape.

Two

RANCHING OUT WEST

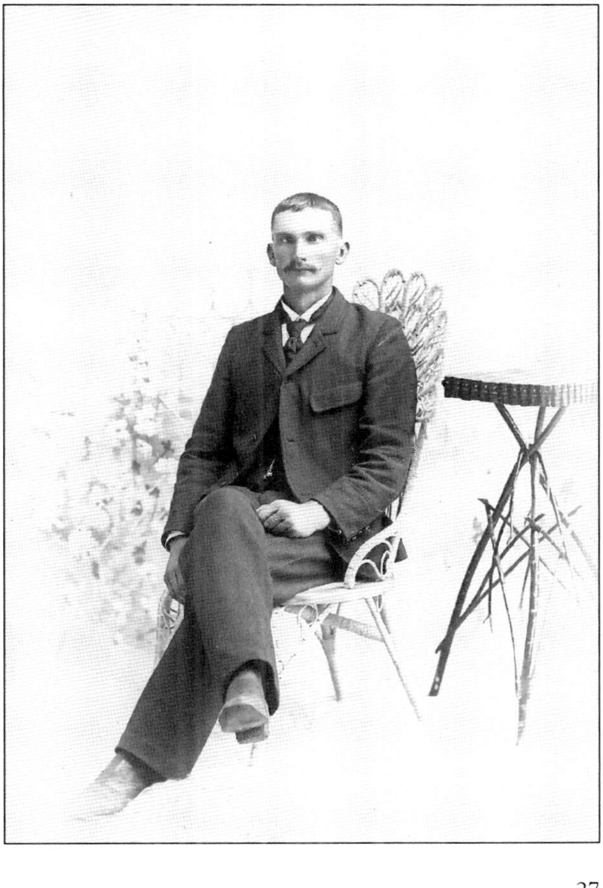

Ranching in Crane County was one of the main occupations settlers originally undertook. Robert Diogenes "Dodge" McGee pioneered one of the first ranches in the county alongside his wife, Katherine (Dunne) McGee. Although it was originally called Quarter Circle RD Ranch, it currently operates under the name J Bar Ranch and has stayed in the same family since 1904. (Courtesy of Calvin and Suzahn Smith.)

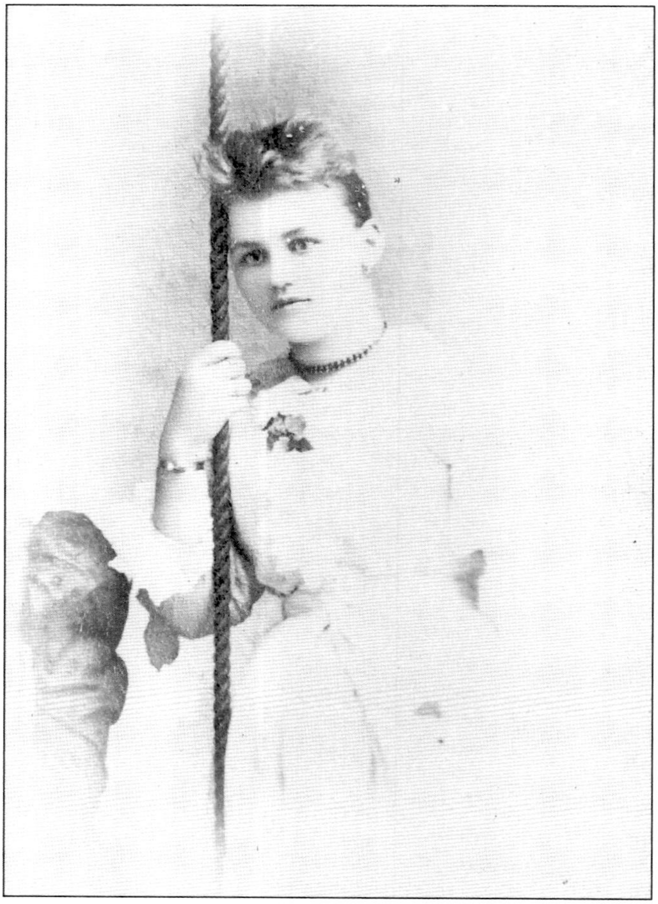

Katherine "Kate" McGee (left) and Robert Diogenes "Dodge" McGee, along with their son Jay D. McGee, traveled to what would later be formed into Crane County. A wedding for Robert McGee's brother initially brought the family to the area, but they further decided to stake a homestead and began ranching near his brother's land. (Courtesy of Calvin and Suzahn Smith.)

Cowboys for the McGees' ranch rest while they break for a meal. From left to right, they are Jae Clark, C.M. Edwards (of Midland), George Clark, Jay McGee, and M.F. Clark. With hard work and the blessings of much-needed rain, West Texas ranches like the J Bar thrive through the labor of men such as the ones pictured here. (Courtesy of Calvin and Suzahn Smith.)

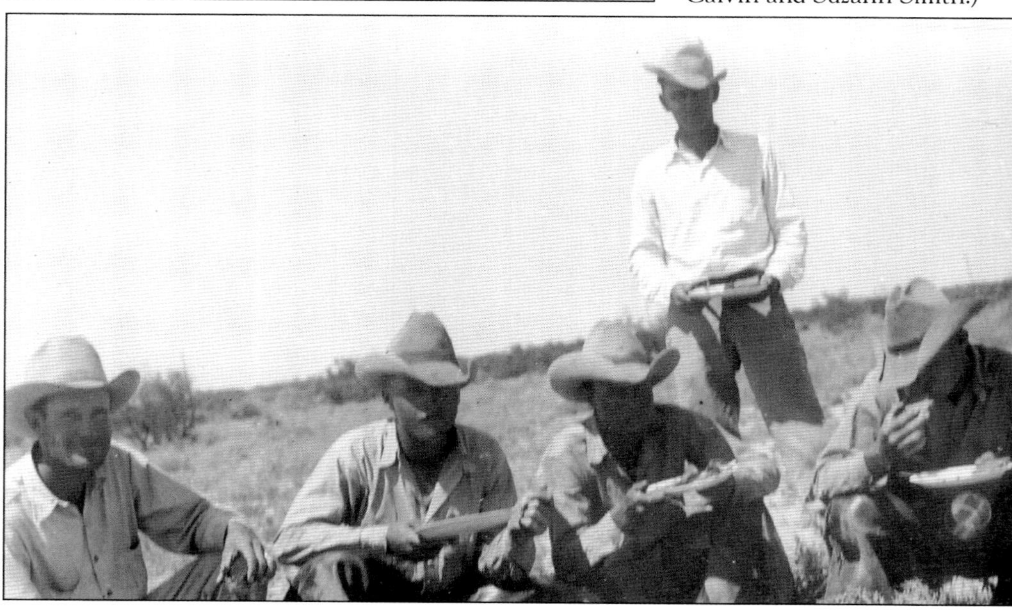

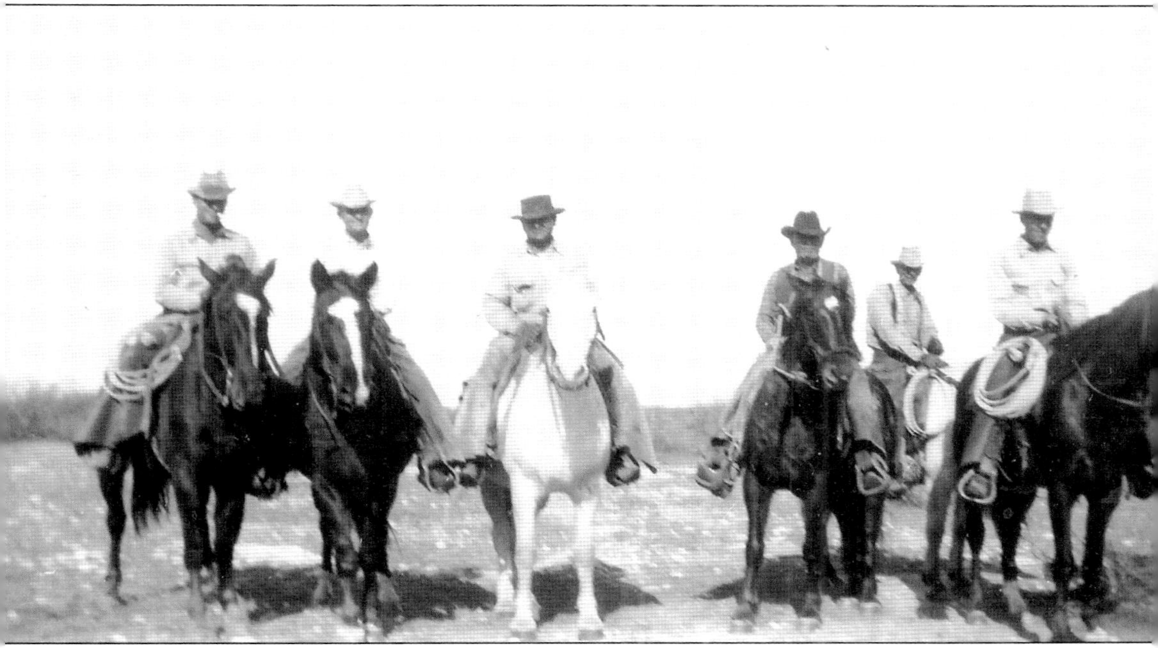

Saddled up for work in the pasture, from left to right, Dub Edwards, Cal Smith, Tige Henderson, ? Hutchins, Jay McGee, and Harold Smith pause for the camera. Katherine and Robert McGee's son Jay McGee attended school in Odessa while he was growing up and eventually married June Lucille Rhodes, whom he met there. They moved to the ranch and continued work as the second generation of the J Bar Ranch. (Courtesy of Calvin and Suzahn Smith.)

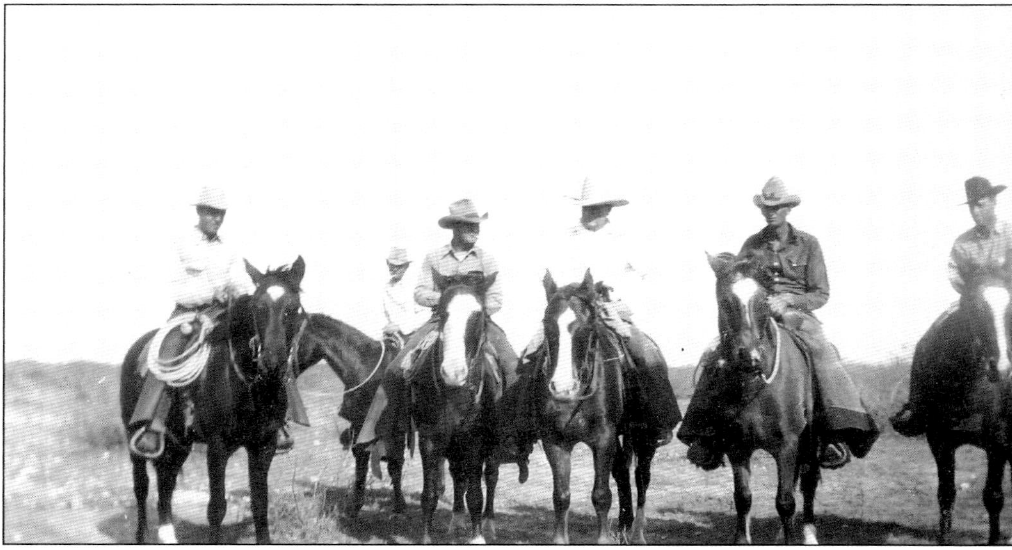

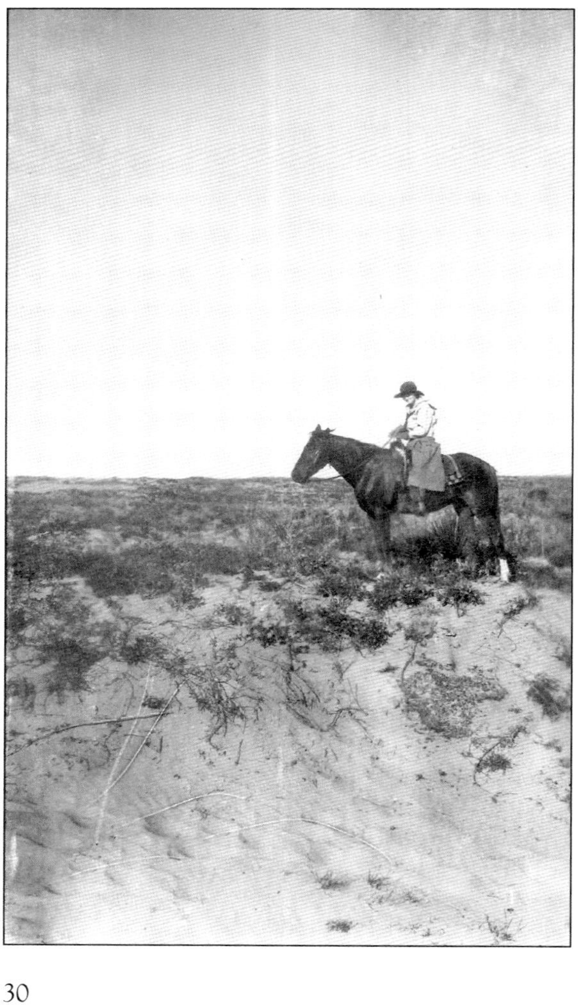

This photograph provides a glimpse into the real ranching life most Americans today can only dream about. Committed to accomplishing hard work day in and day out, these cowboys were the reality Hollywood oftentimes attempts to portray. Identified here are, from left to right, Harold Smith, Johnny Henderson, Tad Henderson, Buck Kelton, Snort Trent, and unidentified. (Courtesy of Calvin and Suzahn Smith.)

A photograph of June McGee captures the true spirit of a working woman. This image of her represents one of many wives of ranchers who have worked by their husband's side regardless of what needed to be done. In addition to helping out with the cattle when the men were shorthanded, the J Bar women provided food for the family and all the cowboys. (Courtesy of Calvin and Suzahn Smith.)

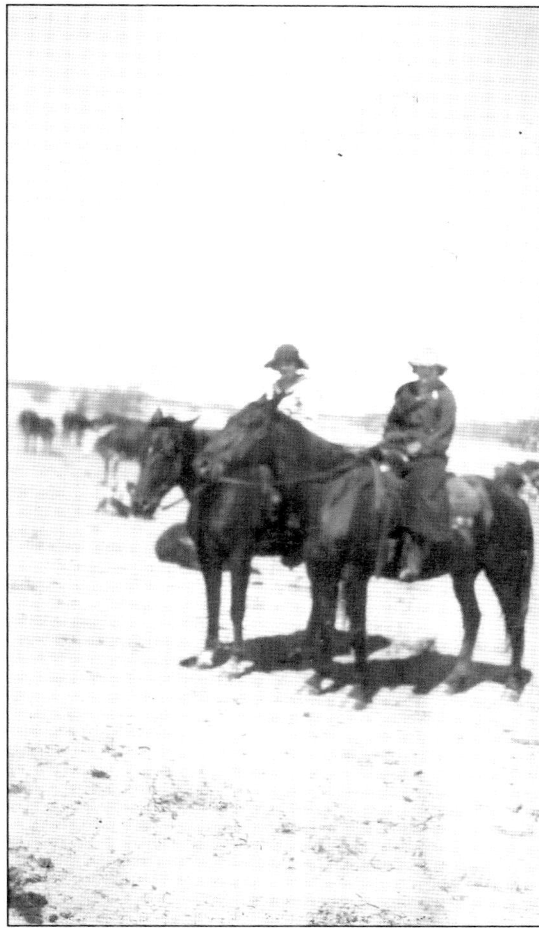

June McGee (left) and an unidentified woman (right) stand among the cattle in the sandy terrain. The land of J Bar Ranch is representative of most Crane County ranches. Besides the McGees, some of the other Crane ranching families were remembered by Acie Williford (Bond) Smith, who said, "Jay and June neighbored with lots of area ranch families: Homer and Marvin Henderson, F.E. Waddell, E.K. Bowman, George and F.M. Clark, Tom Tripp, Marvin Hooper, Buck Kelton, P.J. Lea, T.C. Barnsley, J.B. Tubb, Ewell McKnight . . . just to name a few." Acie Williford Bond, June's great niece, married Harold Rhodes Smith and initiated the third generation of J Bar. (Both, courtesy of Calvin and Suzahn Smith.)

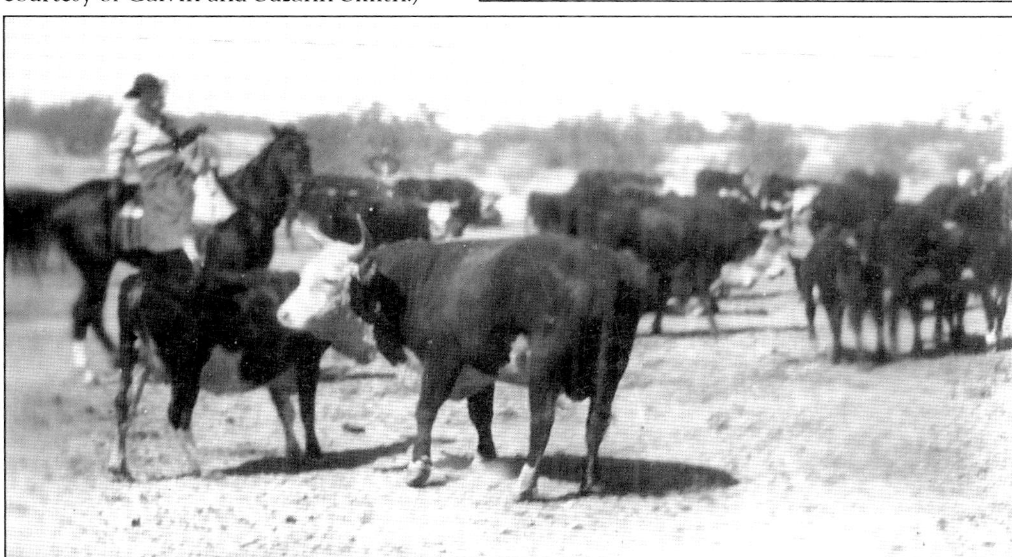

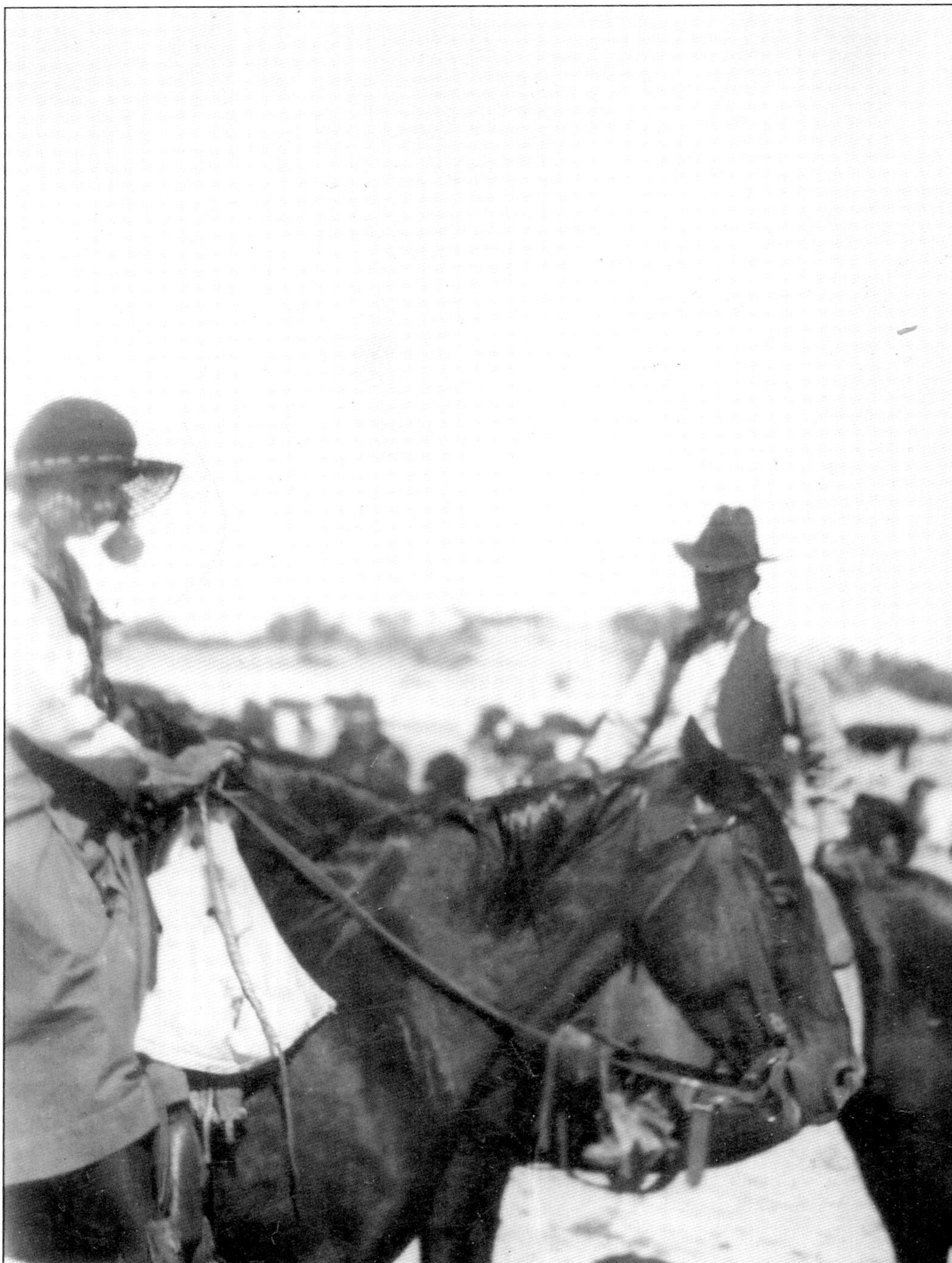

A c. 1920s photograph of June and Jay shows them rounding up their cattle. Acie Williford Smith acknowledged, "Jay was like other ranchers of the time and would stock his J Bar Ranch with 300–500 head of cattle to make a living, often adding extra herds by pasturing or leasing." J Bar had Hereford cattle, as seen in the background of this photograph. (Courtesy of Calvin and Suzahn Smith.)

The people in this photograph are unidentified, but the image calls to mind the camaraderie that ranch hands often share. Rough labor in the sun through the most intense heat of the day and the physical demands of ranch employment go a littler smoother when there is a fellow hand to endure them with. (Courtesy of Calvin and Suzahn Smith.)

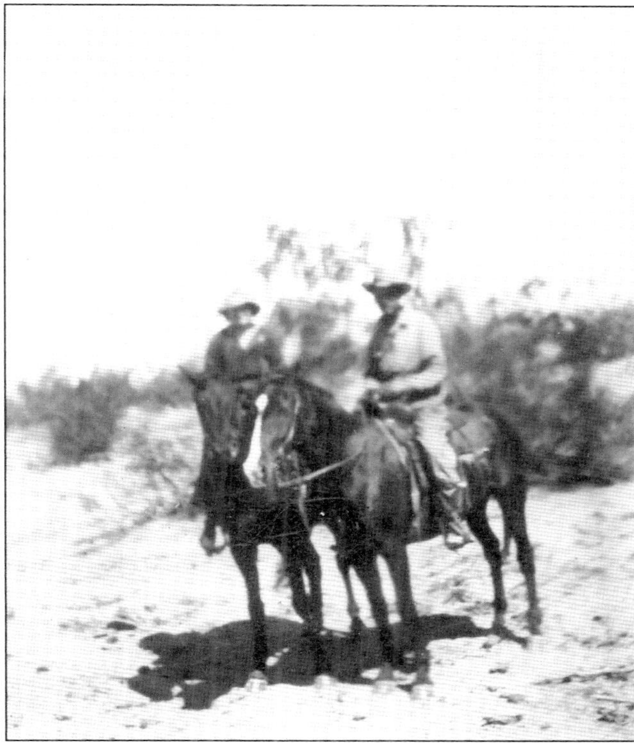

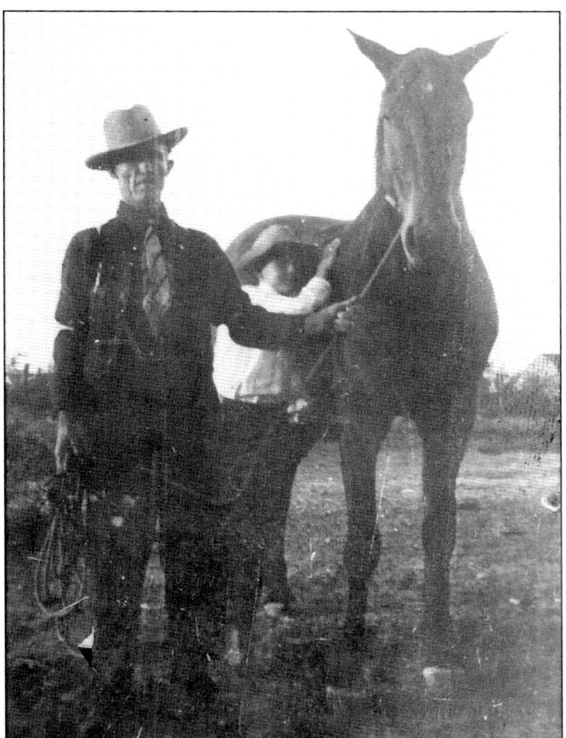

A man identified as Mr. Bowman and Harold Rhodes Smith stand alongside a statuesque horse. The height of the horse would have been measured in four-inch increments called "hands" from the ground to the highest point of the withers. (Courtesy of Calvin and Suzahn Smith.)

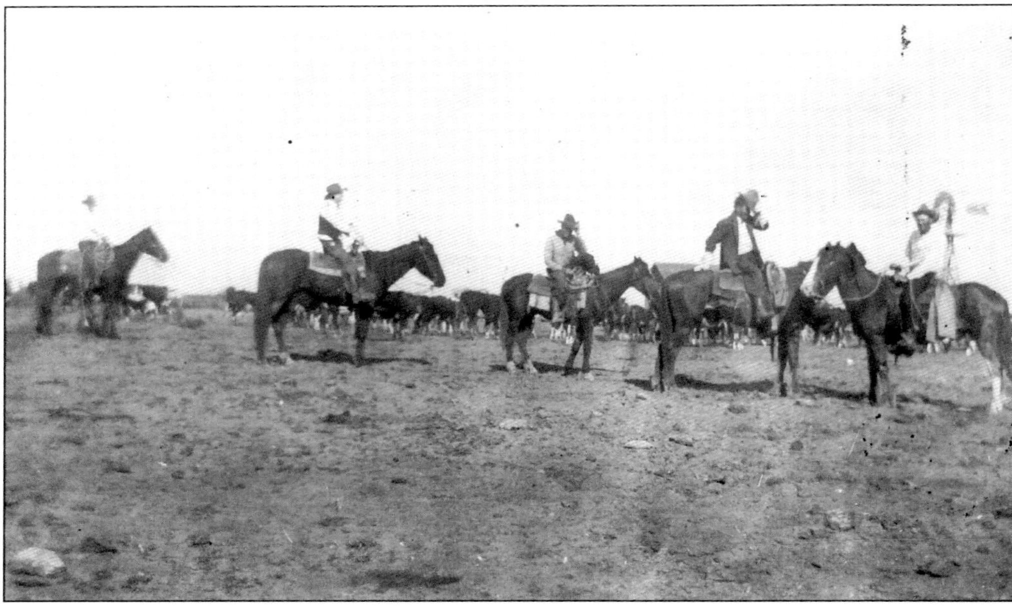

Horses were extremely vital to a man in the days before automobiles and especially so for running a cattle ranch. Generally, quarter horses are used for ranching because of their eagerness to work the cattle. The stamina and drive with which they have been bred qualify them for moving quickly and easily through the cattle. Larger horses were used for tasks such as plowing and hauling. The men in this photograph are unidentified. (Courtesy of Calvin and Suzahn Smith.)

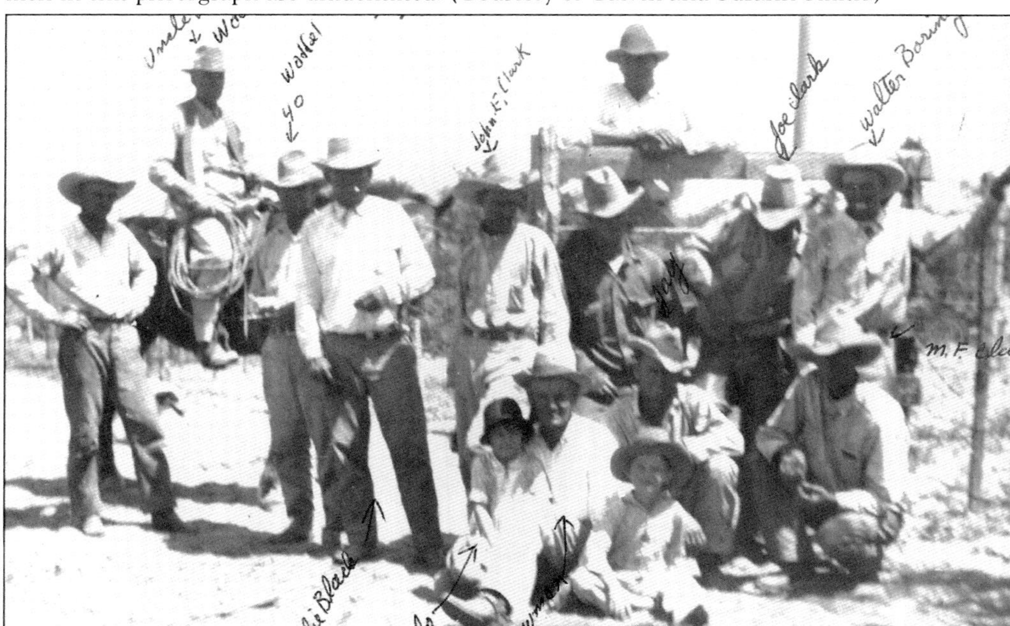

The cowhands in this 1927 photograph are, from left to right, (first row) Billy Jo ?, E.R. Bowman, unidentified, Jay McGee, and M.F. Clark; (second row) unidentified, Will Waddell, ? Waddell, Charlie Black, John E. Clark, two unidentified, Joe Clark, and Walter Boring. (Courtesy of Calvin and Suzahn Smith.)

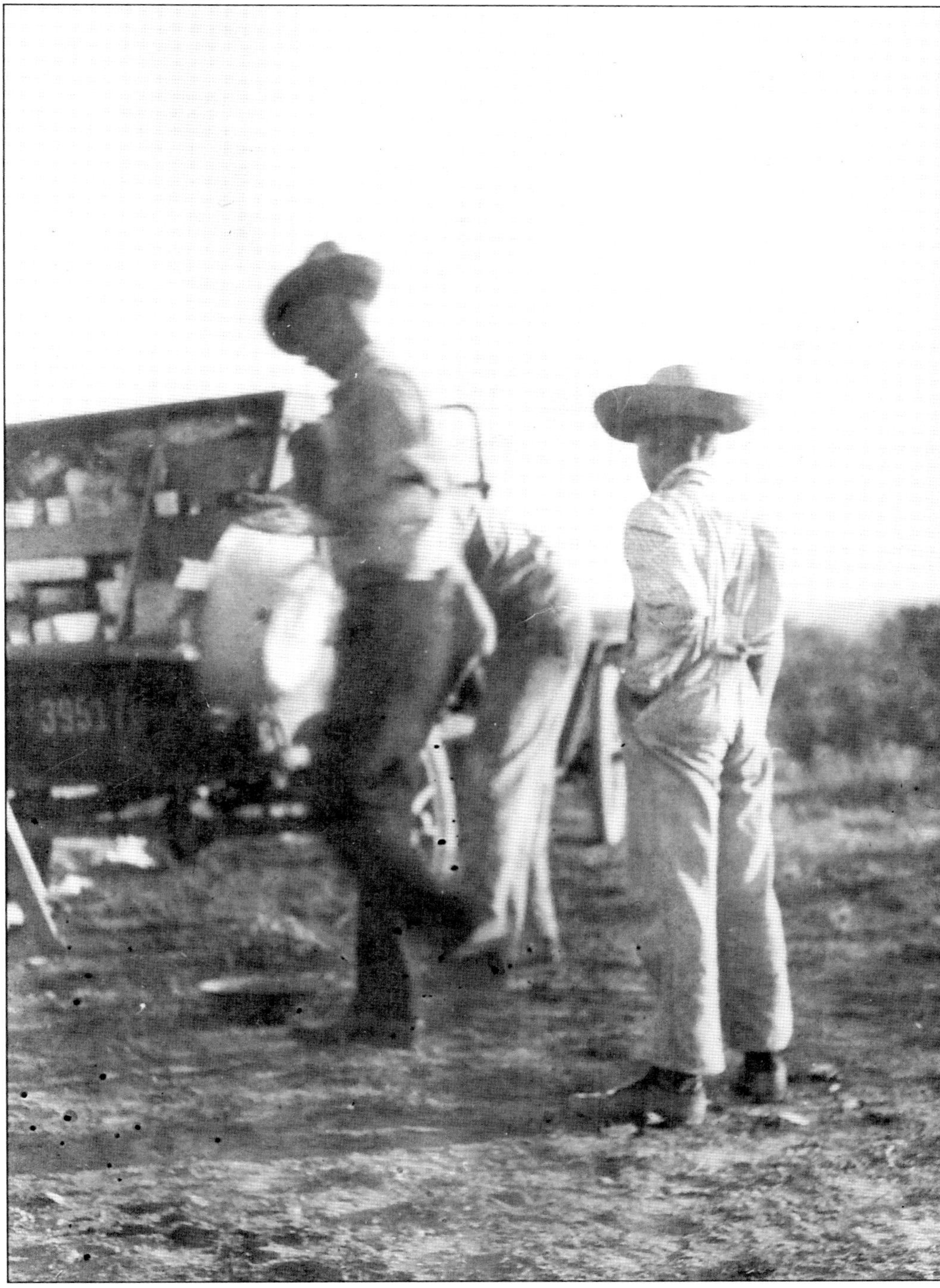

Packing up camp after working cattle, Jay McGee (left) carries a wash basin to a chuck box being pulled by a Ford Model T. The cook would have used the chuck box (back left) to store and transport all the food that needed to be hauled to camp and cooked for meals. (Courtesy of Calvin and Suzahn Smith.)

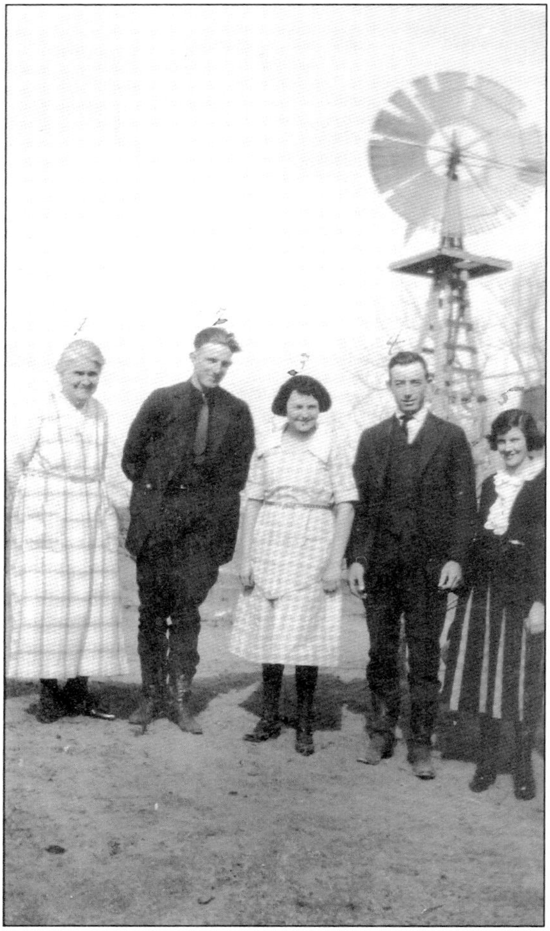

From left to right are Katherine McGee, Jack Cowden, June McGee, Buck York, and Bessie ?, enjoying each others' company as they stop for a photograph in front of the windmill. Fellow ranchers often helped each other out and pioneered the neighborly hospitality that has since characterized the Crane community. (Courtesy of Calvin and Suzahn Smith.)

Pictured below is the McGee family in front of a porch with R.D. McGee (left). The hard life that agricultural jobs entail is easily seen on the faces of these men and women. Not all people find themselves cut out for the kind of work livestock calls for, but the McGees and the Smiths have persevered through the harshness of the business for over 100 years. (Courtesy of Calvin and Suzahn Smith.)

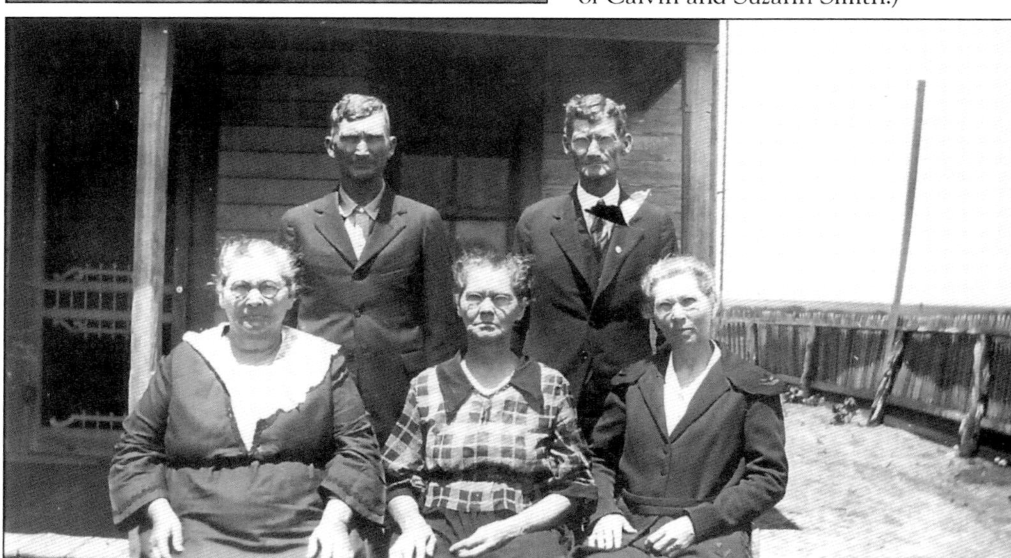

Jay and June McGee are pictured around 1931 standing in front of their vehicle. Acie Williford Smith once reminisced, "Jay was a very generous man to his friends and family, especially treating June like his queen." This couple is a sweet likeness of the many ranchers and their wives throughout the county, and the country, who support each other through the highs and lows of their livelihood. (Courtesy of Calvin and Suzahn Smith.)

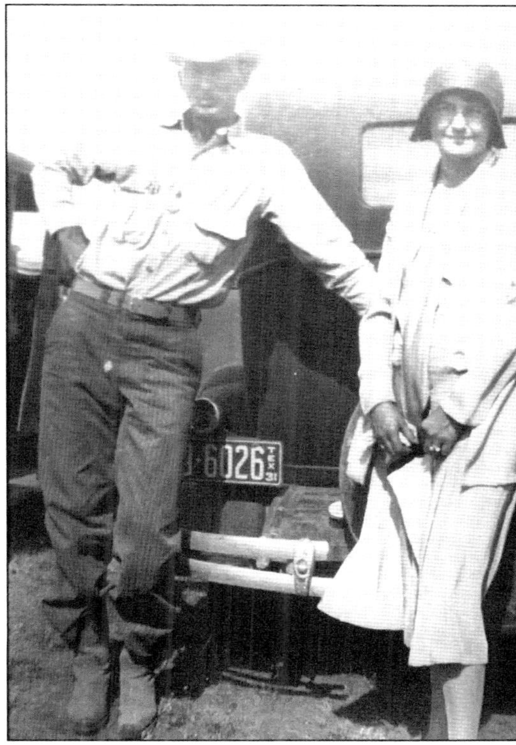

Jay McGee works on the engine of a car while cattle gather in the background. The 20th century saw the coinciding of automobiles and work in a pasture, and ranchers everywhere can attest to the value of being able to drive out to work on cows or fence rather than saddling up every time. (Courtesy of Calvin and Suzahn Smith.)

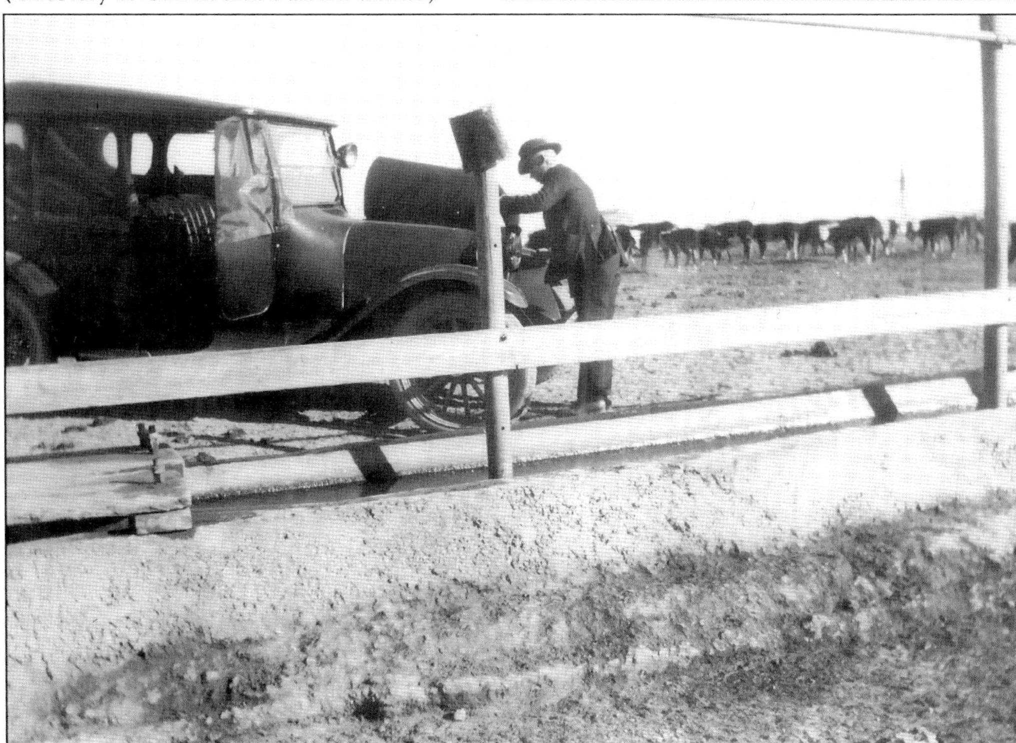

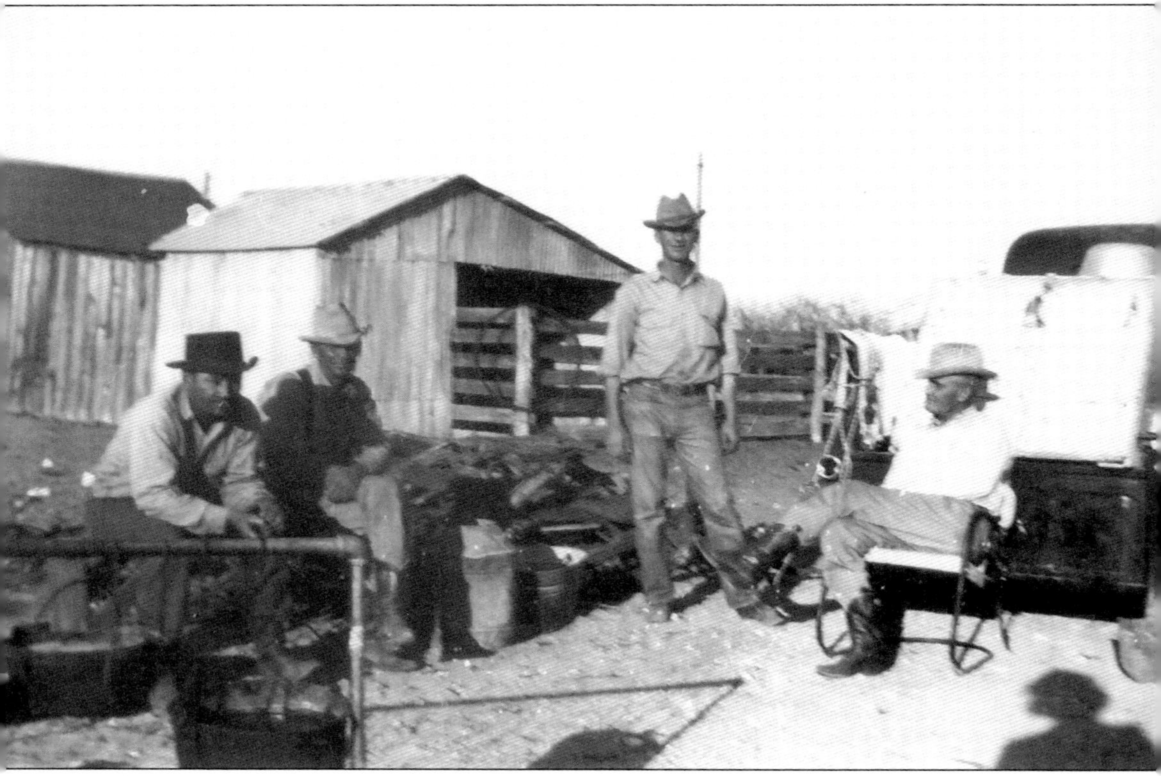

The men rest for a meal while their dutch ovens cook over an open fire. From left to right are Tige Henderson, Jay McGee, Andrew Douthet (cook), and Calvin Monroe Smith. Calvin Monroe Smith was married to June McGee's sister Nicie Lillian Rhodes, and they raised their two boys, Harold Rhodes Smith and William Calvin Smith, to cherish working on the ranch as well. (Courtesy of Calvin and Suzahn Smith.)

One of the women takes a photograph while Jay McGee and Calvin Monroe Smith lean against the bed of a pickup truck. Their boots are tucked in to keep their pants out of the mud, their hats are on for protection from the sun, and they are surrounded by all the kinds of things familiar to even current Crane residents; essentially, these guys are the spitting image of early Texas. (Courtesy of Calvin and Suzahn Smith.)

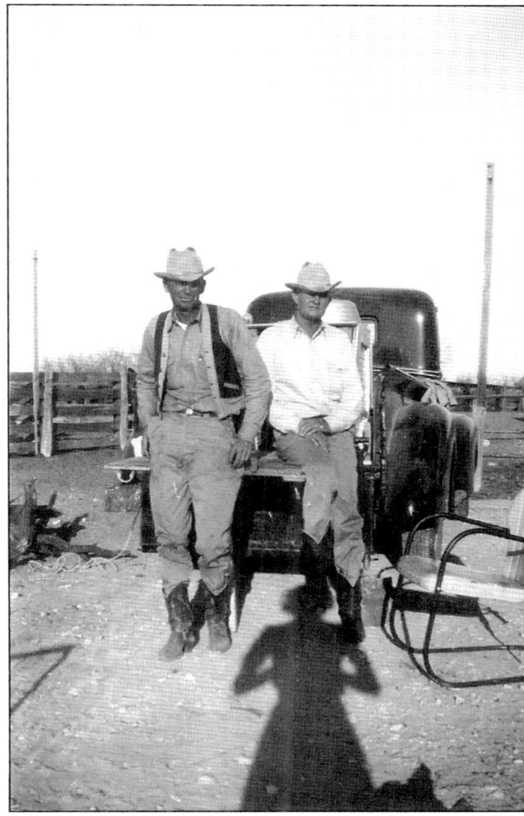

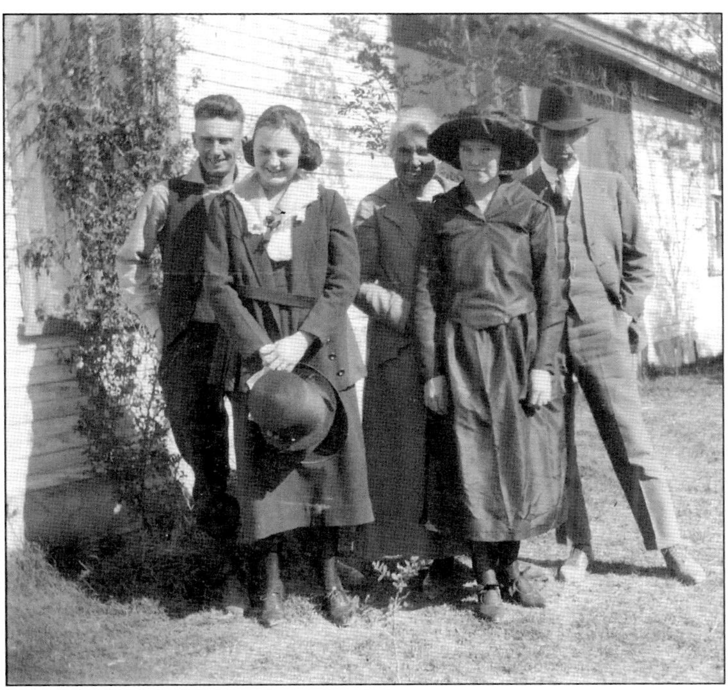

From left to right, Jay, June, and Katherine McGee, Donna Hammett, and Lawerence Webb stand by the house at the J Bar in Crane County. This photograph shows how happy and hospitable the McGees were. Williford Smith once stated, "June and Jay never had children. They loved having June's two nephews stay with them as often as her sister and husband, Nicie Lillian (Rhodes) and Calvin Monroe Smith, would let them." (Courtesy of Calvin and Suzahn Smith.)

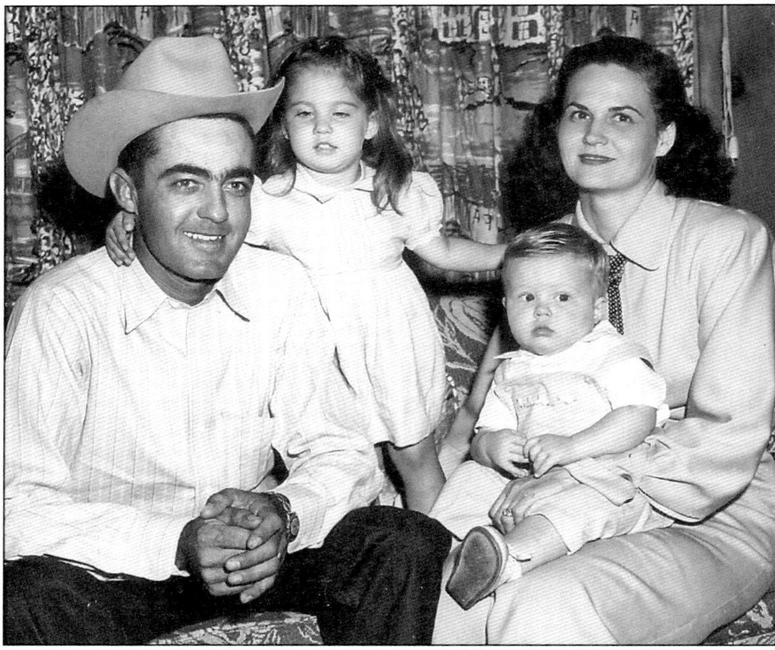

Acie Williford Bond, June McGee's great niece (far right), married Harold Smith (far left), and they had a daughter, Carol June (second from left), and a son, Willie Bond (third from left). The Smiths built a house next to Jay and June McGee on the J Bar Ranch and comprised the third generation of the ranch's history. (Courtesy of Calvin and Suzahn Smith.)

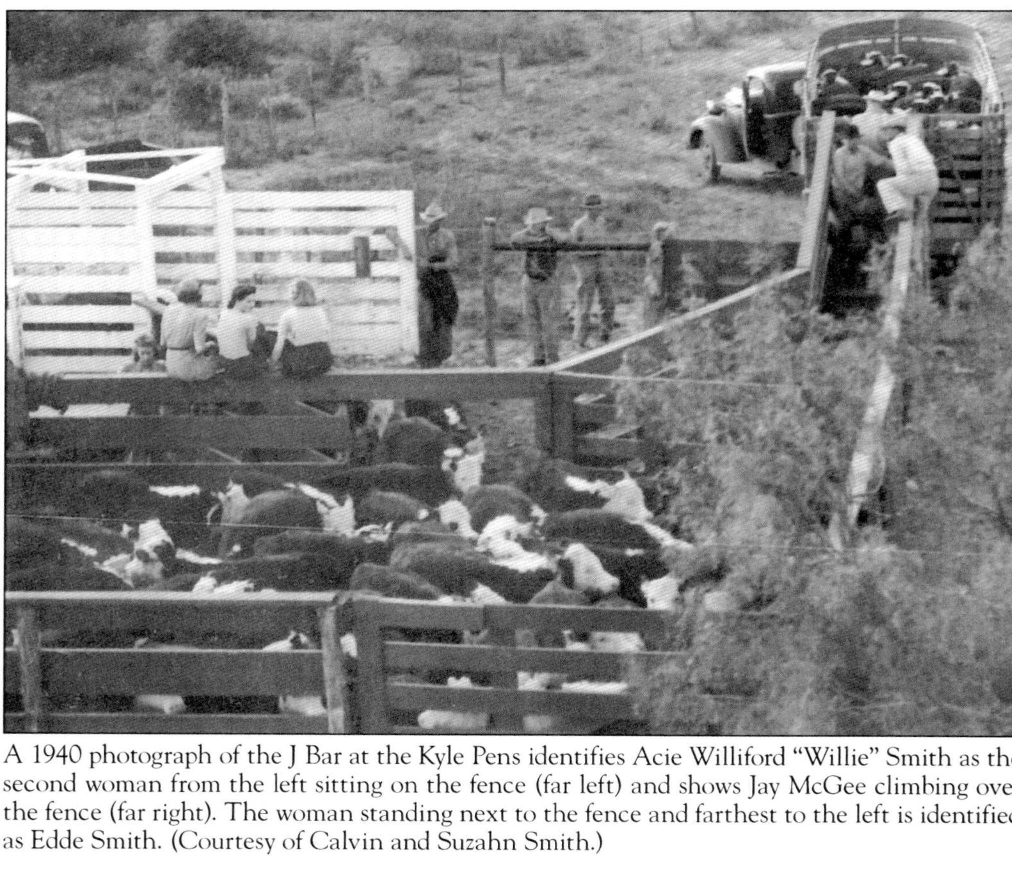

A 1940 photograph of the J Bar at the Kyle Pens identifies Acie Williford "Willie" Smith as the second woman from the left sitting on the fence (far left) and shows Jay McGee climbing over the fence (far right). The woman standing next to the fence and farthest to the left is identified as Edde Smith. (Courtesy of Calvin and Suzahn Smith.)

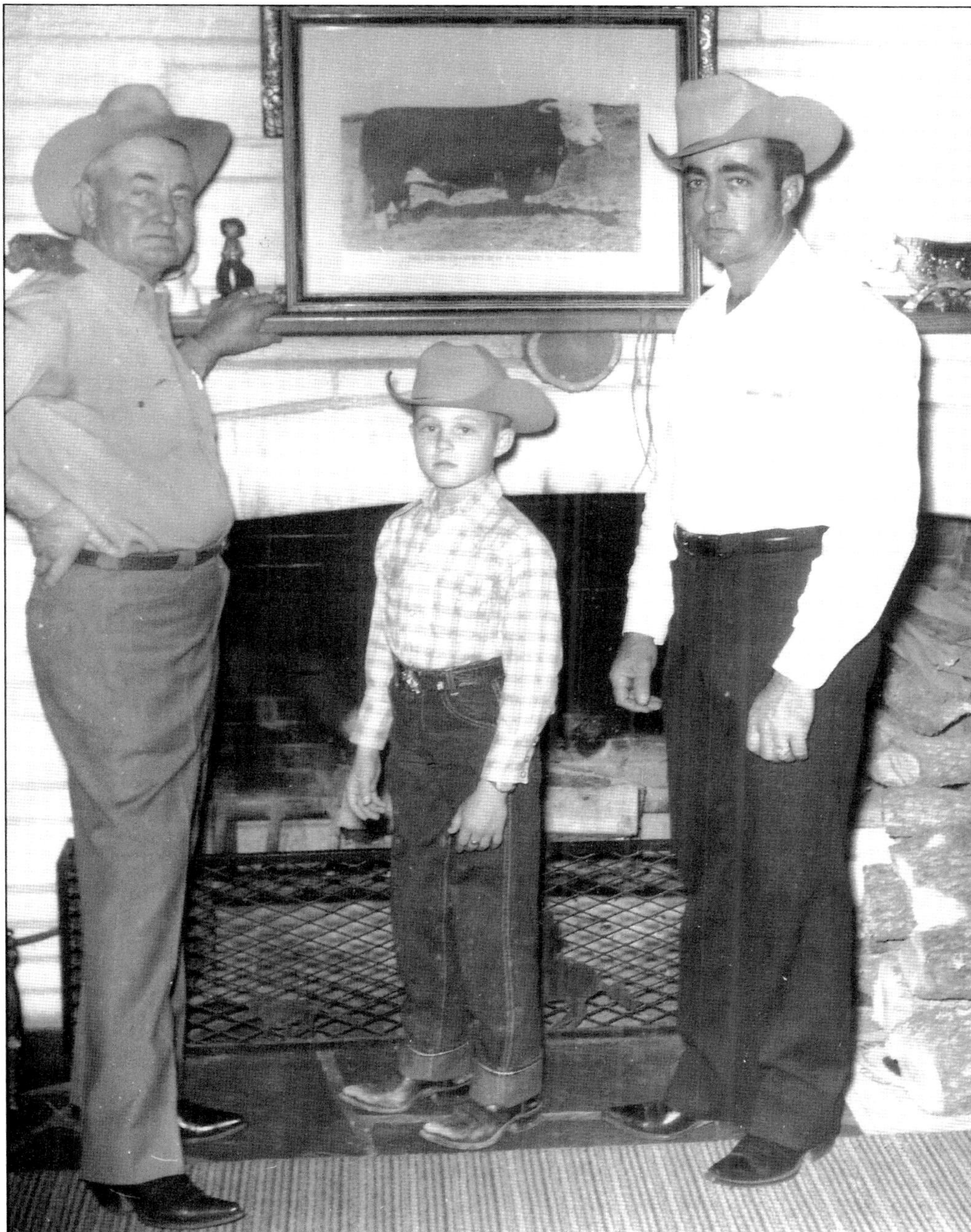

From left to right are Calvin Monroe Smith (married to one of June McGee's nieces), Calvin Bond Smith (Harold's son), and Harold Rhodes Smith (Calvin Monroe Smith's son). They are standing in the den of Calvin Monroe Smith's home. Together, these three men represent three of the six generations that have kept up the J Bar Ranch. (Courtesy of Calvin and Suzahn Smith.)

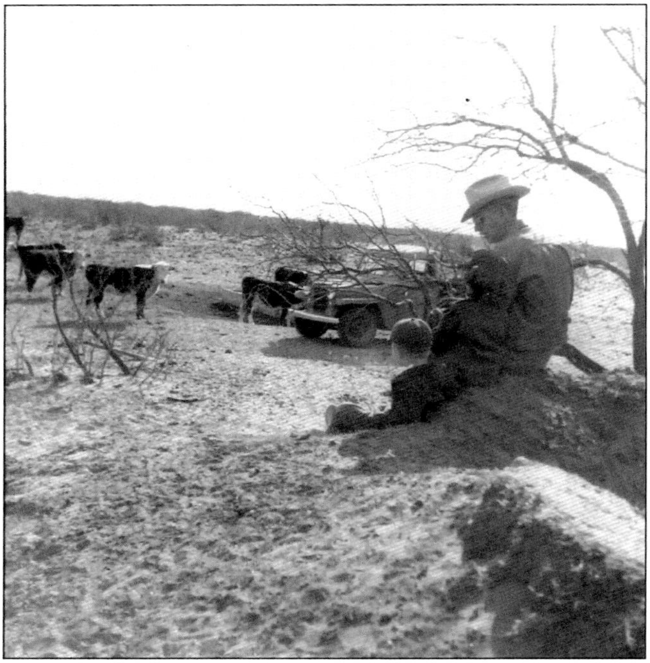

Jay McGee sits with his niece and nephew Carol and Calvin Smith around 1950 as they all overlook their Hereford cattle grazing near their jeep in the pasture. Ranching is a very family-oriented occupation and, as is obvious with the J Bar Ranch, takes everyone working together in order for it to be successful. (Courtesy of Calvin and Suzahn Smith.)

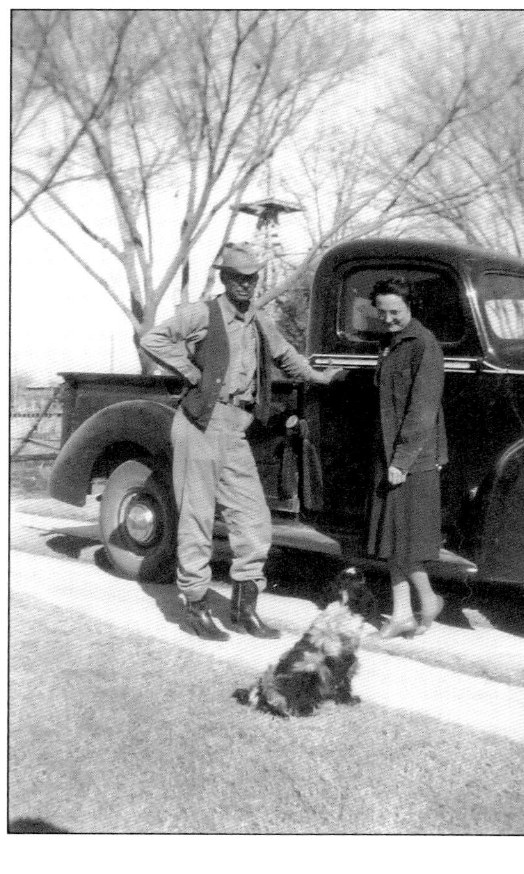

Jay and June McGee and their dog, Buddy, stand next to their Ford pickup at the J Bar headquarters in the 1950s. No ranch is complete without at least one faithful dog to keep its eyes on the place. Ranchers usually keep a well-trained canine, if not for a working dog then at least for a good companion. (Courtesy of Calvin and Suzahn Smith.)

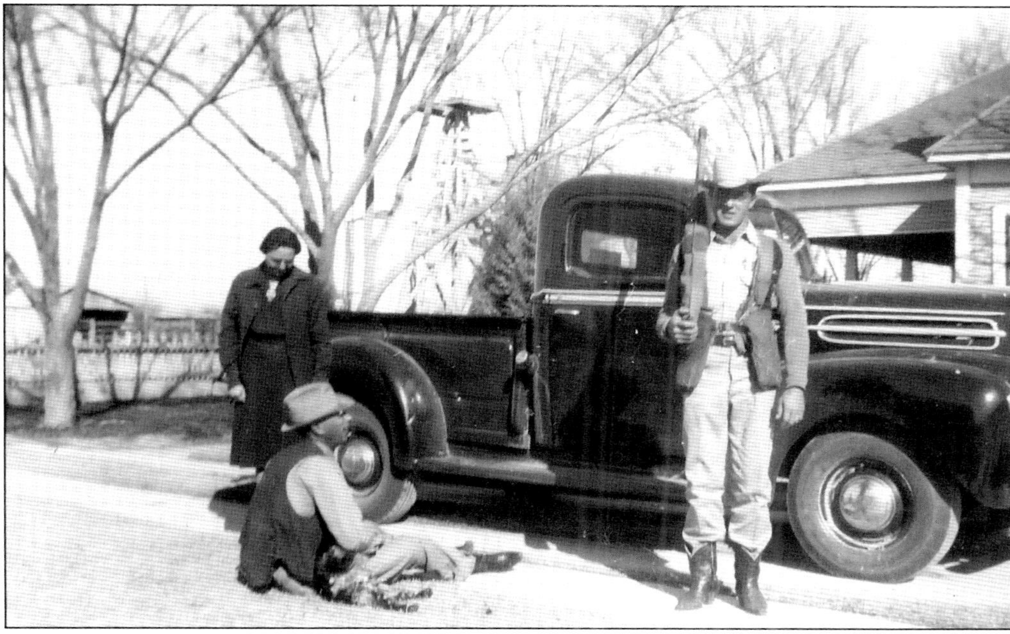

Harold Smith (far right) stands ready for quail hunting, and Jay McGee (second from left) pets his dog, Buddy, while June McGee (far left) looks on affectionately. Good as a sport and useful for putting food on the table, quail hunting for area residents is also a nice opportunity to relax with friends or family in the pasture. (Courtesy of Calvin and Suzahn Smith.)

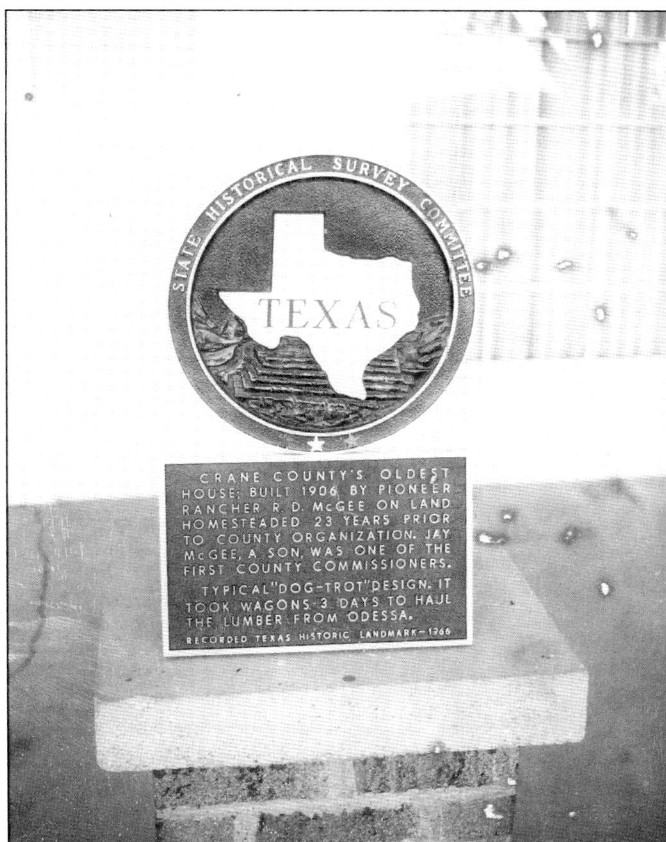

Dubbed Crane County's oldest house, the Texas State Historical Committee officially granted the J Bar Ranch home with an historical marker in 1966. Built by Robert Diogenes McGee in 1906, the J Bar house was constructed with lumber, which took three days to be hauled in from Odessa by horses and wagons. (Courtesy of Calvin and Suzahn Smith.)

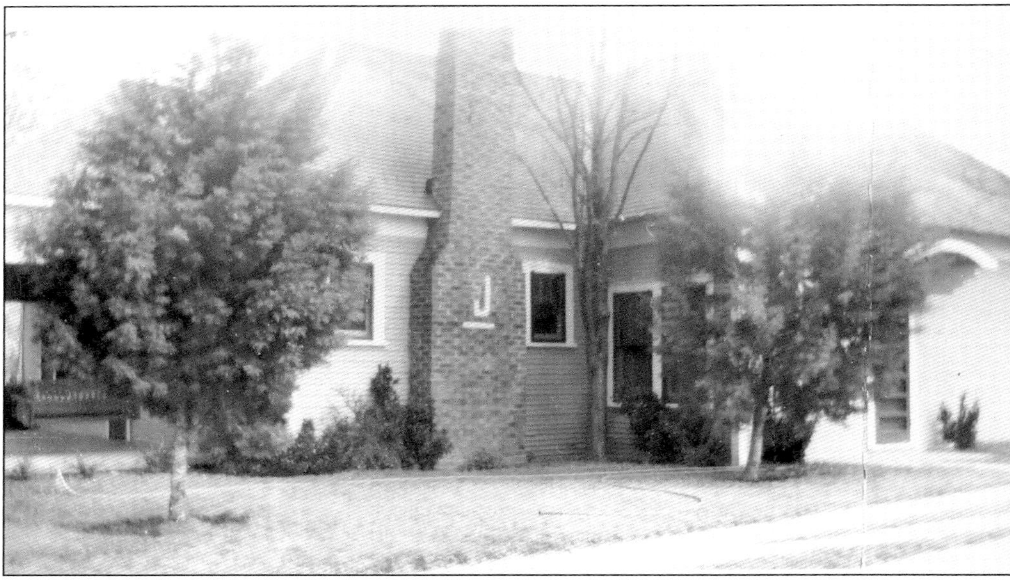

The McGees' ranch house, complete with the J Bar brand on the bricks of the chimney, has been standing for more than 100 years. A 1940 photograph of the J Bar Ranch houses (below) shows Jay McGee's house on the left and a home built by Harold Smith next to the original home on the right. The successive generations of the ranch are as follows: Robert Diogenes and Katherine McGee; Jay D. and June Lucille McGee; Harold Rhodes Smith and Acie Williford Smith; Calvin Bond Smith and Lillian Suzahn Smith; Jason Calvin Smith and Lynn Dee Marie Smith; Justin Rhodes Smith and Amanda Leigh Smith; and Jordan Jay Smith. (Courtesy of Calvin and Suzahn Smith.)

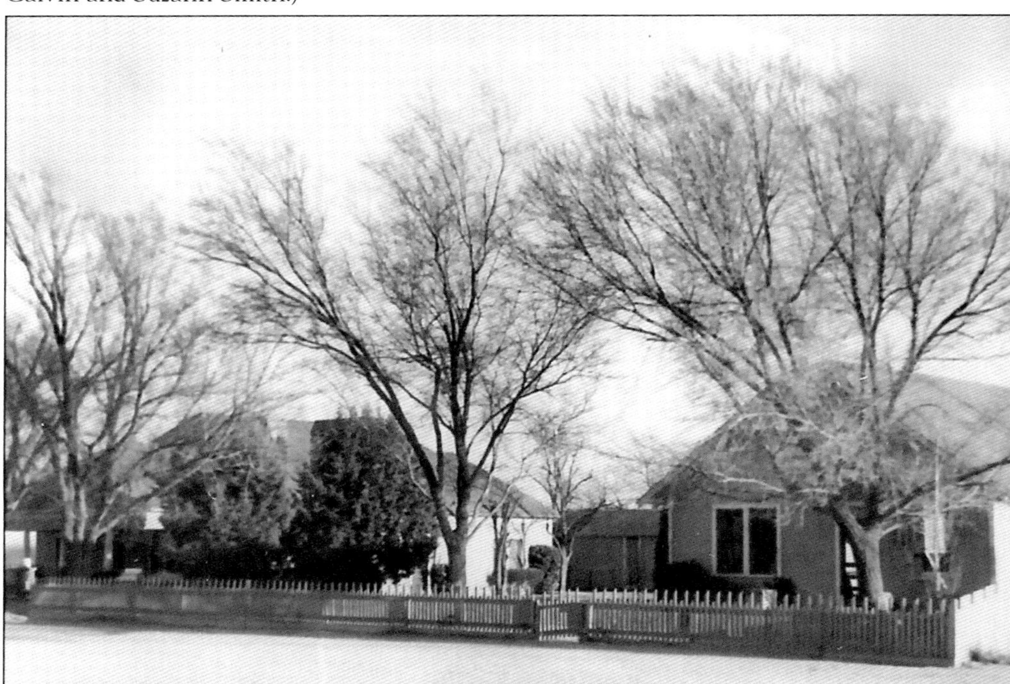

Three

Black Gold

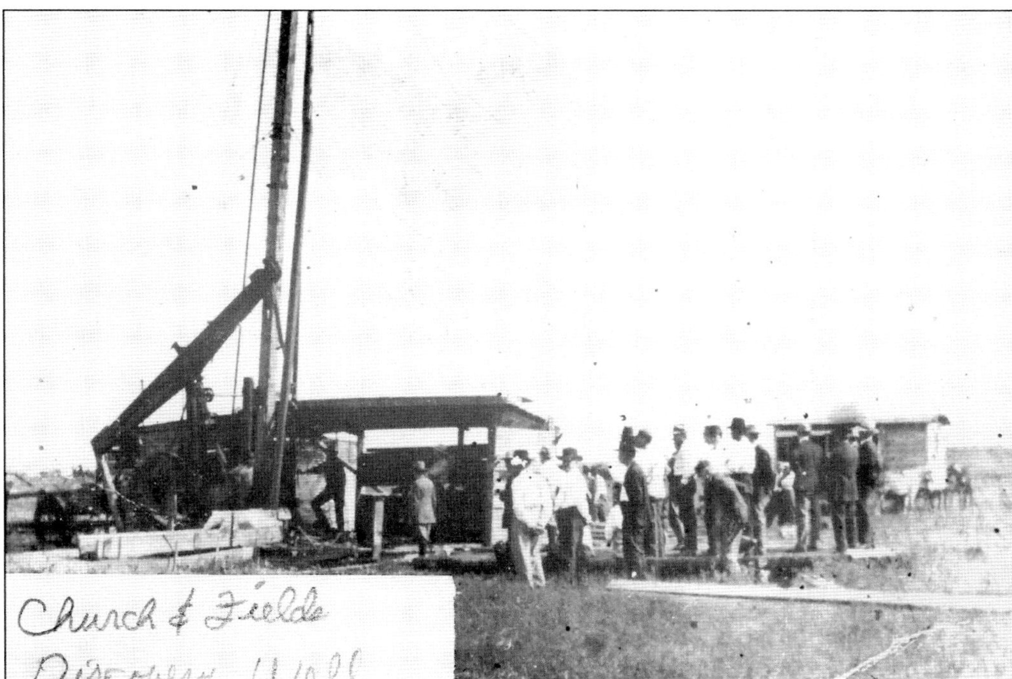

The Church and Fields oil well on the McElroy Ranch was the first successful drill in the county. George M. Church and Robert Fields partnered up after acquiring a permit on the McElroy University Lands and celebrated its first yield in March 1926. Along with Reagan and Upton Counties, Crane County is home to a majority of the original oil production in the Permian Basin.

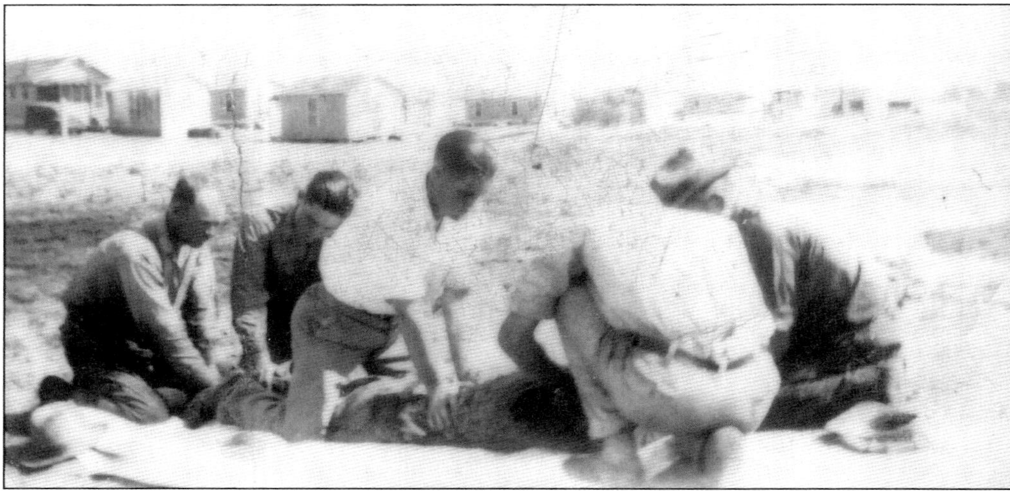

Even amid advances in modern technology, oil and gas industries continue to and always have posed hazards. Staying prepared for the worst at the Humble Oil and Refinery Corporation camp in 1927, this photograph of the first aid team captured, from left to right, Vay Roberts, D.D. Dendy, Ross Smith, ? Burns, ? Brown, and Waggoner Roach.

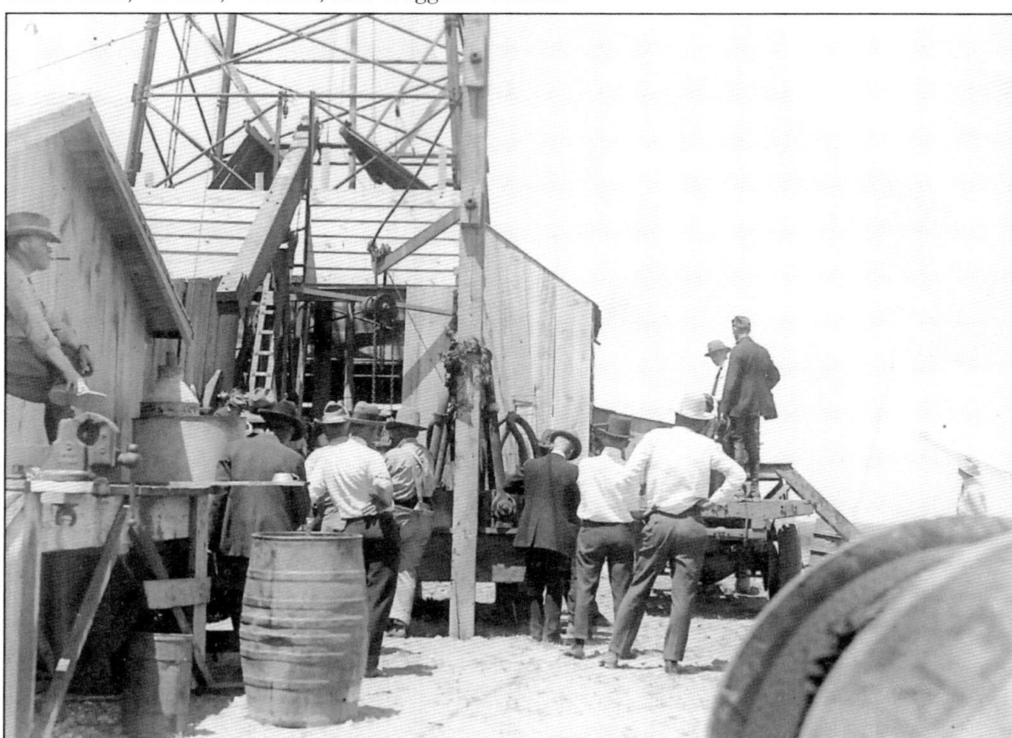

Pictured here is the first well of the Texas Development Corporation on the Jax Cowden Ranch. Although it was spudded on April 3, 1924, the site was leased on November 9, 1923. Amid the typical configuration of an oil well, a man rests against the pump house to smoke a cigar while several men gather around the pump jack and two other men inspect operations from a trailer parked next to the derrick.

The first well of the Gulf Oil Corporation in Crane County, this well sparked the beginning of a major employment opportunity for many citizens in the following years. A gusher spews from the rig pictured here as a man identified as Mr. Kid rushes to tend to the well's successful flow of oil. The descendants of former Gulf Oil Corporation employees still remember the early days of the oil boom and living in the camps with their parents. Even though these camps are a thing of the past, the stories are just as alive as the industry is today. People came for different reasons, but many oilfield employees were primarily baseball players, and the different companies had teams that held tournaments with each other.

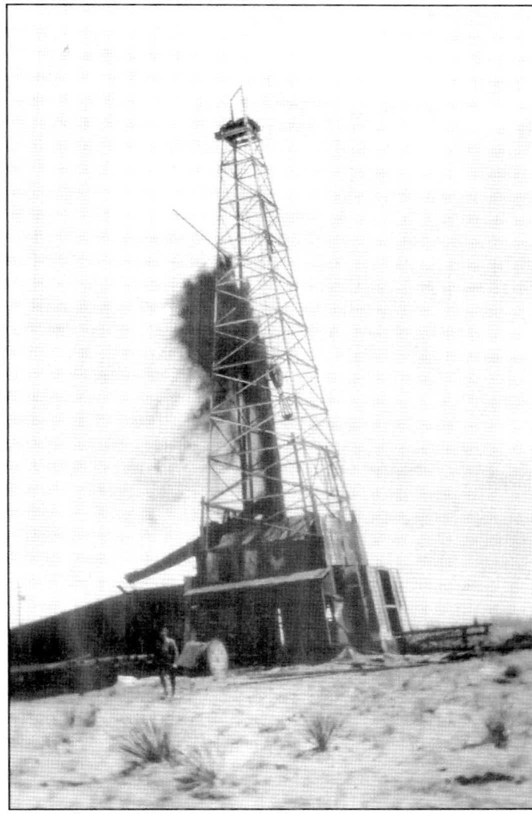

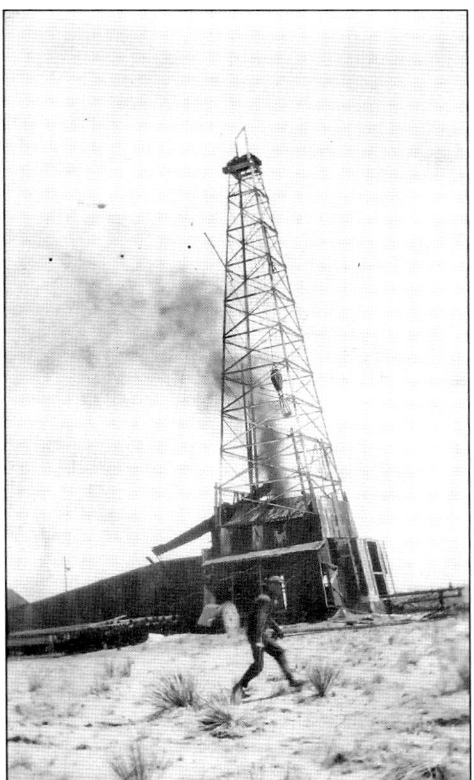

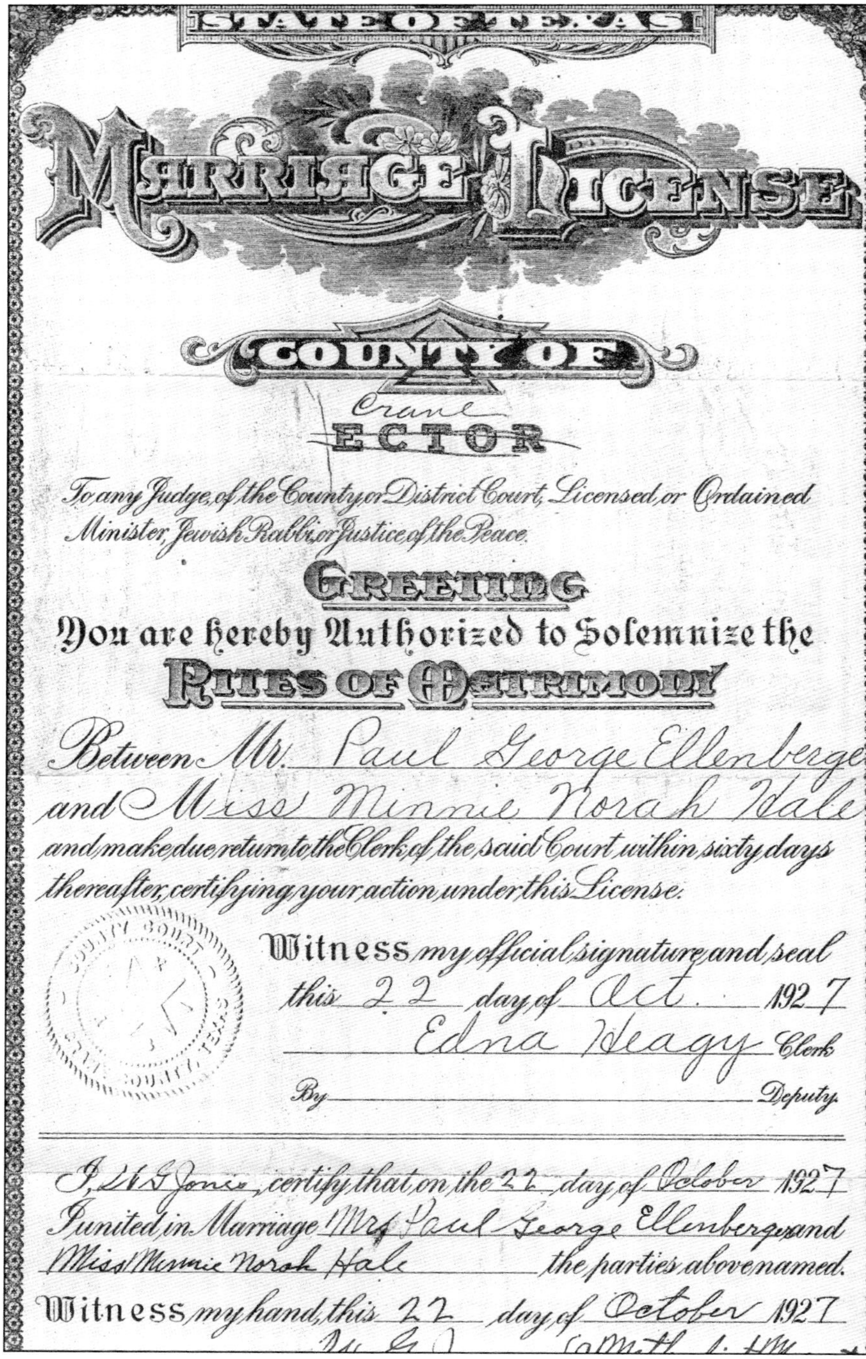
STATE OF TEXAS

MARRIAGE LICENSE

COUNTY OF

Crane

~~ECTOR~~

To any Judge, of the County or District Court, Licensed or Ordained Minister, Jewish Rabbi, or Justice of the Peace.

GREETING

You are hereby Authorized to Solemnize the

RITES OF MATRIMONY

Between Mr. Paul George Ellenberger
and Miss Minnie Norah Hale
and make due return to the Clerk of the said Court within sixty days thereafter, certifying your action under this License.

Witness my official signature and seal
this 22 day of Oct. 1927
Edna Heagy Clerk
By ____________ Deputy

I, W G Jones, certify that on the 22 day of October 1927
I united in Marriage Mr Paul George Ellenberger and
Miss Minnie Norah Hale the parties abovenamed.
Witness my hand, this 22 day of October 1927

A marriage license from Ector County, the next county to the north, was found useful in the newly formed Crane County simply by marking out "Ector." Crane County officially organized in August 1927, two months before Minnie Norah Hale and Paul George Ellenberger married. On September 3, 1927, county officials' elections were held, and the place where future Crane couples united in marriage started to form its own entity.

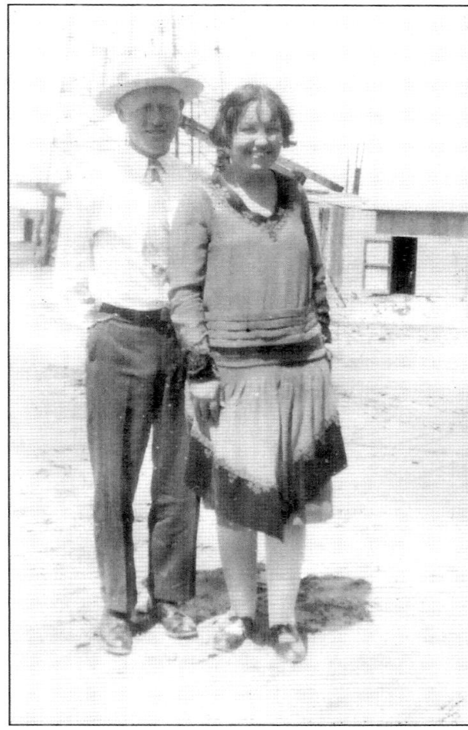

Many Texas couples moved to small towns like Crane and began careers out of the era's promising oil boom. Pictured on the right are newlyweds Paul George Ellenberger and Minnie Norah Hale on the State University Lease for Humble Oil and Refinery Corporation in Crane County. Ellenberger was a farm boss, and Mrs. Ellenberger served as a first aid nurse for the Humble camp. Crane County oilfield camps nurtured family life and fellowship. On October 12, 1928, Mrs. Ellenberger holds her two-week-old baby, Sarah Elizabeth (below). An invitation that read "We'll shower her with gifts of love, / On Tuesday, August, Twenty-eighth, / At the Gulf camp, in the Recreation Hall, / Come at two thirty, and don't be late" welcomed guests to a baby shower held in honor of the mother-to-be.

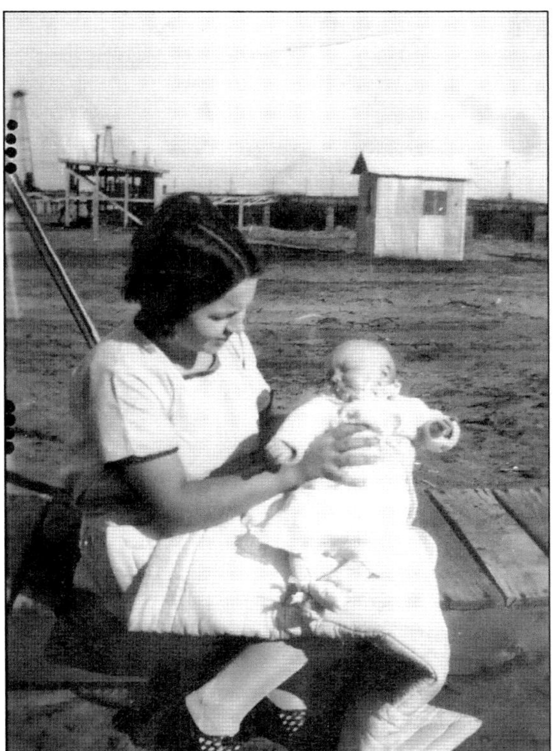

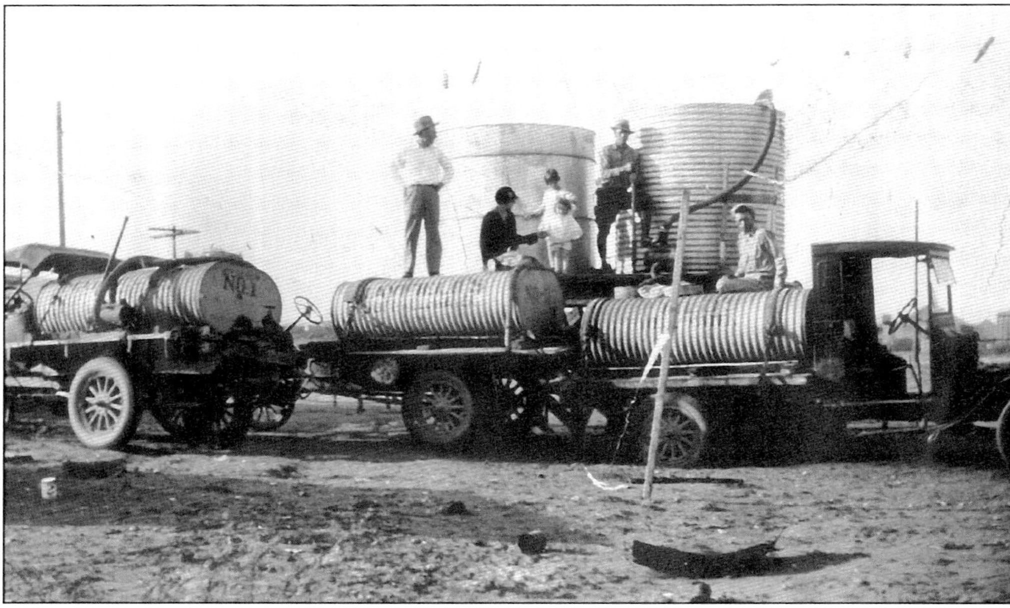

A c. 1920s photograph of K.V. Melton's water storage and delivery truck crew reminds present-day Cranites how much of a blessing plumbing and water availability is for convenience. The crew potentially delivered water to the camps for use in the homes of the residents. A man's wife and their two children stand on top of the truck next to the water tanks.

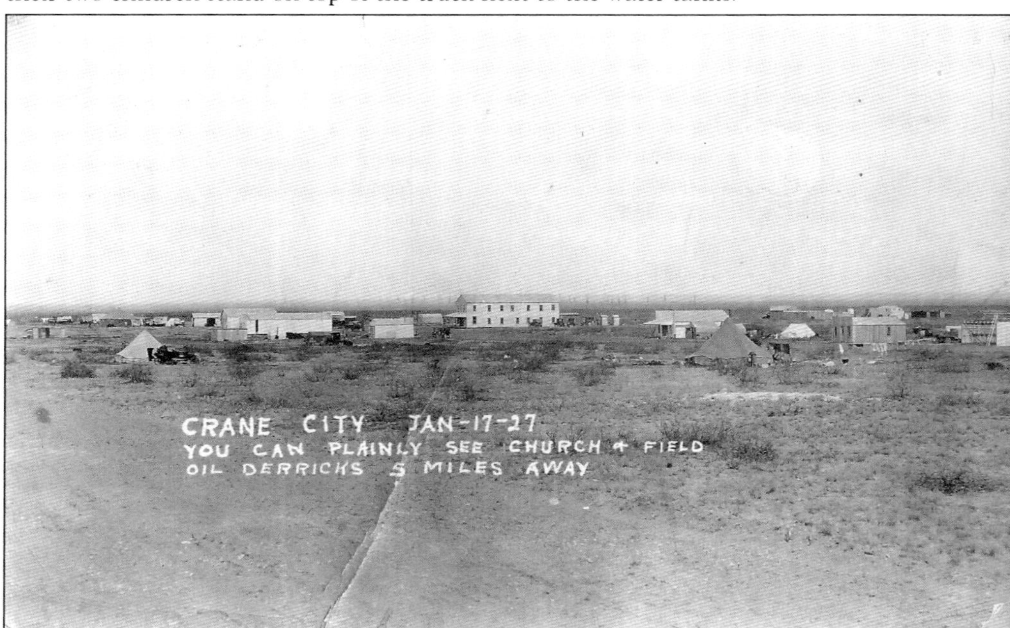

Crane began on the outskirts of the oil fields and literally started in tents, as far as the residents were concerned. This photograph reads, "CRANE CITY JAN—17—27 YOU CAN PLAINLY SEE CHURCH AND FIELD OIL DERRICKS 5 MILES AWAY." As the rigs pump in the background, a lady works outside of her tent washing and hanging up the laundry while a little girl plays in the dirt.

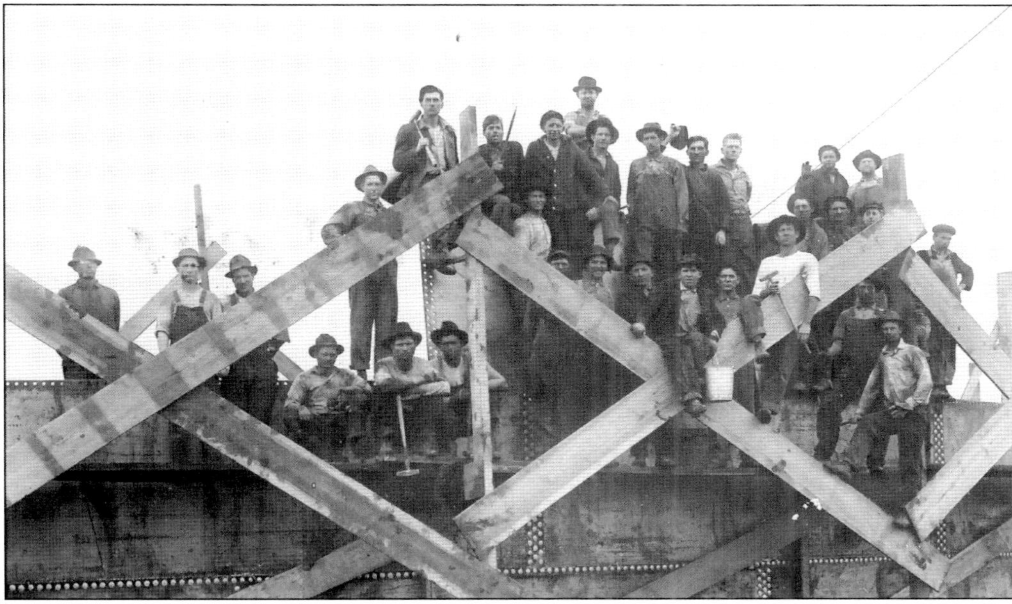

The men of a rig-building crew stop on the scaffolding of their worksite for a photograph. Modern-day derricks are built from steel, but in the beginning of the business, they were all wooden. Many of the first homes in Crane were built from tin and the oil-soaked wood of old derricks and, consequently, several families suffered the loss of their homes at the faintest spark or flame.

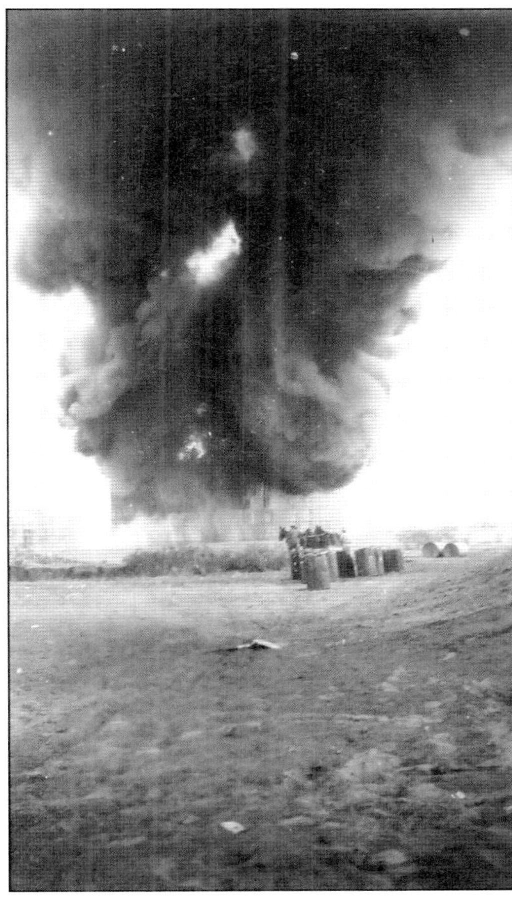

Oil is usually stored in large tanks, like the one pictured here, at what are duly called tank farms. At 2:15 p.m. on May 9, 1928, lightning struck this particular 80,000-barrel oil tank and created the explosion and billowing smoke captured in this photograph. Each barrel (right front) would constitute about 50 gallons of the "rich Texas tea."

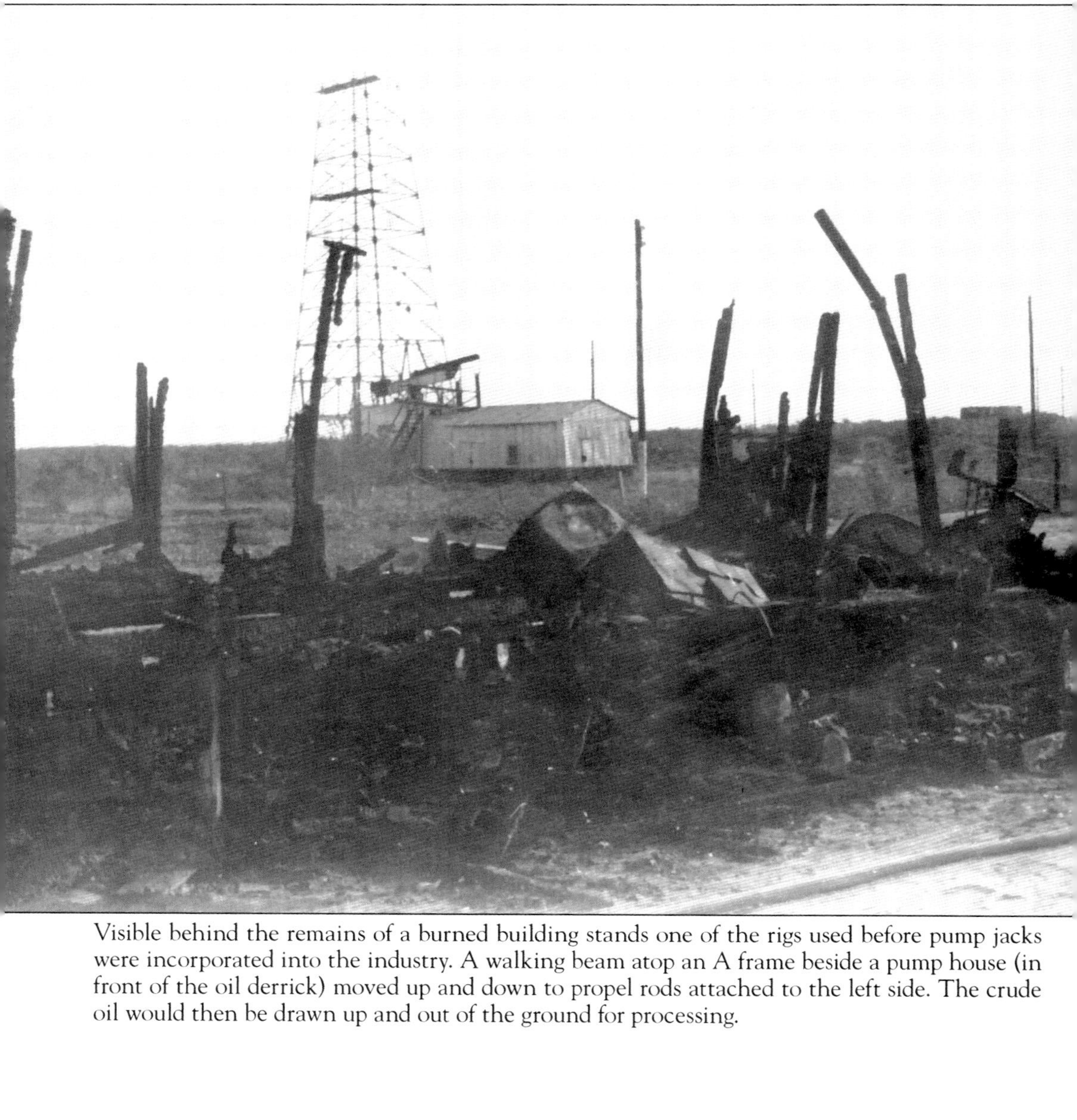

Visible behind the remains of a burned building stands one of the rigs used before pump jacks were incorporated into the industry. A walking beam atop an A frame beside a pump house (in front of the oil derrick) moved up and down to propel rods attached to the left side. The crude oil would then be drawn up and out of the ground for processing.

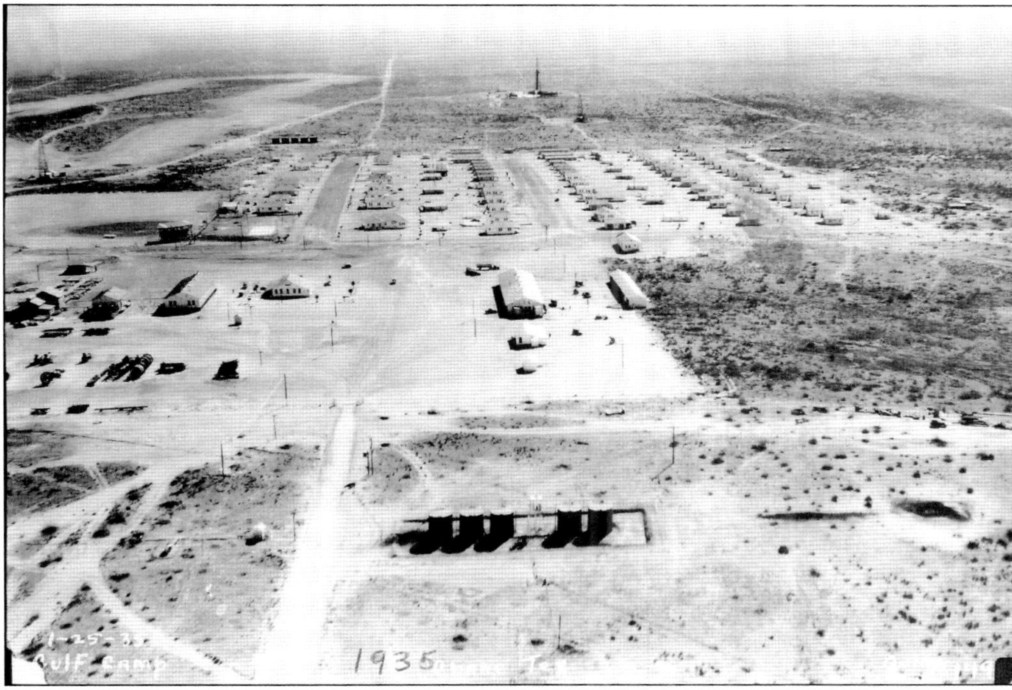

Taken on January 25, 1935, this aerial shot shows Gulf Camp in its original location (off of present-day Rankin Highway). Housing is visible in the back center, an oil derrick stands in the far back, a warehouse resides in the center, the central work station is seen at the far left, and holding tanks are discernible in the front of the photograph.

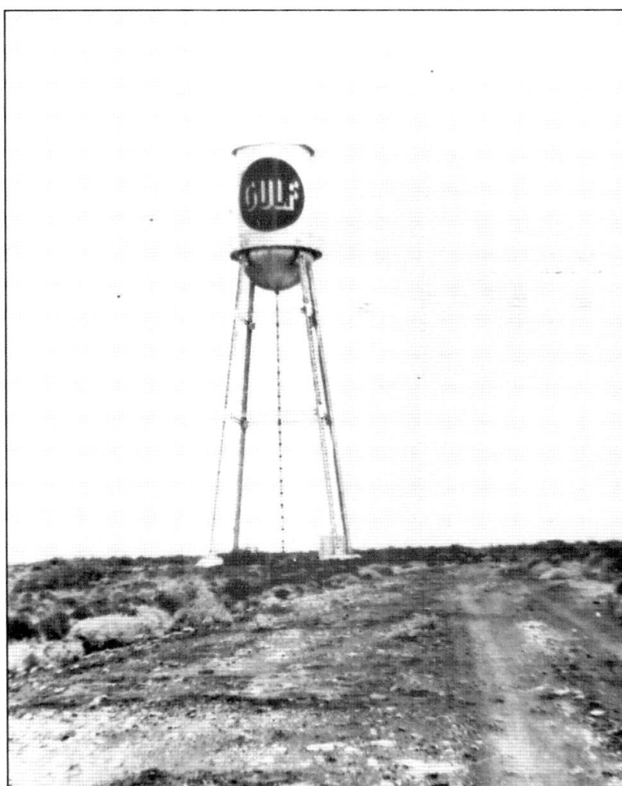

At a later date, camp was relocated to Roark, Twenty-first, Twenty-second, Twenty-third, and Twenty-fourth Streets. A water tower for the residents of the camp in the new site displays the company logo amid the big West Texas sky. A story floated around town about how four boys, two of whom were Gene Cowden and Art Looney, allegedly blew up one of the legs and had to pay for the damages.

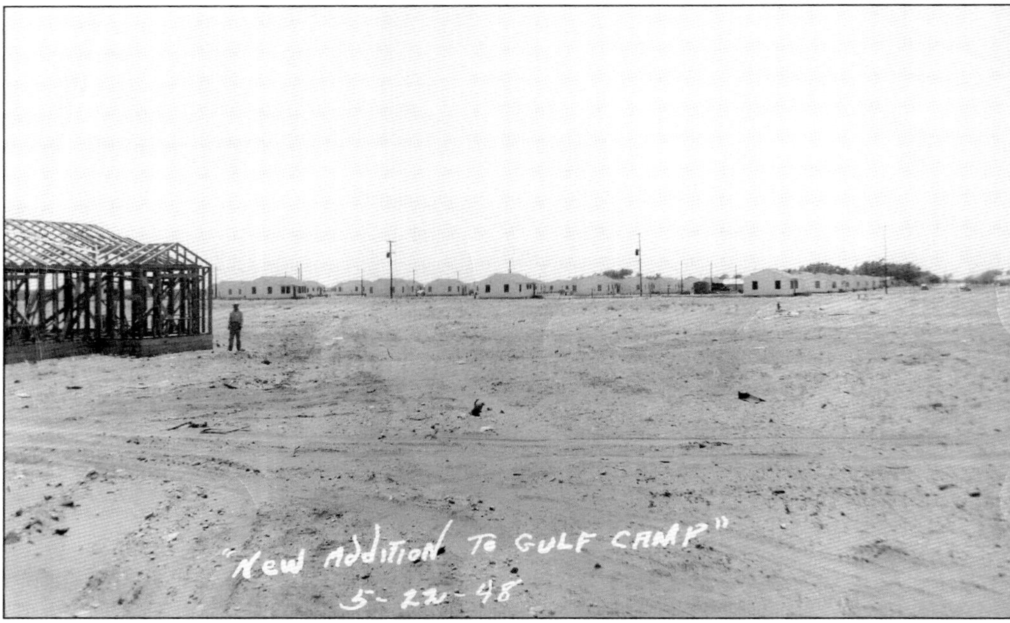

Photographs of new buildings under construction at the Gulf Camp captured several men working on two unfinished projects. A man stands next to the frame of one new addition (above), and four men work on the incomplete roof of a new brick office building (below) on May 22, 1948. The location of this Gulf Camp currently serves as the neighborhood of present-day Crane residents, some of whom still live in remodeled versions of the very same houses where Gulf residents dwelled. These shotgun houses were by no means extravagant, but the humble homes, for the most part, served their purpose as a safe haven from the elements. Some children of Gulf employees still remember their mothers covering up windows and cracks around the doors with dampened sheets during dust storms in hopes that less sand would blow in.

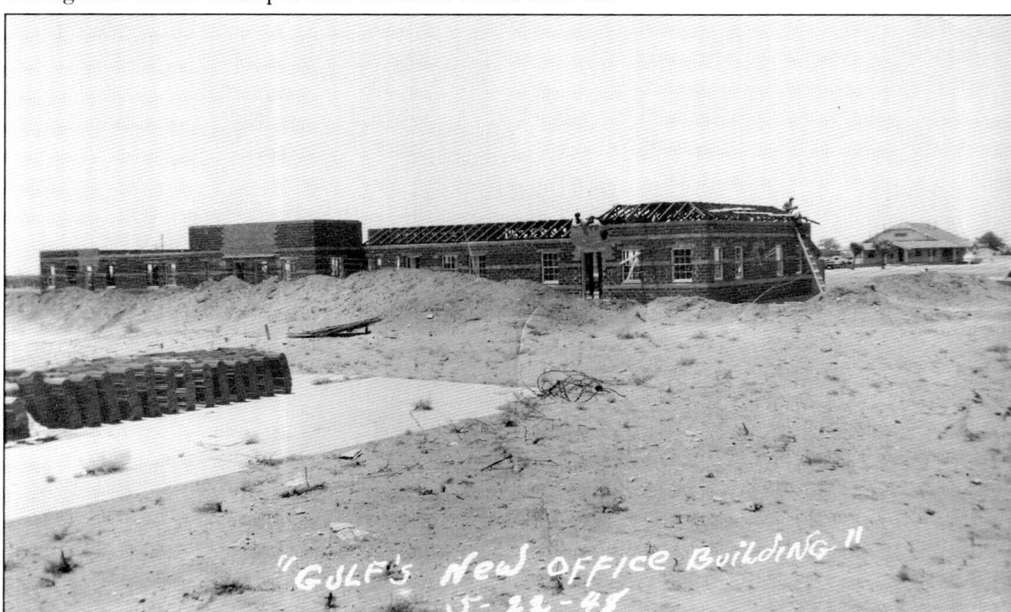

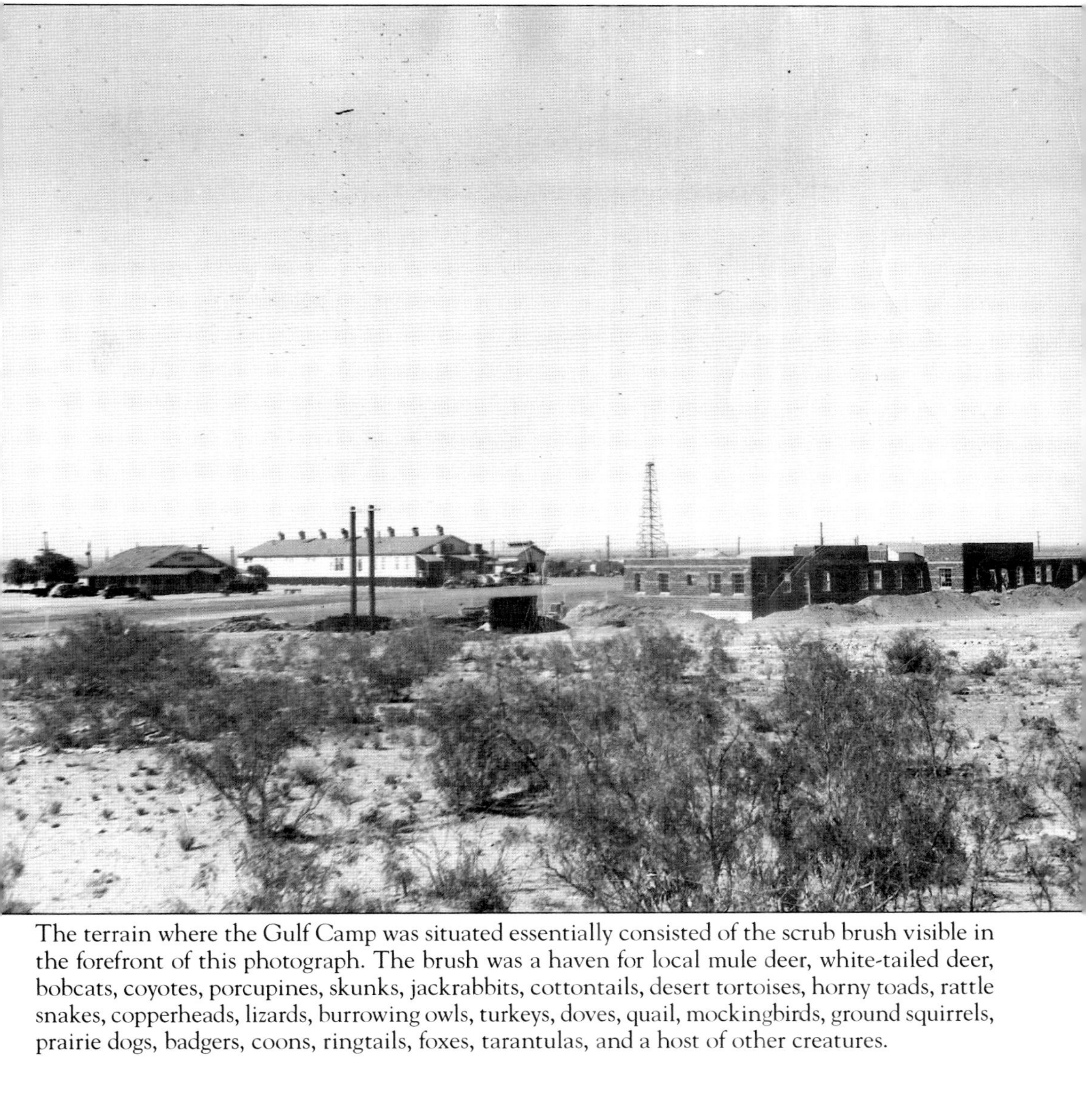

The terrain where the Gulf Camp was situated essentially consisted of the scrub brush visible in the forefront of this photograph. The brush was a haven for local mule deer, white-tailed deer, bobcats, coyotes, porcupines, skunks, jackrabbits, cottontails, desert tortoises, horny toads, rattle snakes, copperheads, lizards, burrowing owls, turkeys, doves, quail, mockingbirds, ground squirrels, prairie dogs, badgers, coons, ringtails, foxes, tarantulas, and a host of other creatures.

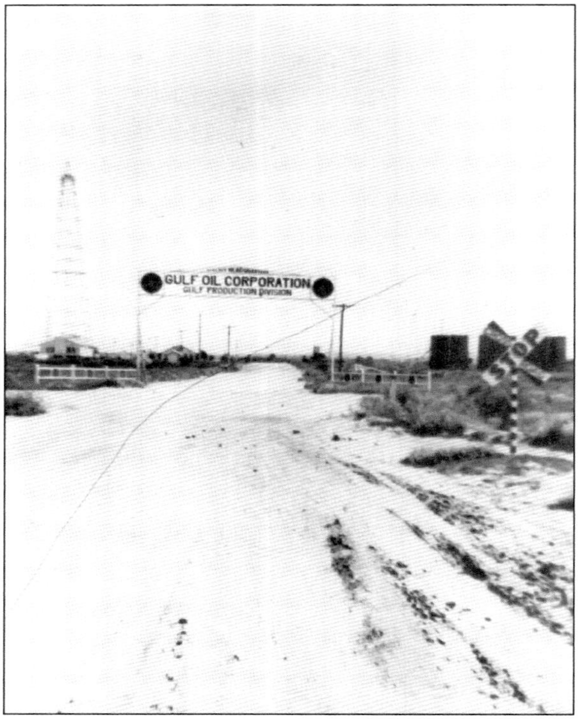

A photograph of the Gulf Oil Corporation entrance in Crane County shows oil tanks in the back right, an oil derrick on the left, and several small buildings amongst electrical poles. Taken after the company had grown in the area and relocated to McElroy Ranch land, this photograph dates from 1948.

Identified in this early-1950s photograph of a Gulf Camp reunion are Bud Horne, Chief Hendricks, Jumbo Williams (below Bud Horne), Buck Lewis, P.O. Vines, John Woody, Jack Mills, and Lee Turner. Being in the camps was obviously more than an occupation; rather, it was a rugged way of life for the committed families that called it home.

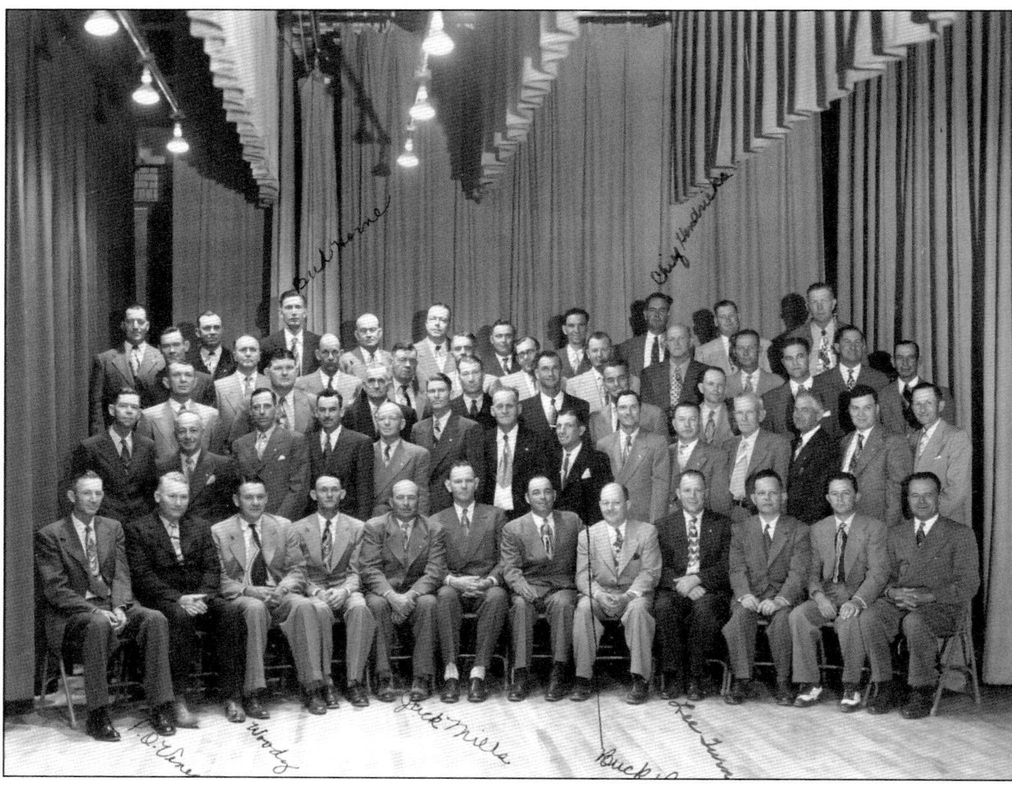

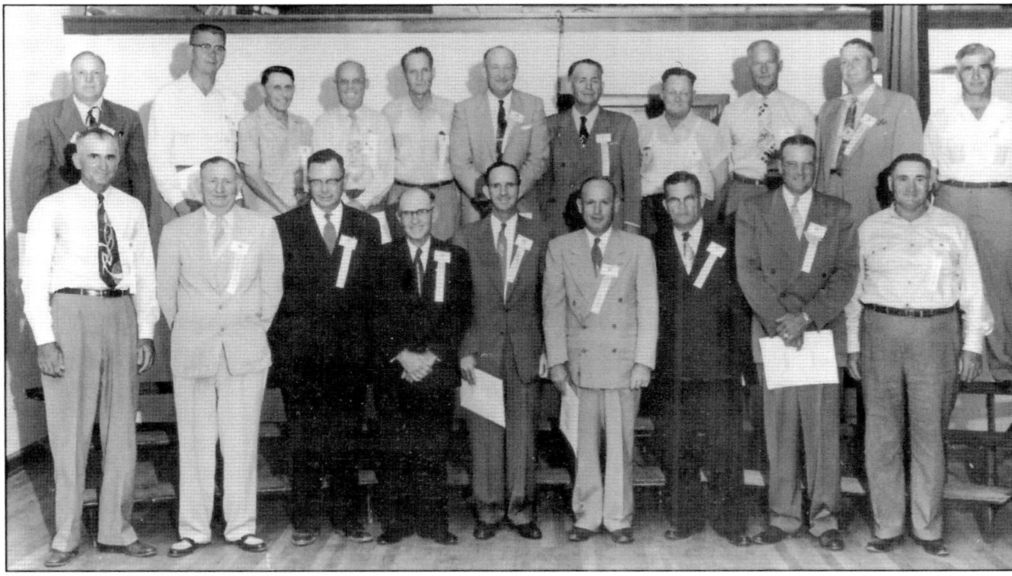

Two rows of Gulf employees in 1949 standing from left to right are (first row) Gordon Wood, unidentified, O.L. Chenevich, O.M. Rustin, two unidentified, ? Hussey, unidentified, and Seed Coker; (second row) Jim Snelson, two unidentified, Red Mills, three unidentified, Frank Lakin, A.L. Higdon, Josh Johnston, and Jim Zarafonetis.

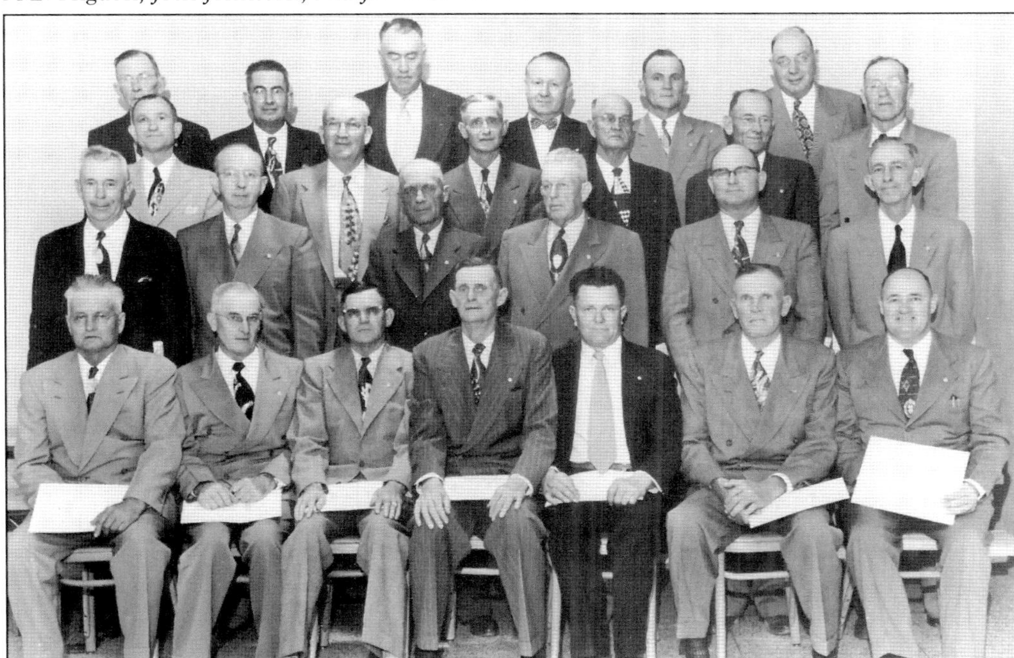

Gulf Corporation employees posing for a photograph on an unknown date are, from left to right, (first row) Hershel Evans, M.A. Daniels, E.E. McLauren, J.H. Huggins Sr., O.Y. Idom, and two unidentified; (second row) Tom Caldwell, E.A. Crites, Charles "Chief" Hendrix, Fred Hays, A.M. Murrell, and unidentified; (third row) Martin Boone, ? Davis, G.B. Ingram, and three unidentified; (fourth row) all unidentified.

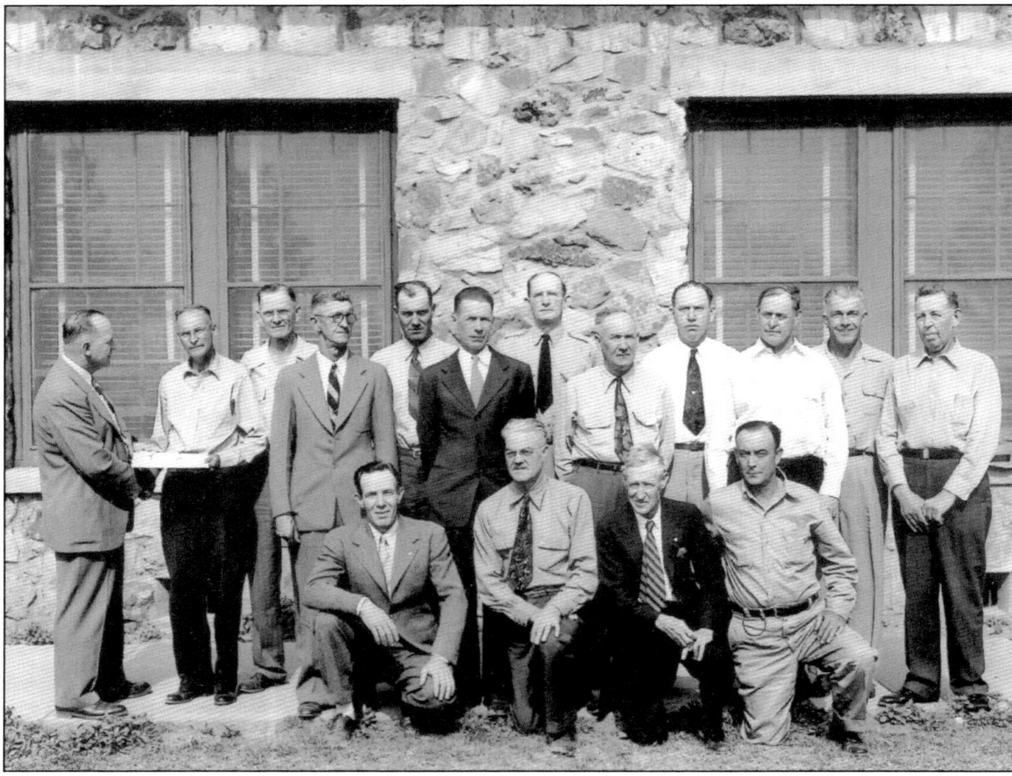

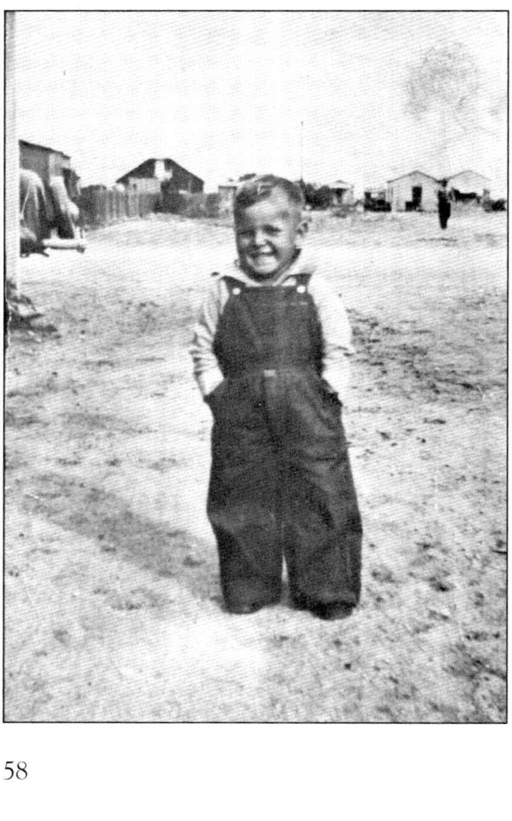

This photograph shows all of the McElroy Gulf Camp employees on an unknown date. They are, from left to right, (first row) three unidentified and Thomas Garrett; (second row) Bill Todd, Jim Branam, Dewey Holcomb, Red McAfee, Realons Maynard, and Leanard B. Henderson; (third row) Bill Havin, John Hayes, Emmett Miller, Rube Smith, unidentified, and Fred Murray.

A newspaper clipping reminds readers of the good old days in the oil camps. Hayes Damron's little boy Doug Damron is all grins as he poses for the camera in his overalls. Like many other Crane dads, his father worked in the oilfield and raised his family with small-town values. In good humor, a friend of Doug ran this "wanted" photograph of him in the Crane newspaper. (Courtesy of Betty Damron.)

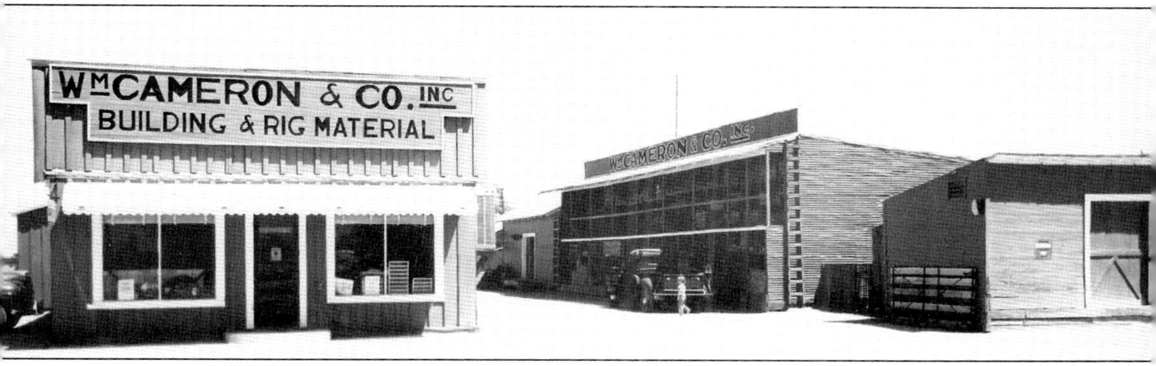

Without the oil and gas industry, small West Texas oil towns would not be able to thrive. Welding businesses, along with others that revolve around the industry, provide the necessary tools and resources for the production and maintenance of pipelines and other operations involved with extracting, processing, storing, and moving oil and natural gas. WM Cameron & Co., Inc., was one of several businesses that have come and gone in Crane throughout the years.

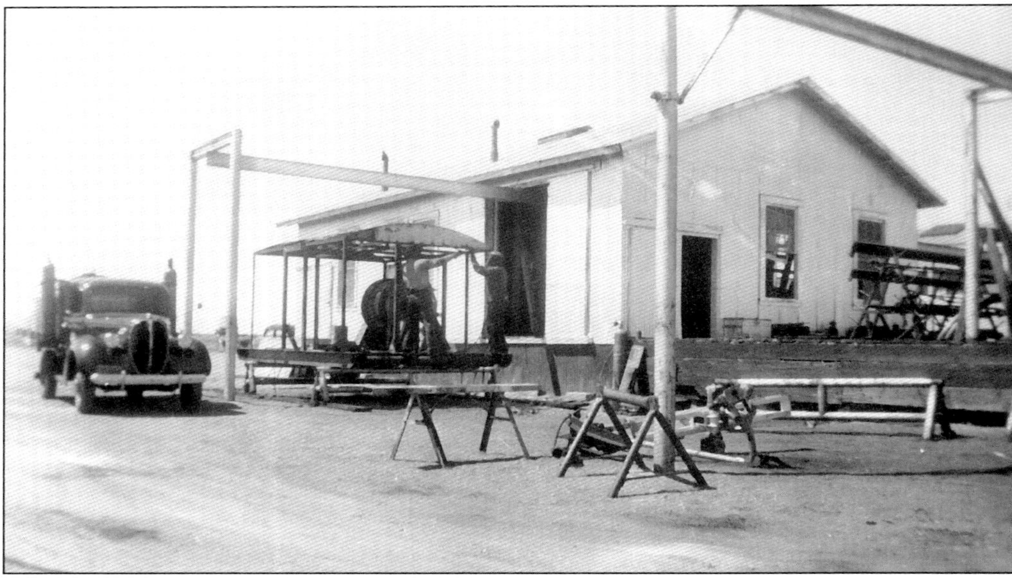

Two men work on the frame of a metal structure at an unidentified location in Crane County. Among their many services, welding businesses were instrumental in constructing pipelines that carried the oil and gas to desired locations. This photograph dates from either the late 1930s or early 1940s. (Courtesy of Betty Damron.)

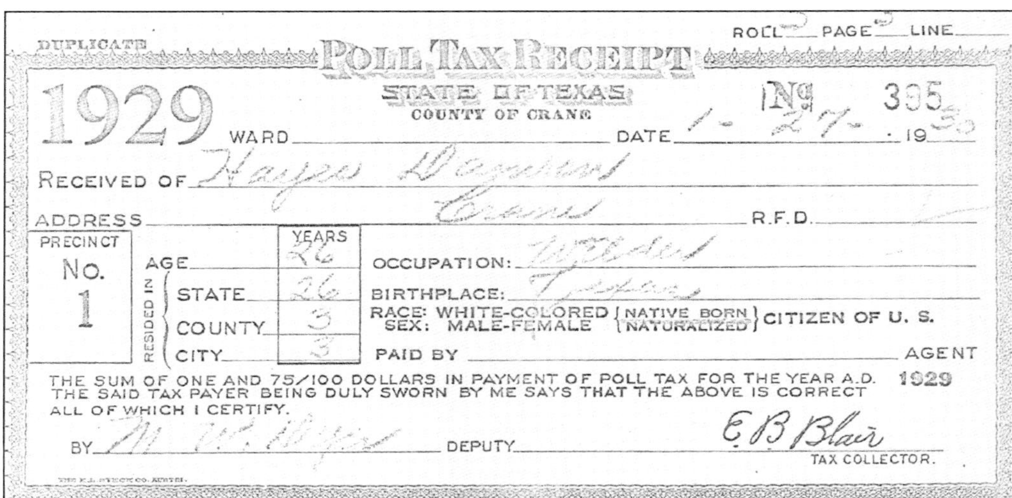

DUPLICATE

ROLL ___ PAGE ___ LINE ___

POLL TAX RECEIPT

1929

STATE OF TEXAS
COUNTY OF CRANE

No 395

WARD ___ DATE 1-27-1930

RECEIVED OF Hayes Damron

ADDRESS Crane R.F.D. ___

PRECINCT No. 1

	YEARS
AGE	26
RESIDED IN STATE	26
RESIDED IN COUNTY	3
RESIDED IN CITY	3

OCCUPATION: Welder

BIRTHPLACE: Texas

RACE: WHITE-COLORED
SEX: MALE-FEMALE
{NATIVE BORN / NATURALIZED} CITIZEN OF U. S.

PAID BY ___ AGENT

THE SUM OF ONE AND 75/100 DOLLARS IN PAYMENT OF POLL TAX FOR THE YEAR A.D. 1929
THE SAID TAX PAYER BEING DULY SWORN BY ME SAYS THAT THE ABOVE IS CORRECT
ALL OF WHICH I CERTIFY.

BY ___ DEPUTY E B Blair
TAX COLLECTOR.

A poll tax receipt from Crane County for welder Hayes Damron reminds voters today about the Jim Crow laws, which made voting a privilege only for those who had the means with which to pay for it. Signed by tax collector E.B. Blair, this receipt dates from January 27, 1930. (Courtesy of Betty Damron.)

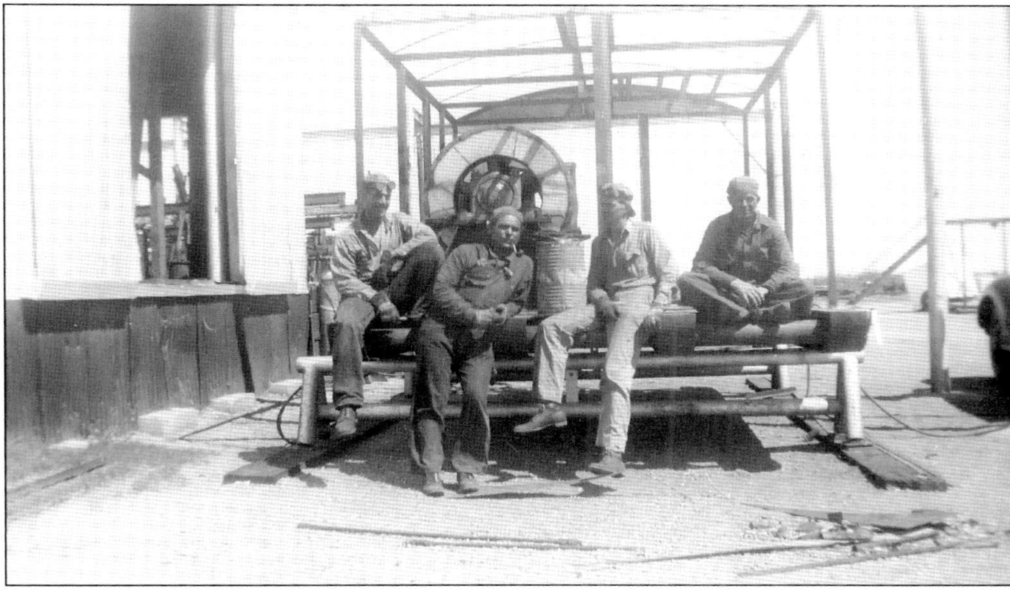

Hayes Damron (second from the left) owned Damron Welding before his son Doug Damron took it over. Local resident Spud Curfew remembers a welder Damron once hired who was missing one of his hands. Having a hook instead, this man was able to handle the hot metal welders that others needed to let cool first, and in one instance, he accidentally welded a pipe to his hook. (Courtesy of Betty Damron.)

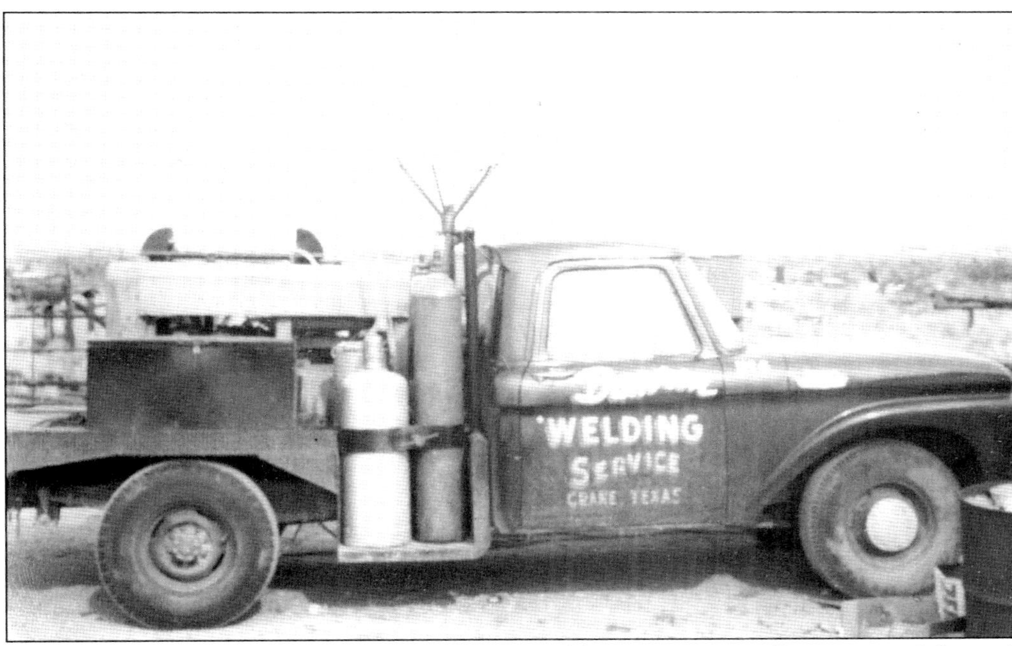

A photograph of the welding truck for Damron Welding gives an excellent image of the tools necessary to complete a job, such as two large bottles in the center that hold oxygen and acetylene for cutting steel, a toolbox on the left (keeping things like a torch), welding rods, hoses, gloves, hoods, extra tips, and a slag hammer. The welding machine itself is visible at the back left.

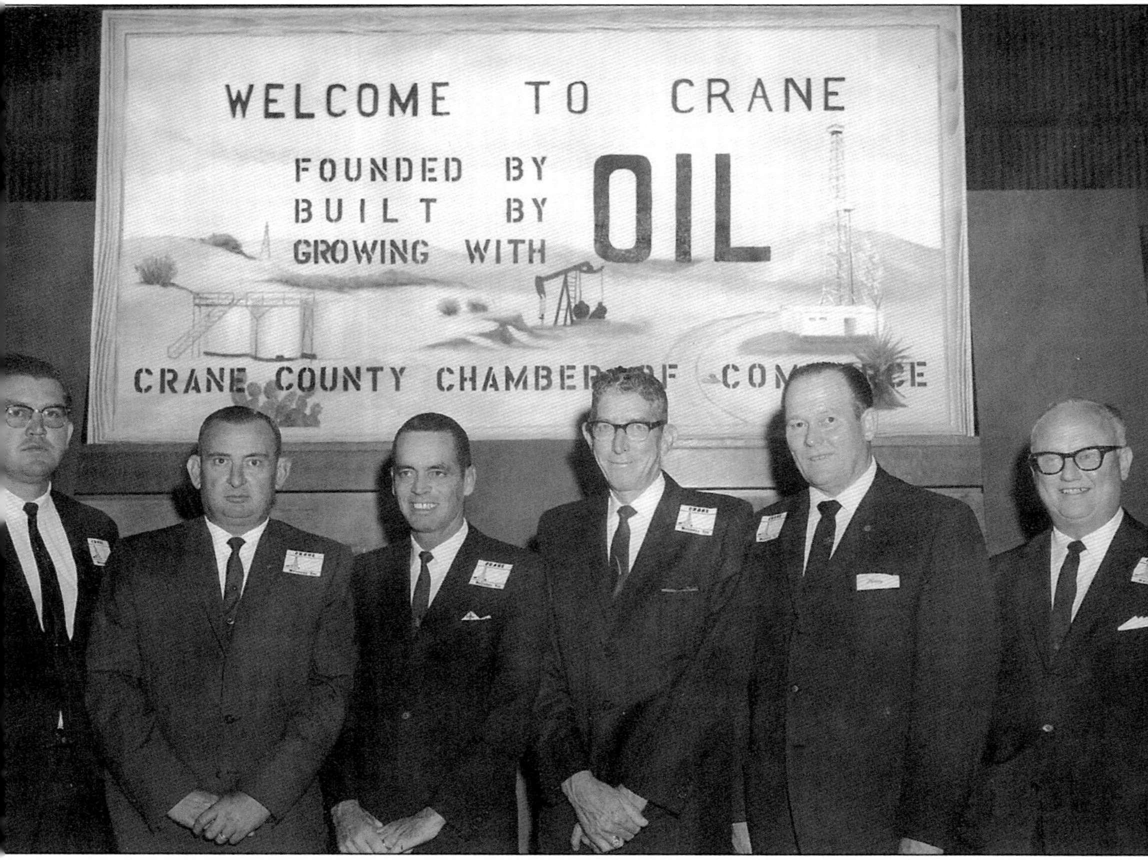

The chamber of commerce held a banquet in celebration of the oil industry that has sustained Crane County since its inception. Standing in front of a sign that proudly affirmed "WELCOME TO CRANE—FOUNDED BY OIL, BUILT WITH OIL, GROWING WITH OIL" are, from left to right, Bill Payne, R.H. McManus, Harold Pettit, C.A. Caroll, Henry Ingles, and Ken Spencer.

Four

Business Before Pleasure

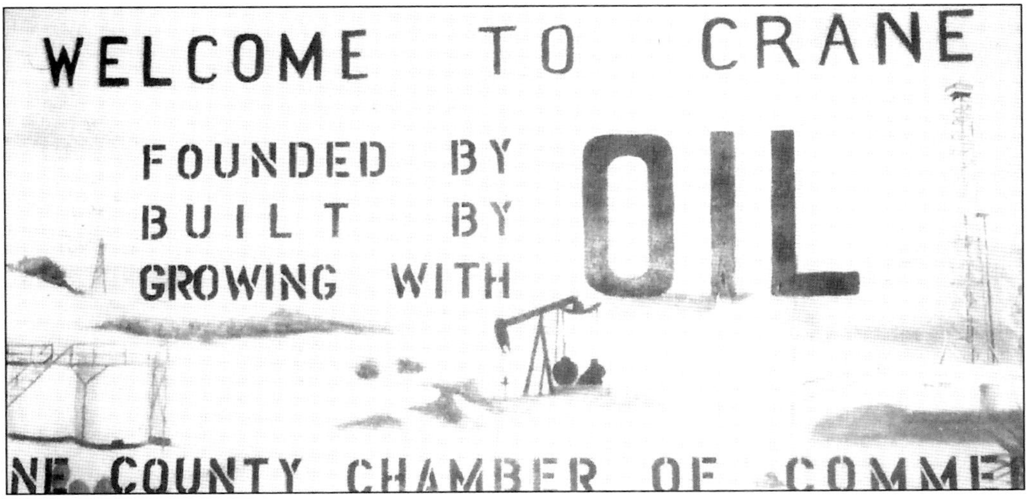

Crane County has always been sparsely populated, but a new age began in the region after the discovery of oil. The Crane County Chamber of Commerce subsequently created this mural to explain the importance of oil to Crane's history. The chamber of commerce proves to be a valuable resource for people migrating to Crane County, usually to take advantage of an oil boom. The employees of the chamber of commerce help minimize the culture shock many new citizens might feel by pointing them toward local attractions and activities. (Courtesy of the Crane County Chamber of Commerce.)

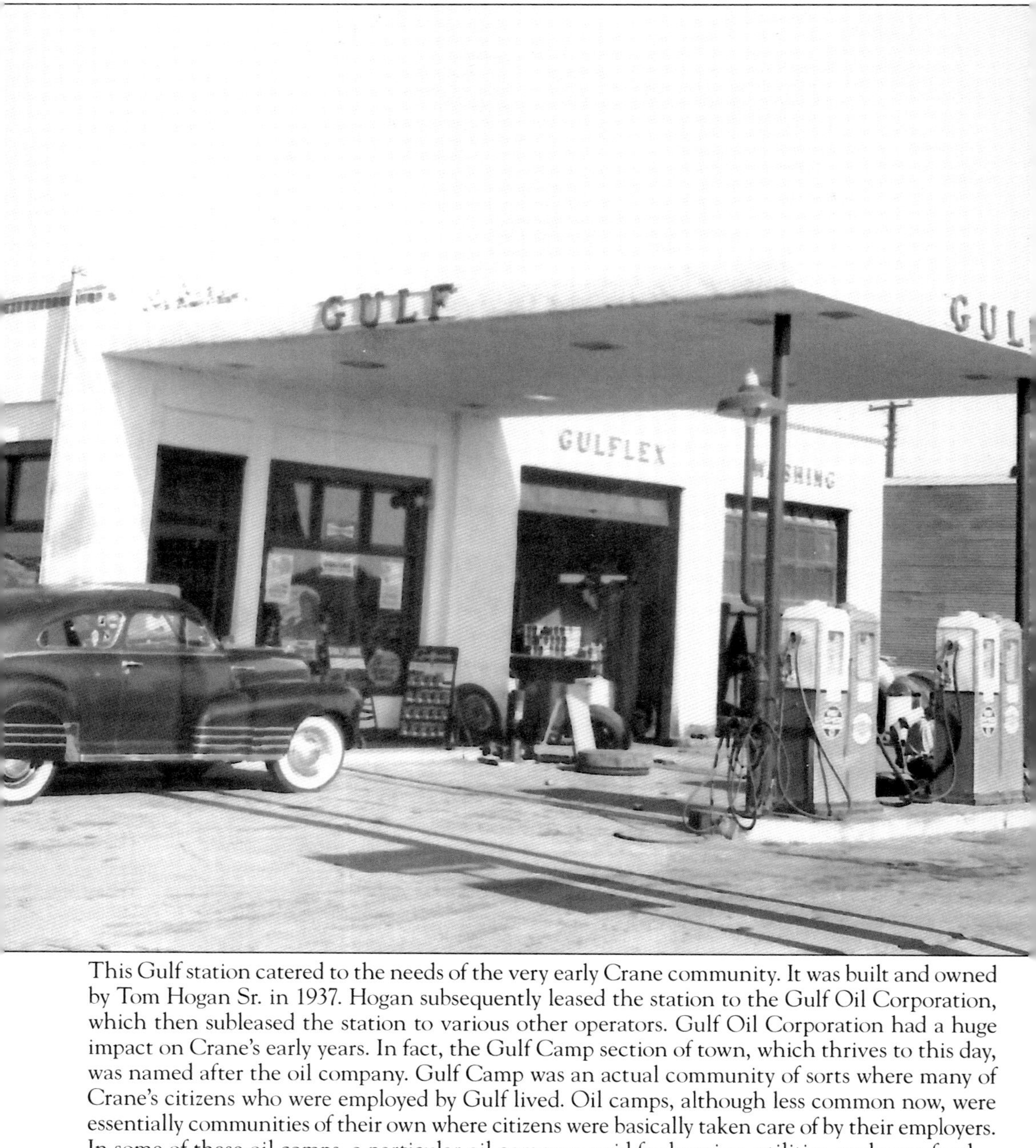

This Gulf station catered to the needs of the very early Crane community. It was built and owned by Tom Hogan Sr. in 1937. Hogan subsequently leased the station to the Gulf Oil Corporation, which then subleased the station to various other operators. Gulf Oil Corporation had a huge impact on Crane's early years. In fact, the Gulf Camp section of town, which thrives to this day, was named after the oil company. Gulf Camp was an actual community of sorts where many of Crane's citizens who were employed by Gulf lived. Oil camps, although less common now, were essentially communities of their own where citizens were basically taken care of by their employers. In some of these oil camps, a particular oil company paid for housing, utilities, and even food.

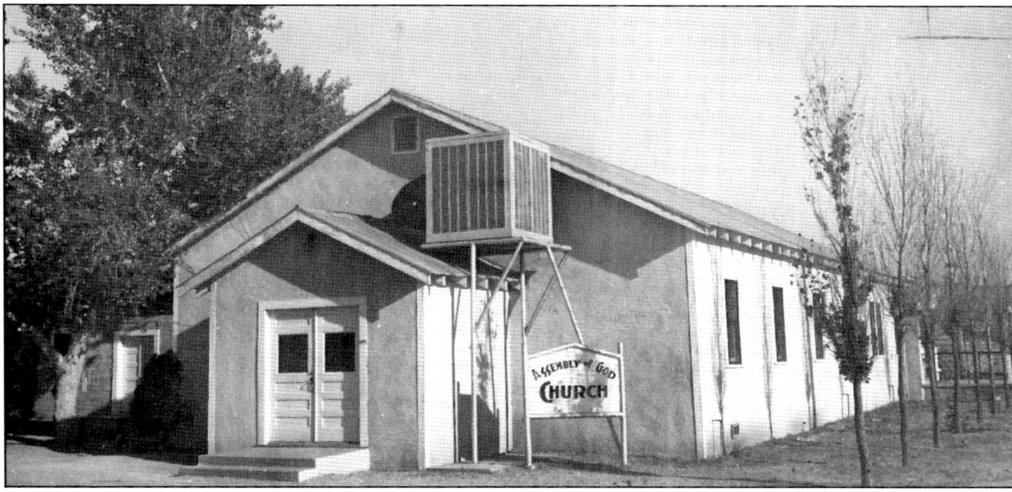

The Assembly of God Church, which was organized in 1934, is pictured here. One of the town's earliest houses of worship, the Assembly of God Church was located at the crossroads of Seventh and Gaston Streets. Today, there is no longer an Assembly of God church in Crane, and the building itself has since been demolished.

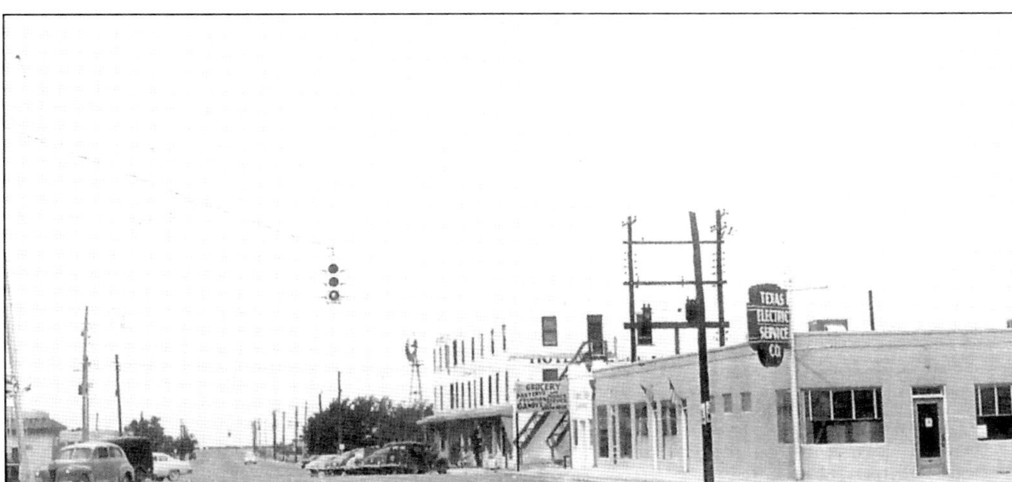

Downtown Crane and its businesses have changed much since the town's early years. The businesses seen in this photograph have all gone the way of history. Most of these structures have since been demolished and replaced with newer, more modern architecture.

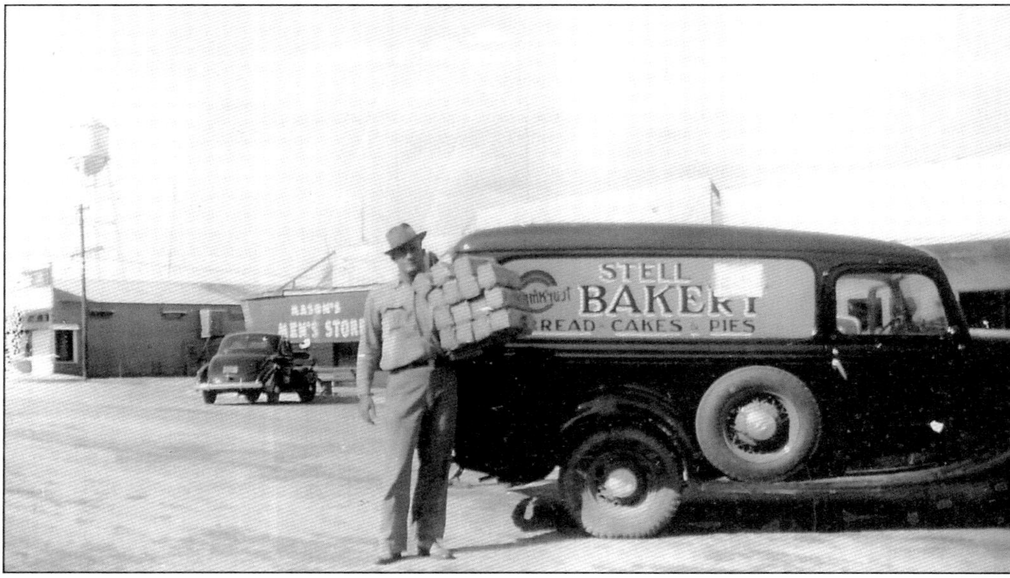

The city streets of Crane once contained a bakery. Throughout the years, bakeries have come and gone. This bakery has likewise gone the way of history. In this photograph, captured more than 70 years ago, the town baker handles an armful of hot bread loaves fresh out of the oven.

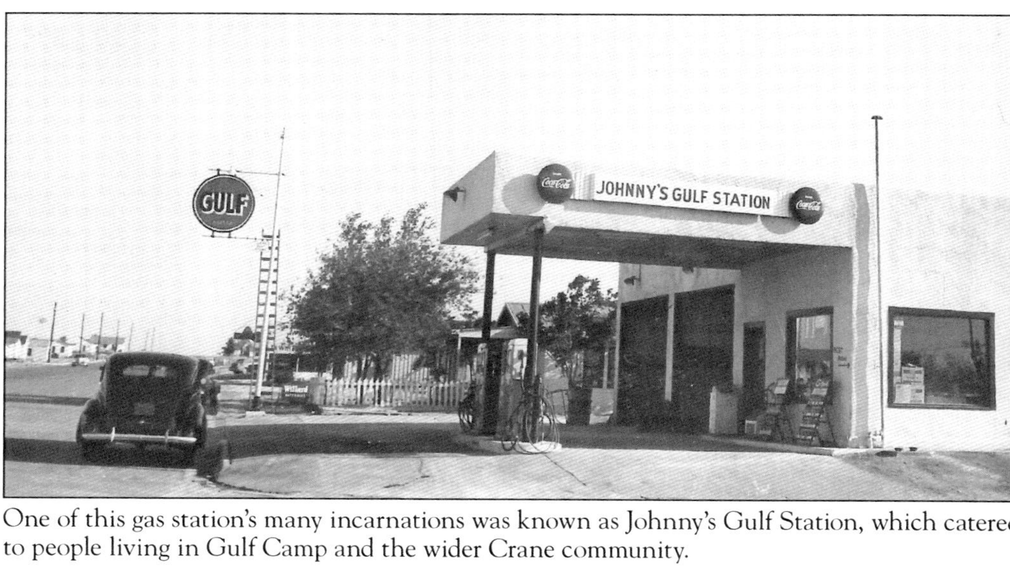

One of this gas station's many incarnations was known as Johnny's Gulf Station, which catered to people living in Gulf Camp and the wider Crane community.

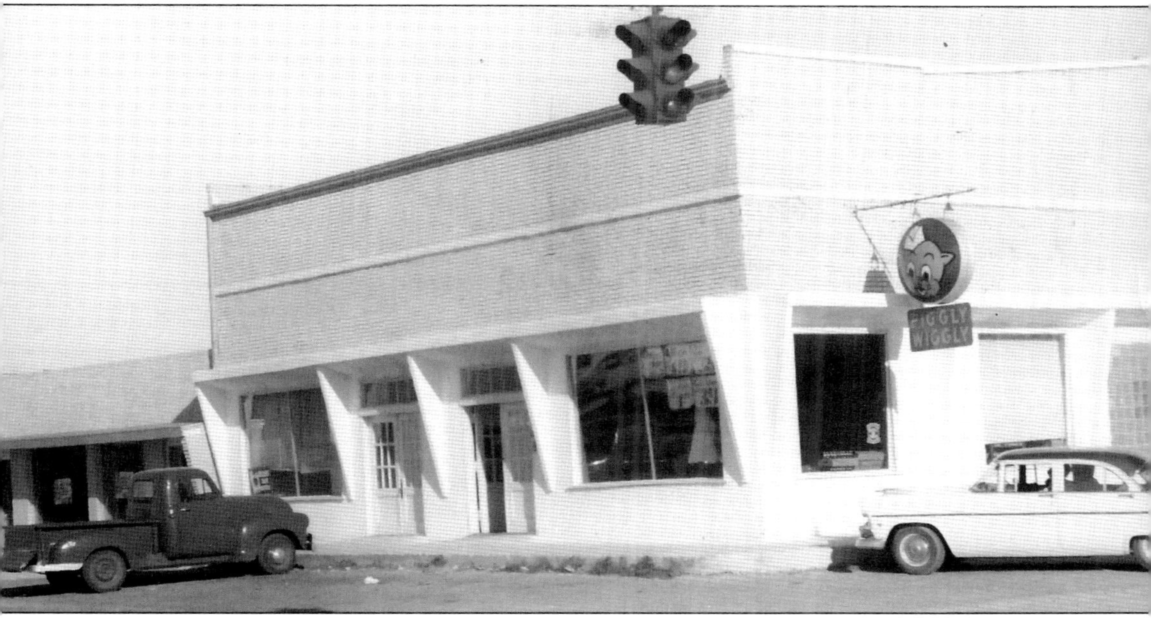

The Piggly Wiggly offered all the sundry items needed for day-to-day living in Crane. This c. 1945 photograph shows the storefront at the time. The Piggly Wiggly was the first self-service grocery store. Prior to the Piggly Wiggly, shoppers would present store clerks with their grocery lists, and the clerks would do the shopping for them. Many at the time predicted that this idea would fail, believing that people would not want to shop for themselves. Today, however, this once-novel idea has become the most common way of grocery shopping in the United States.

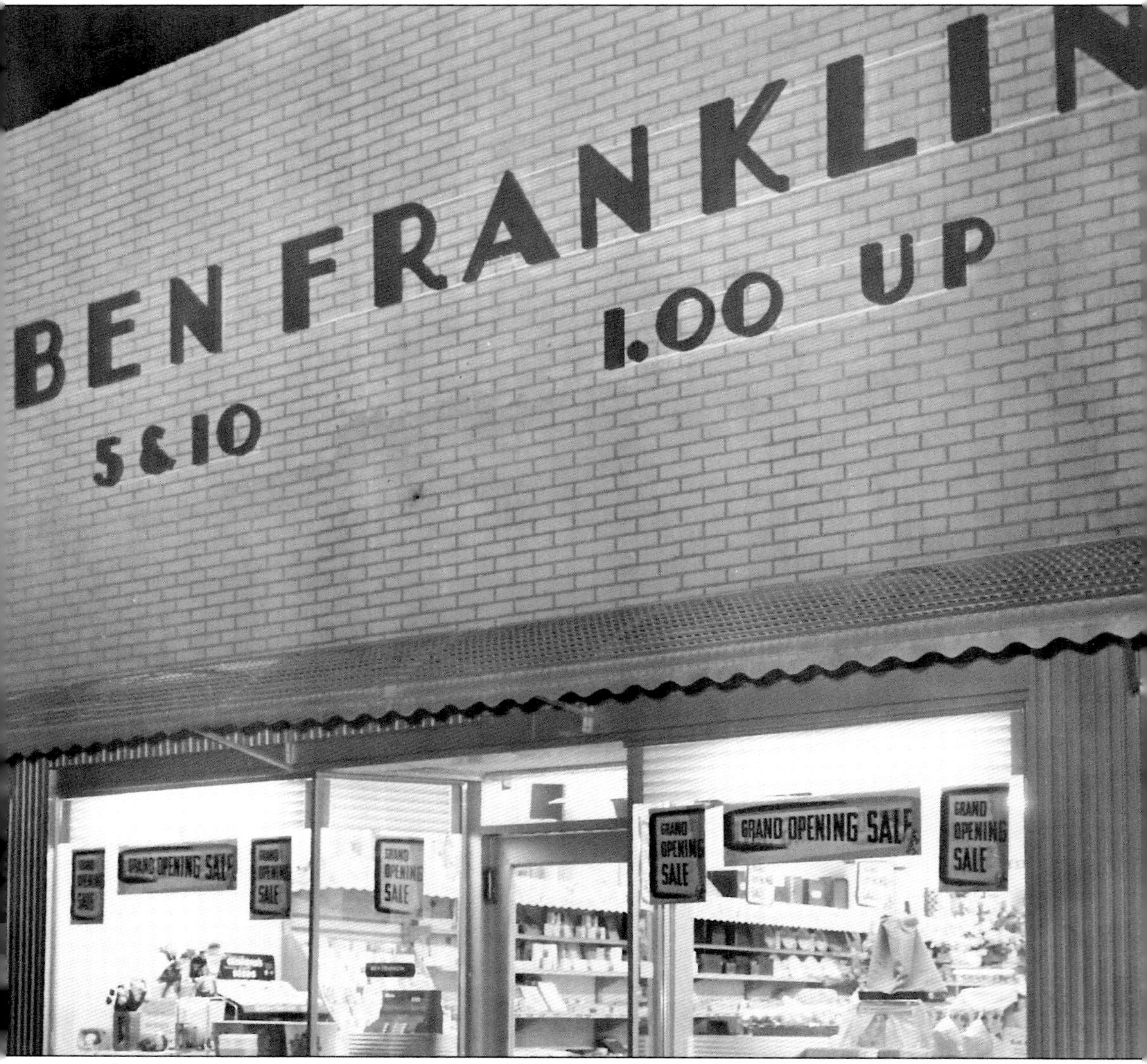

Shown here is the grand opening of Ben Franklin, a department store that has long since vanished from Crane. Ben Franklin is a chain store that can still be found in small towns throughout the United States. Known as five-and-dime stores, shops like this have morphed into dollar stores due to inflation. Unfortunately, nickels and dimes cannot buy much more than a piece of bubblegum today, if that.

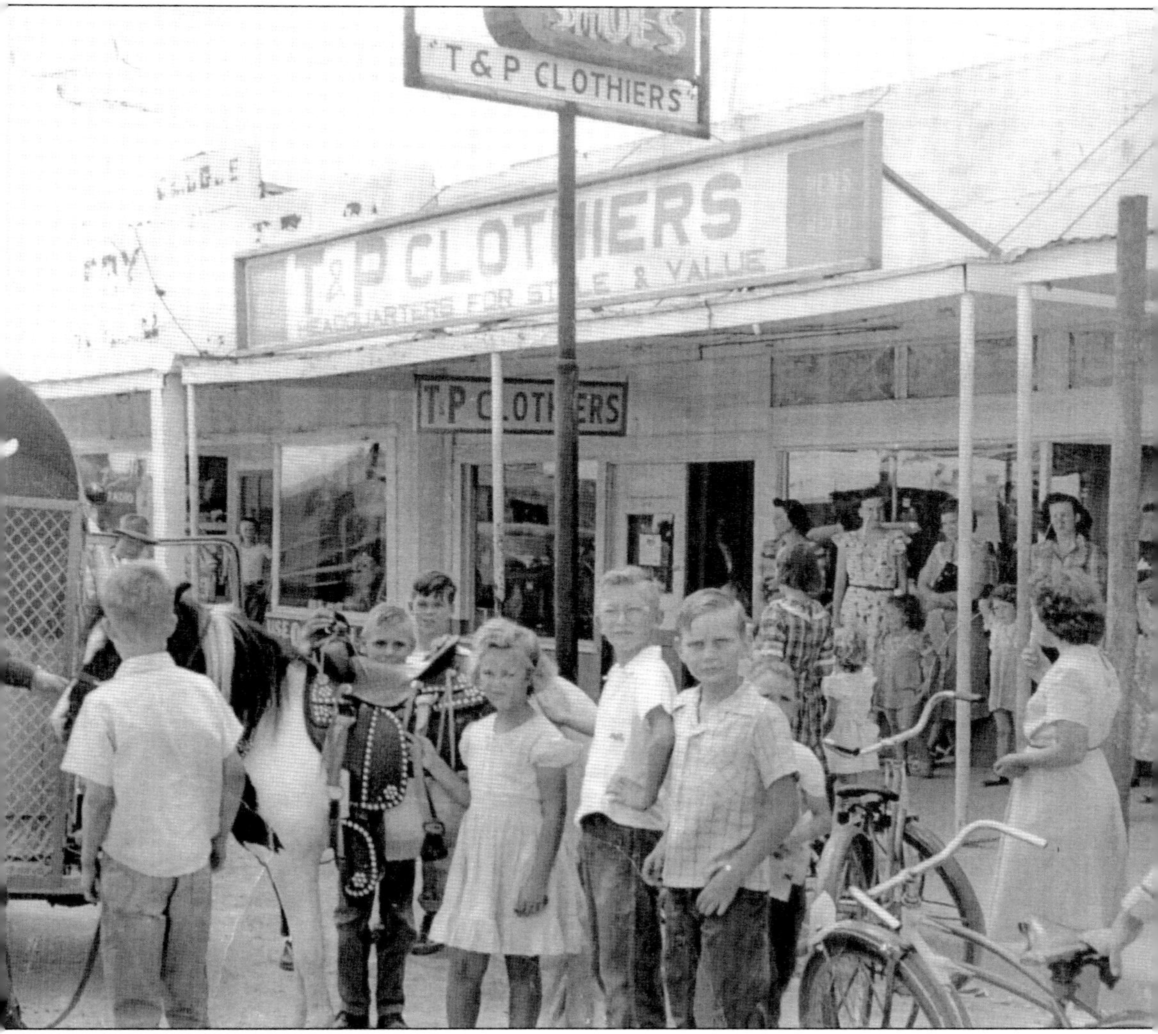

T&P Clothiers was a clothing store loved by Crane citizens for decades. Shown here is the clothing store in its earliest days, as Crane citizens gather at the storefront to enjoy the festive atmosphere of the store's grand opening. An estimated 1,000 people attended the celebration. Many people were drawn to the event by the possibility of getting to pet, or maybe even ride, one of Gene Autry's ponies, which were brought in special for the occasion. T&P Clothiers was named after its founders, Bob Tobin and his partner and brother-in-law Charles Passur. Incidentally, the Passur family operated the first dry goods store in Crane, which opened in 1927.

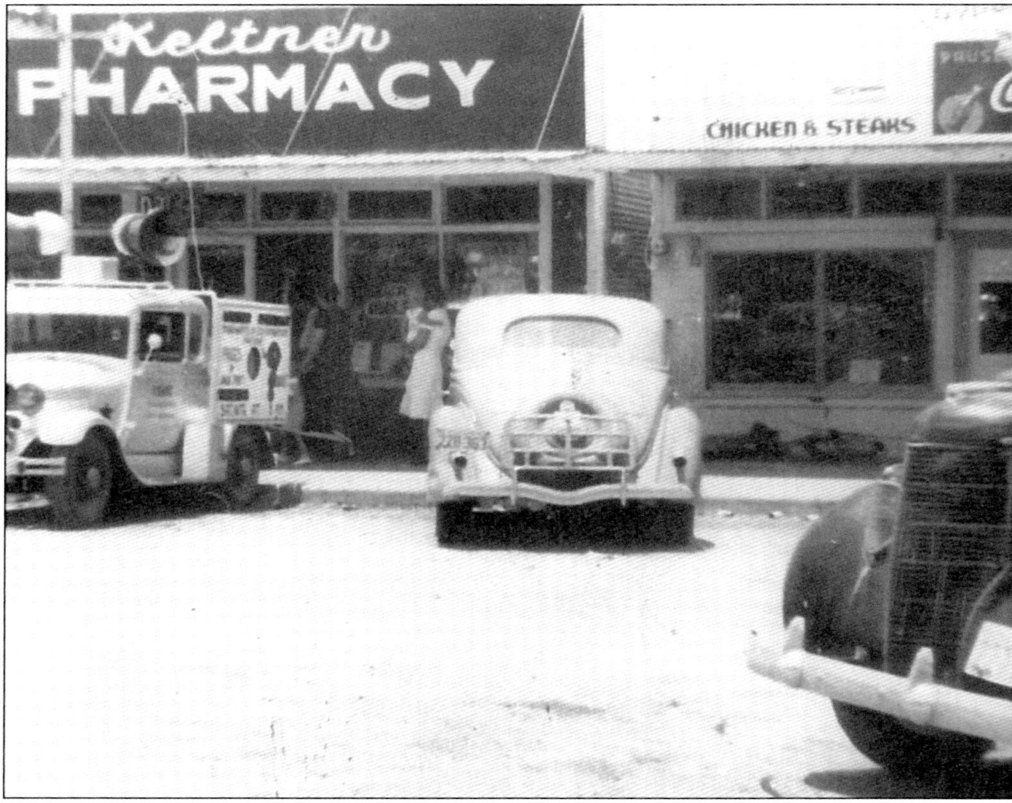

Keltner Pharmacy, one of Crane's former apothecaries from approximately 1942, is shown here. Notice the old vehicle out front with the large speakers mounted on top. These mobile vehicles, similar to modern-day ice cream trucks, were used to broadcast special events, low prices, and announcements across town.

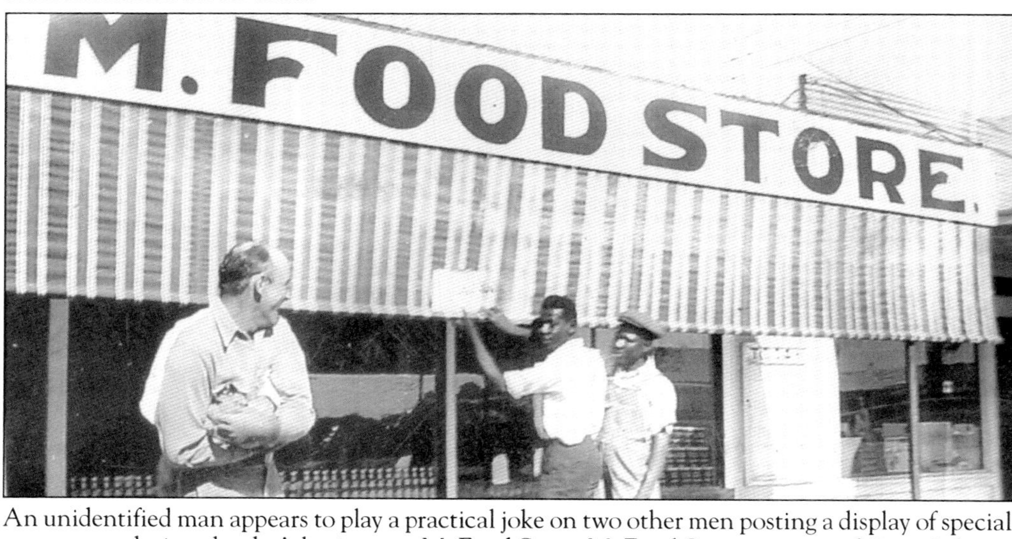

An unidentified man appears to play a practical joke on two other men posting a display of specials to promote during the day's business at M. Food Store. M. Food Store was one of Crane's former grocery stores, operating around 1940.

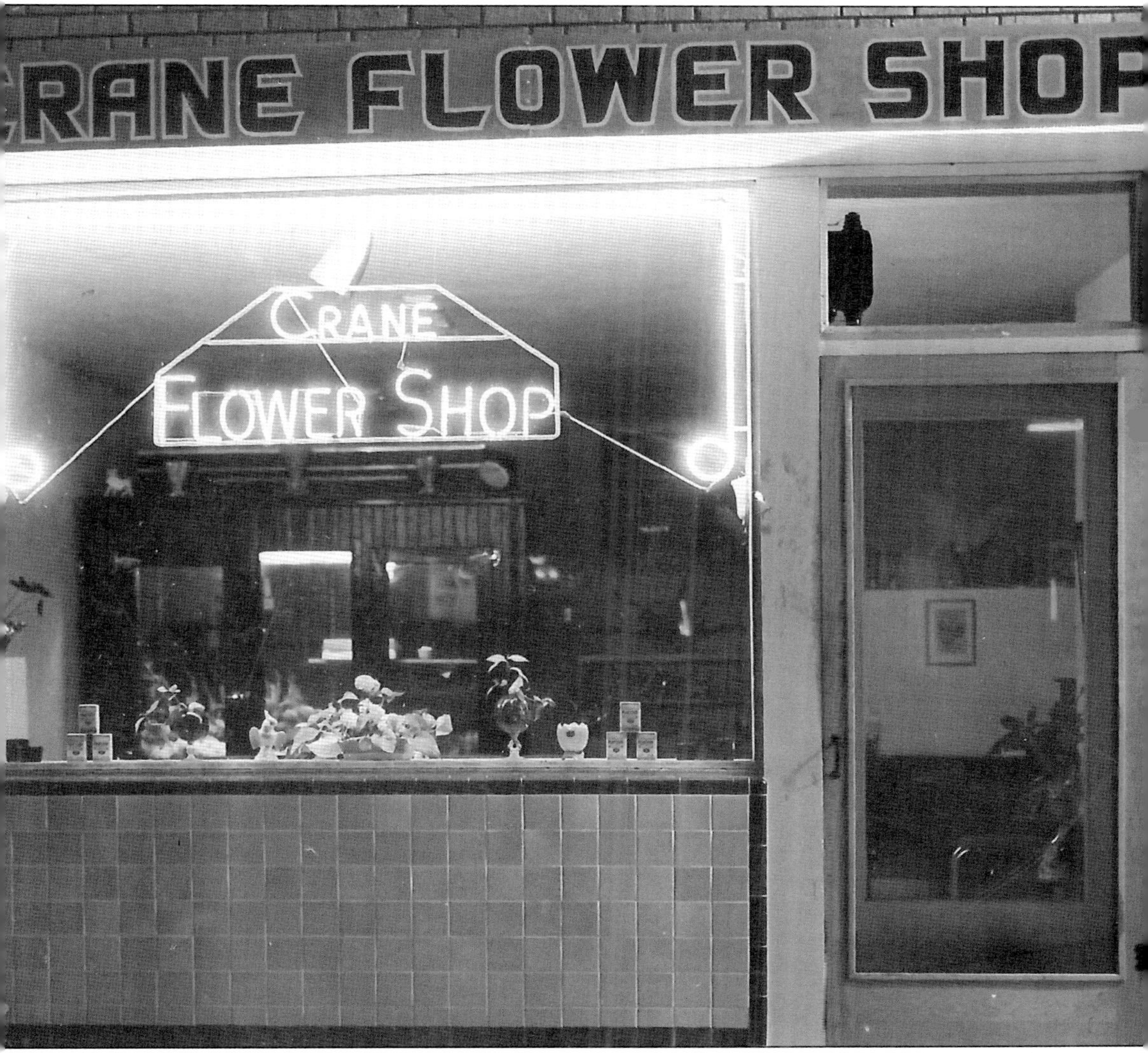

Crane has had several flower shops throughout its history, but the Crane Flower Shop was the primary source for Crane citizens in love or in mourning to purchase beautiful flowers and plants. The business was in operation in Crane for many years before and after this 1948 photograph was taken. Claudia Willis operated the Crane Flower Shop after she purchased it from Ray Hart, the store's previous owner, on December 1, 1948. The shop was later moved, but this image shows the storefront at its previous location on 107 West Fifth Street.

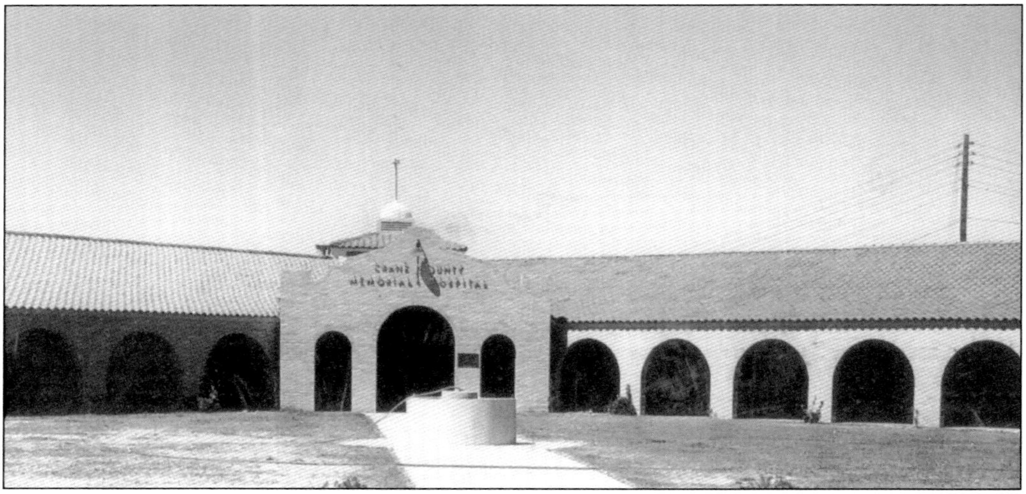

Shown here is the original Crane County Memorial Hospital following its completion on October 3, 1948. Crane Memorial Hospital had 32 beds and cost only $130,000 to construct. The hospital was built as a memorial to World War II veterans of Crane County. The facilities were later replaced with a newer version of Crane Memorial Hospital, which is a 25-bed, licensed critical access hospital serving Crane County and the surrounding areas.

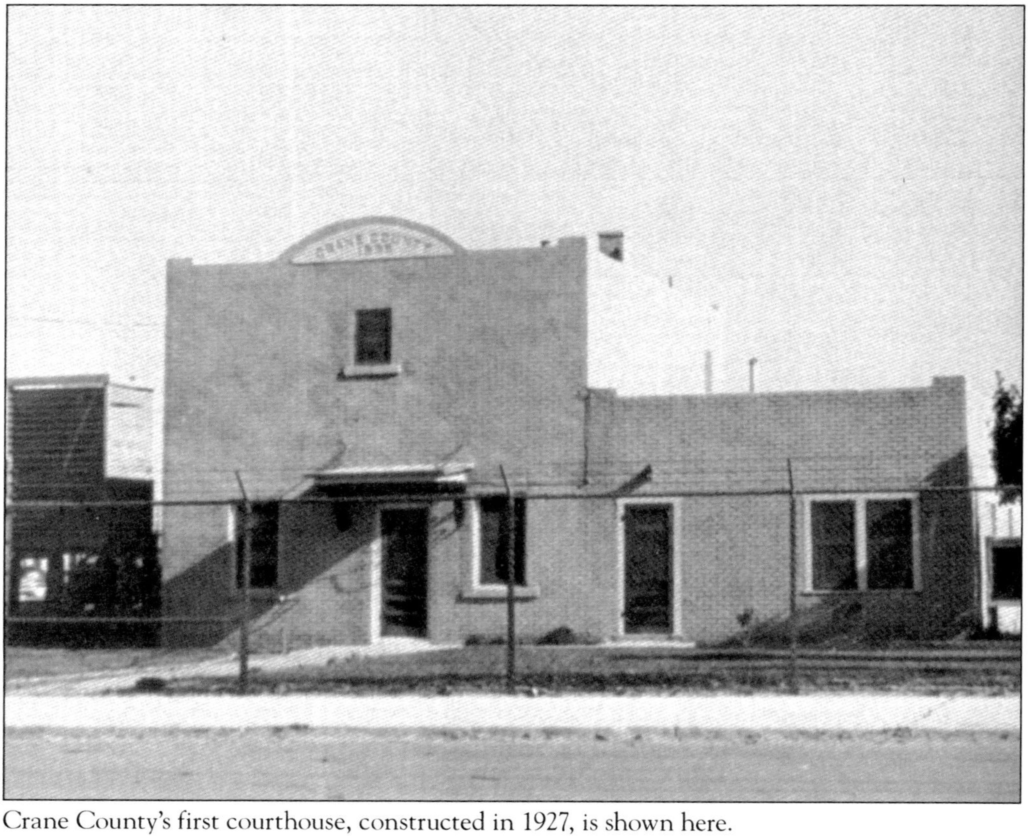

Crane County's first courthouse, constructed in 1927, is shown here.

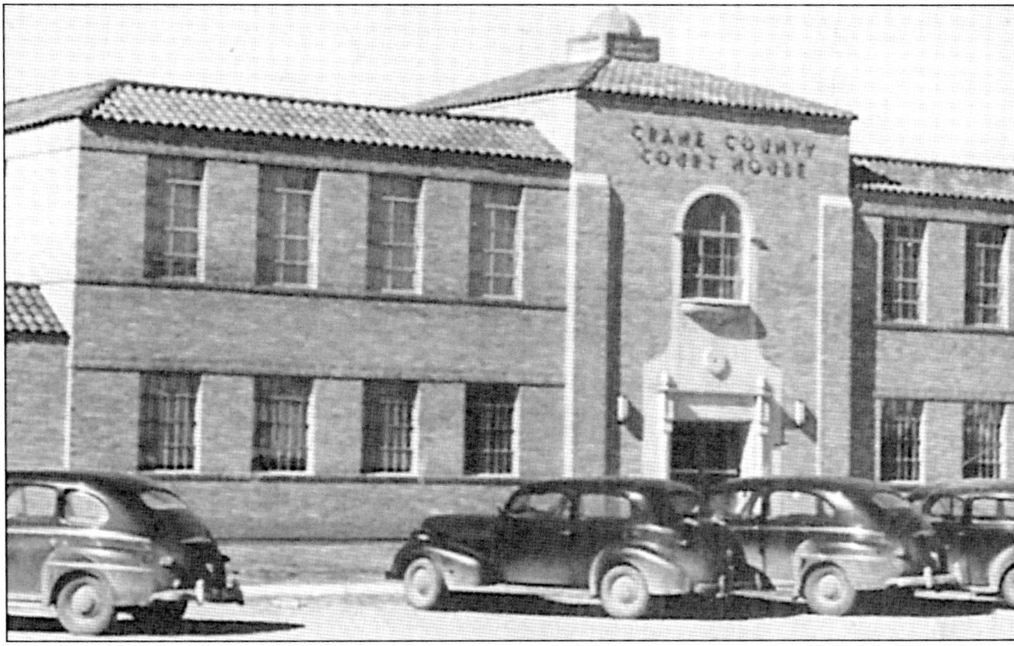

Crane County's second courthouse, which was completed in 1948, is shown here. The courthouse was later remodeled to how it looks today. (Courtesy of the Crane County Chamber of Commerce.)

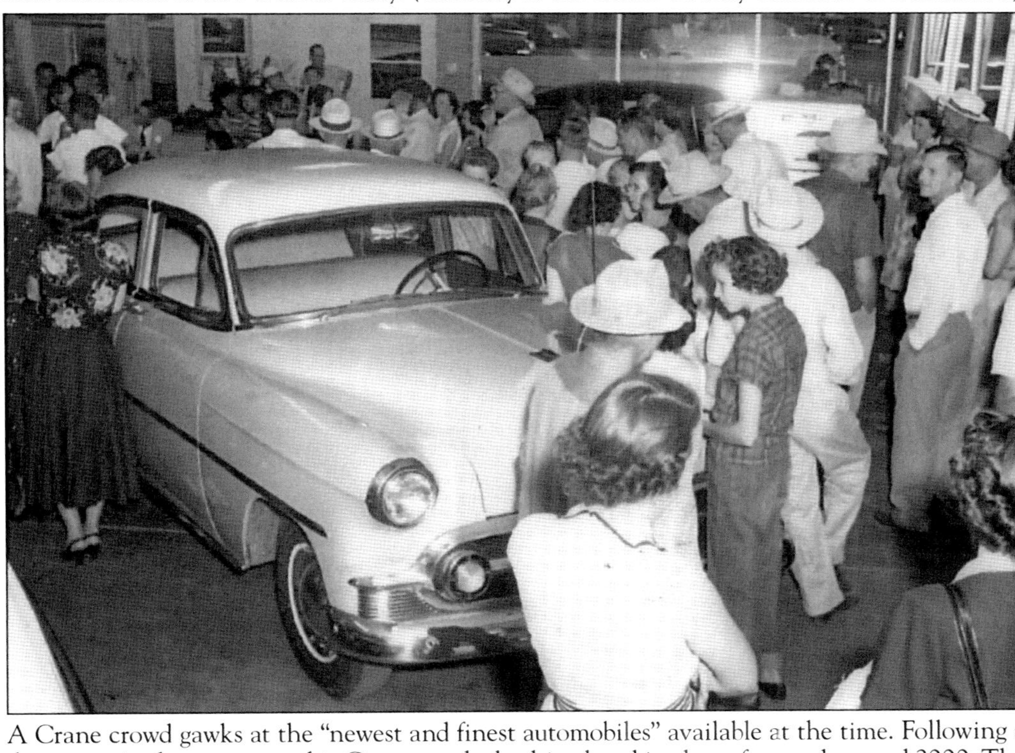

A Crane crowd gawks at the "newest and finest automobiles" available at the time. Following a downturn in the economy, this Crane car dealership closed its doors for good around 2000. The building is no longer in use.

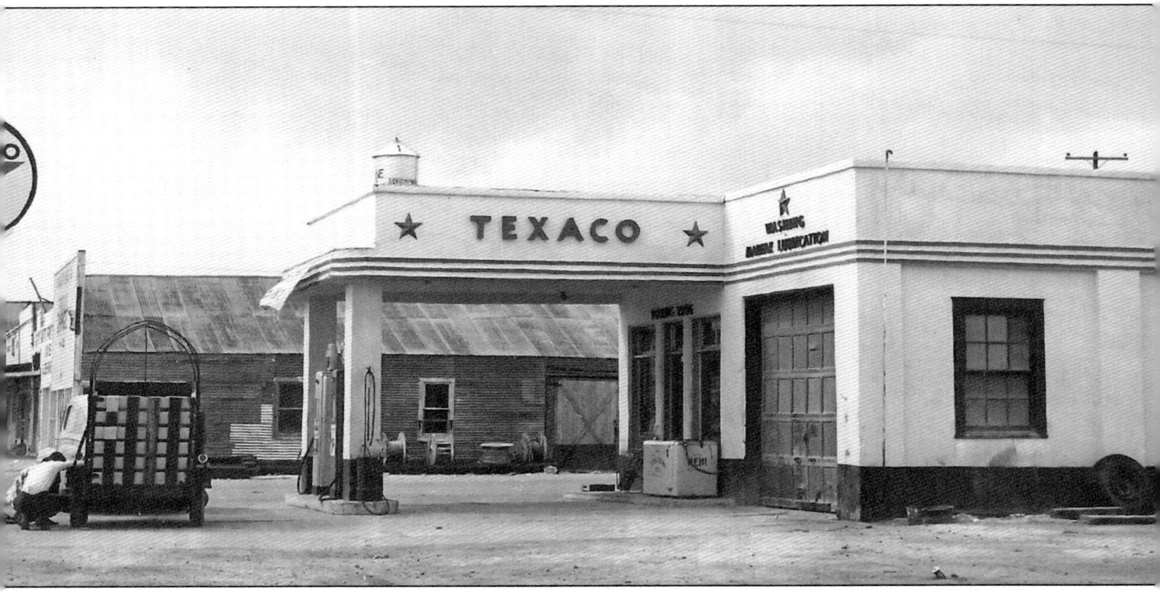

A Texaco gas station in Crane is pictured in the early 1950s. Although some of the original infrastructure from town gas stations still stands, many oil and gas company names have changed several times over the decades. As oil companies grow rich or go bankrupt, many are sold off to financially stronger oil companies, thereby resulting in name changes. With oil, things are always evolving. For example, the methods of extracting the oil beneath the earth proceed to change year after year. However, regardless of other changes, the oilfield subculture remains the same since the early days of "big oil." Certainly, oil is the lifeblood of the Crane County community, and the people of the region are forever thankful for the black gold that puts food on their tables.

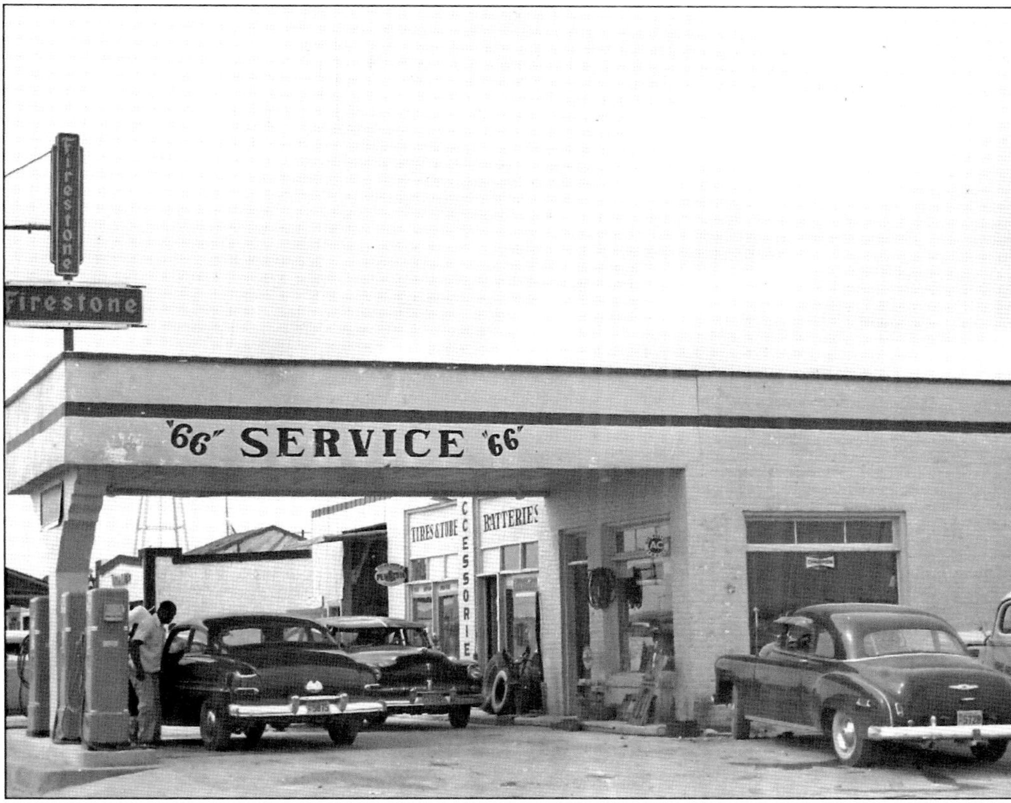

Full-service filling stations were commonplace in Crane all the way into the late 1980s. Shown here is a 66 employee giving a customer the full treatment, which nowadays is a thing of the past.

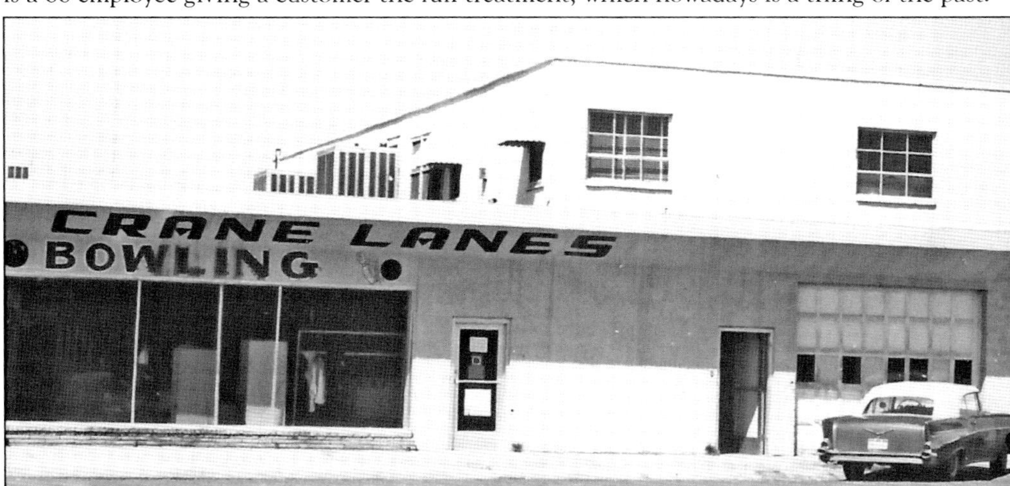

The Crane Bowling Alley, shown here in the 1950s, has since disappeared. Along with the bowling alley, Crane citizens also had, at one point in time, a drive-in movie theater, a skating rink, and a movie theater that allowed admission with money or a couple of Gandy's milk carton tops. Although Crane citizens do not have access to these businesses anymore, most are willing to make the short drive to Odessa or Midland to take care of their entertainment needs.

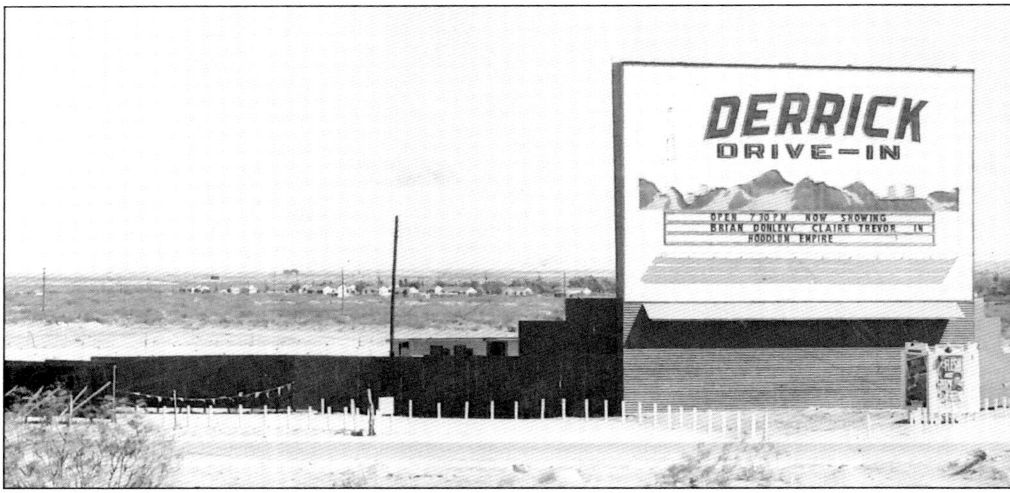

The Derrick Drive-In, shown here in 1953, was a popular hot spot for Crane citizens for many years. Closed in the 1970s, it was located on the southern edge of town. (Courtesy of the Crane County Chamber of Commerce.)

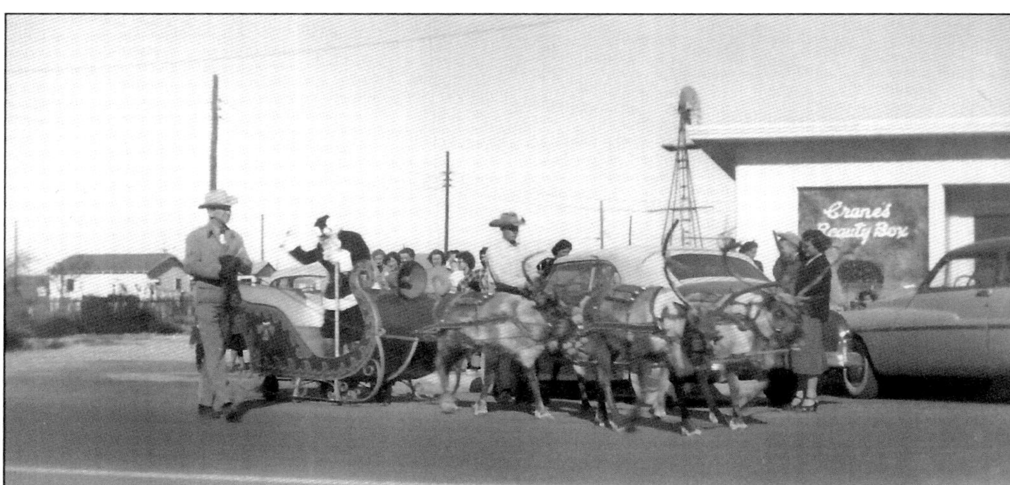

When the oilfields boom, many Crane citizens go to extraordinary lengths to bring an element of fun and amusement to the barren West Texas landscape. Shown in this early-1950s photograph is a herd of reindeer pulling Santa's sleigh through the town common. Crane's Beauty Box, which appears in the background, catered to women wanting to "look beautiful today."

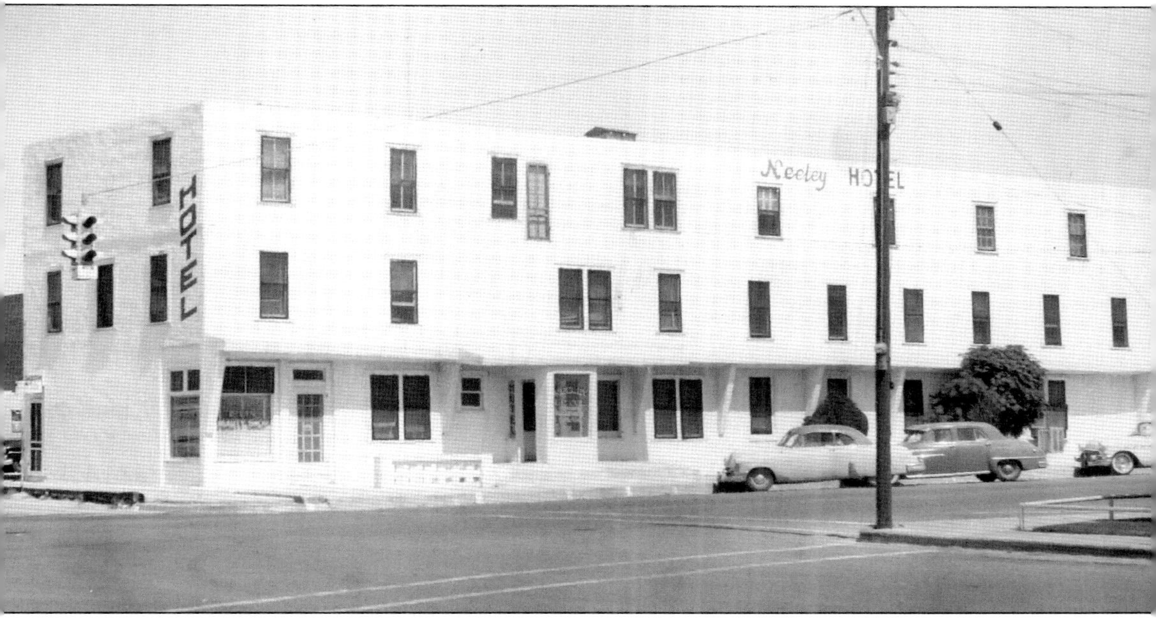

The Neeley Hotel was a rarity in Crane, being the only three-story building within the town's city limits. The hotel, which has long since been demolished, was a famous landmark that harkened back to an earlier, simpler time. The establishment was primarily used by the transient population or by those staying for an extended period of time to take advantage of an uptick in the local oil economy.

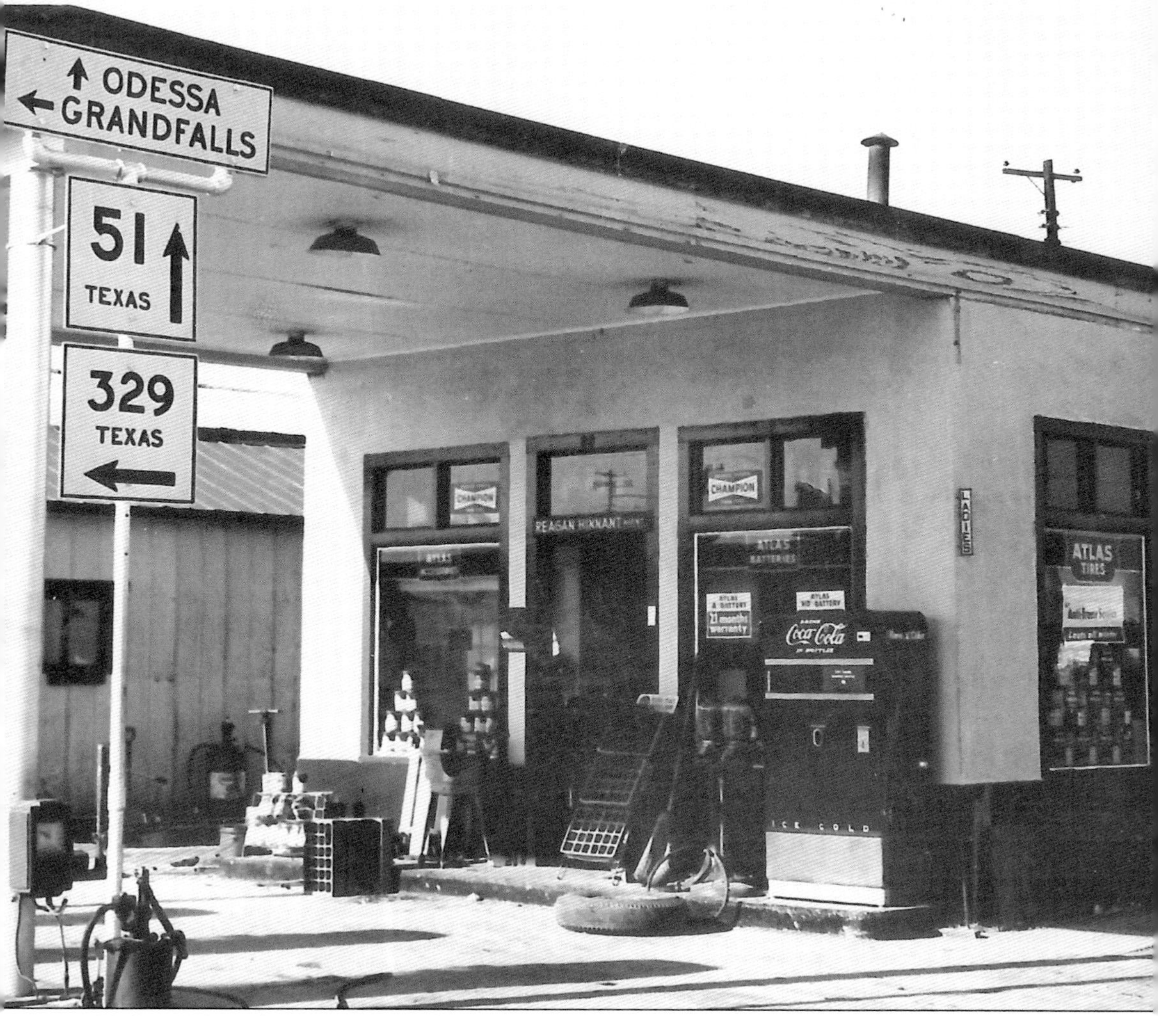

Today, US Highway 385 cuts through the middle of town, leading the traveler (like the man shown here) to one of two places—Odessa if he is traveling north or McCamey if he is traveling south. However, prior to 1959, when this photograph was taken, this highway was known as Texas Highway 51. In 1959, US Highway 385 replaced Texas Highway 51. The highway leading east and west out of town, Texas State Highway 329, is still in use under this designation.

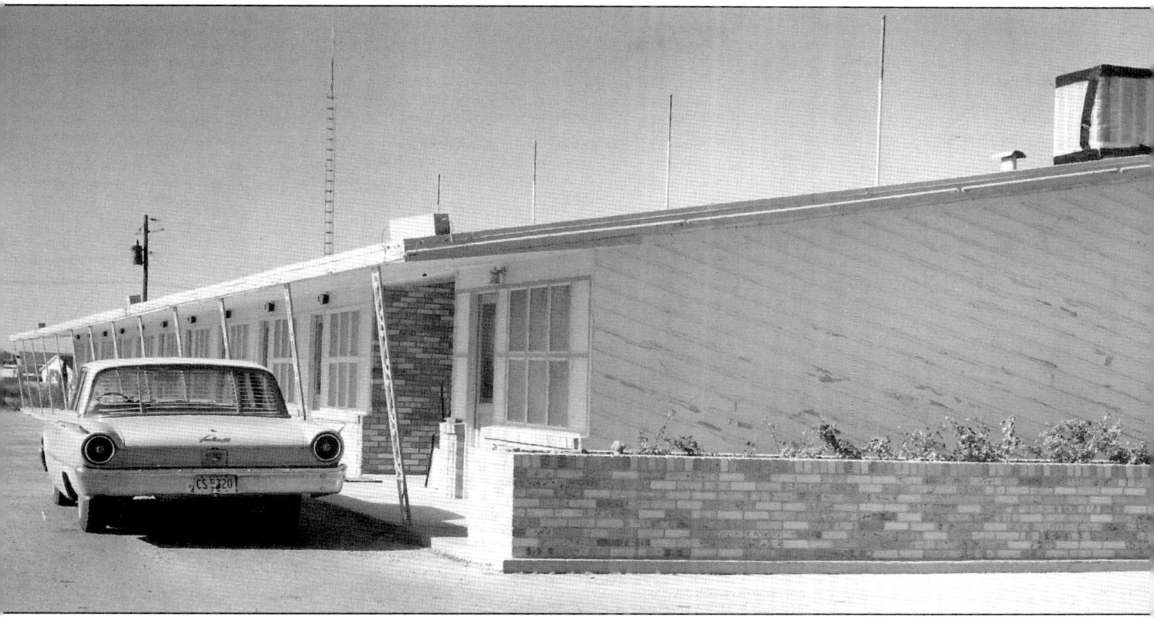

Presently, there is still one hotel for folks passing through Crane to stay in, which is the Best Budget Inn. At the time of this January 1964 photograph, the town hotel to stay in was the Executive Lodge Motel.

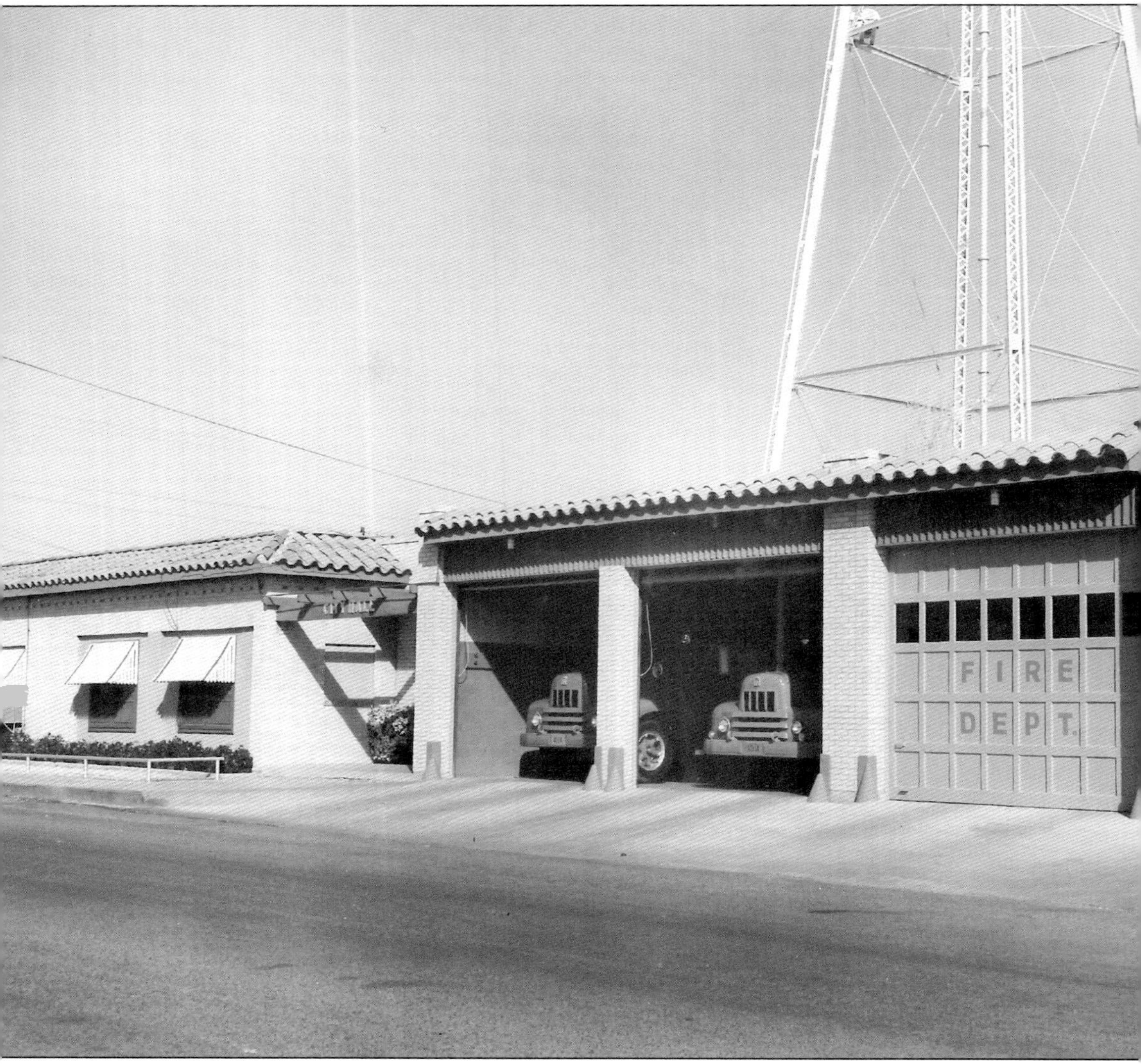

Crane County Fire Department is a volunteer organization. Pictured in 1985, the fire engines are at rest in the garage. Firemen at the department have put out many fires since Crane County's earliest days. In one of the driest counties in the region, brush fires are commonplace, especially in times of extreme drought. At the time of this writing, the residents of Crane County are experiencing one of the worst droughts in recorded history, which increases the responsibilities of the firemen and the frequency with which they are needed.

Today, Crane citizens would be out of luck if they wanted to purchase diamonds within the city limits. However, Sanders Jewelers provided a service where Crane citizens could spend some of their hard-earned cash on their loved ones. In this c. 1983 photograph, folks gather at the storefront to watch the procession of a parade.

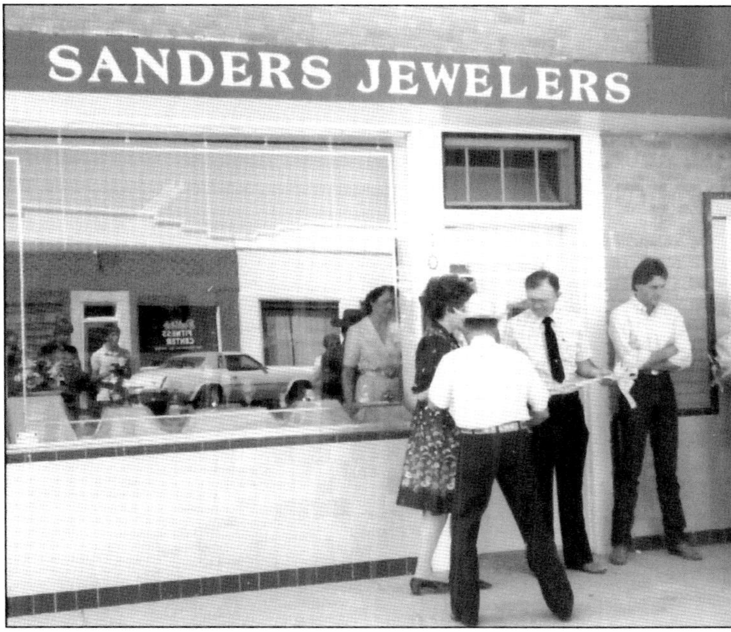

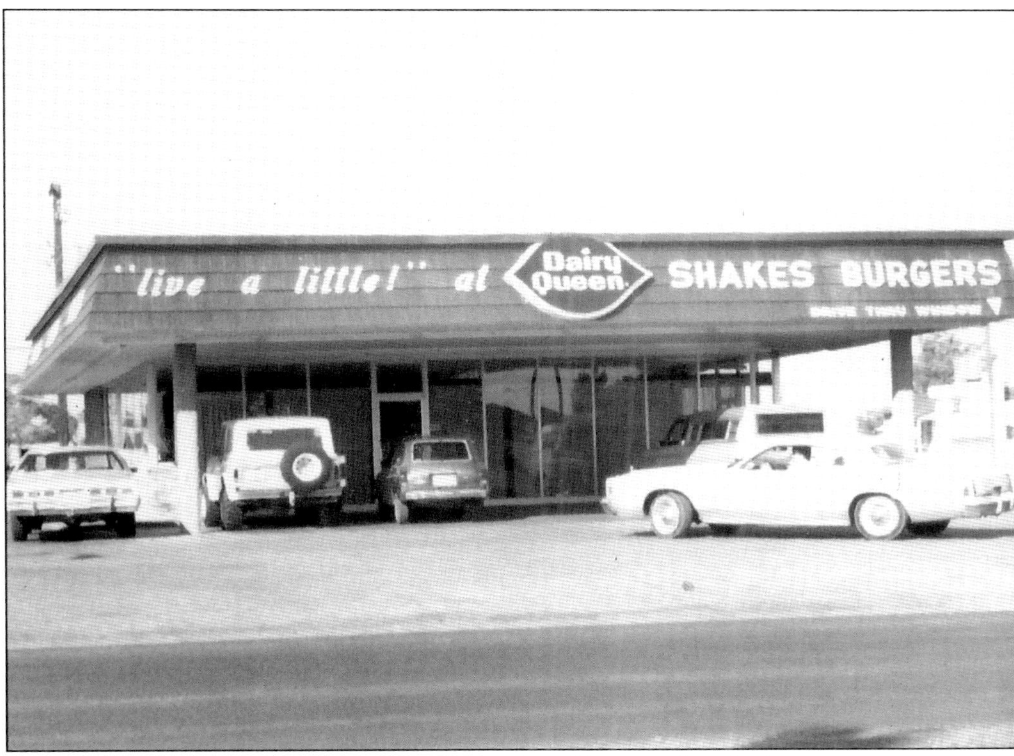

Crane's Dairy Queen has been around for decades, offering a place for Crane citizens to gather, drink coffee, and enjoy a meal with their friends and families. Shown here in September 1983, the restaurant has changed little over the years. Other restaurants, which tend to come and go in Crane, do not seem to possess the staying power of the local Dairy Queen.

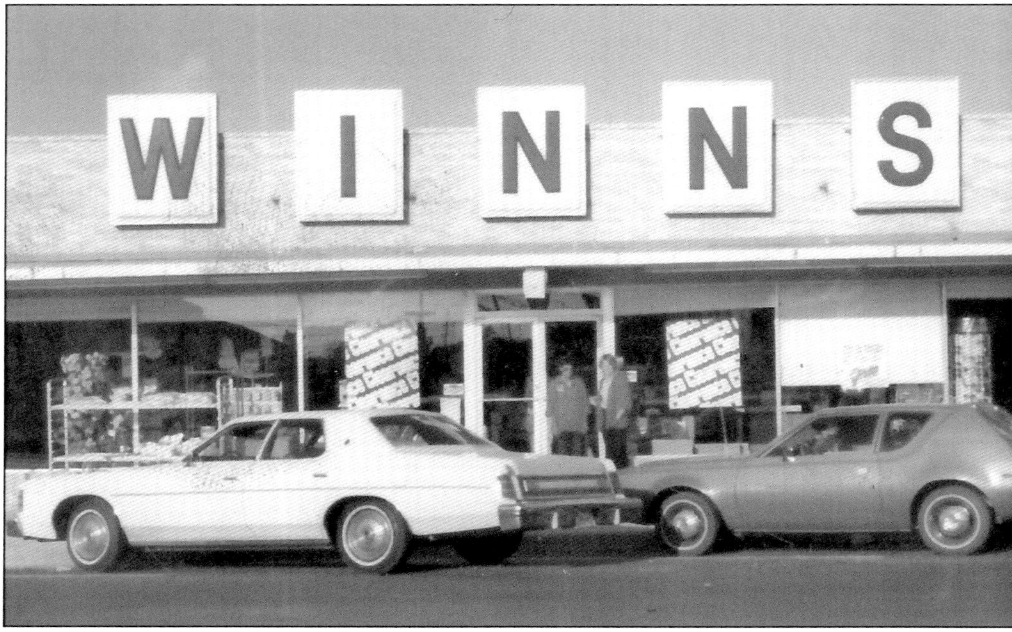

Winn's Department Store was a favored place for children of the 1980s to shop for toys. The store has since been replaced by a dollar store. The rise of the dollar stores is responsible for the vanishing of a lot of businesses like Winn's because of their deep discounts.

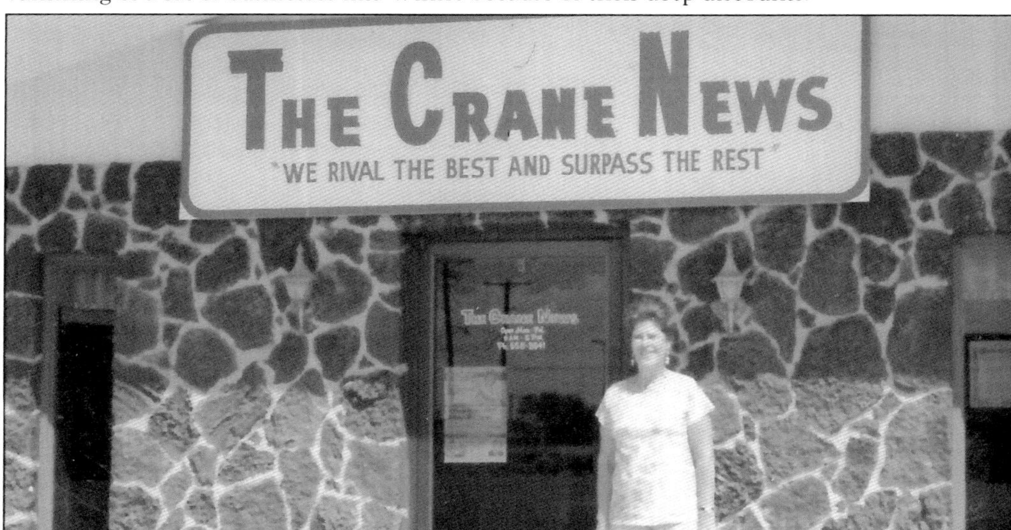

The *Crane News* has been Crane's news source for decades. A weekly paper, its main purpose is to illustrate the goings-on in the local community and wider Permian Basin area. In this 1983 photograph, an unidentified person exits the paper's headquarters on "deadline day." The *Crane News* at this time boasted, "We rival the best and surpass the rest."

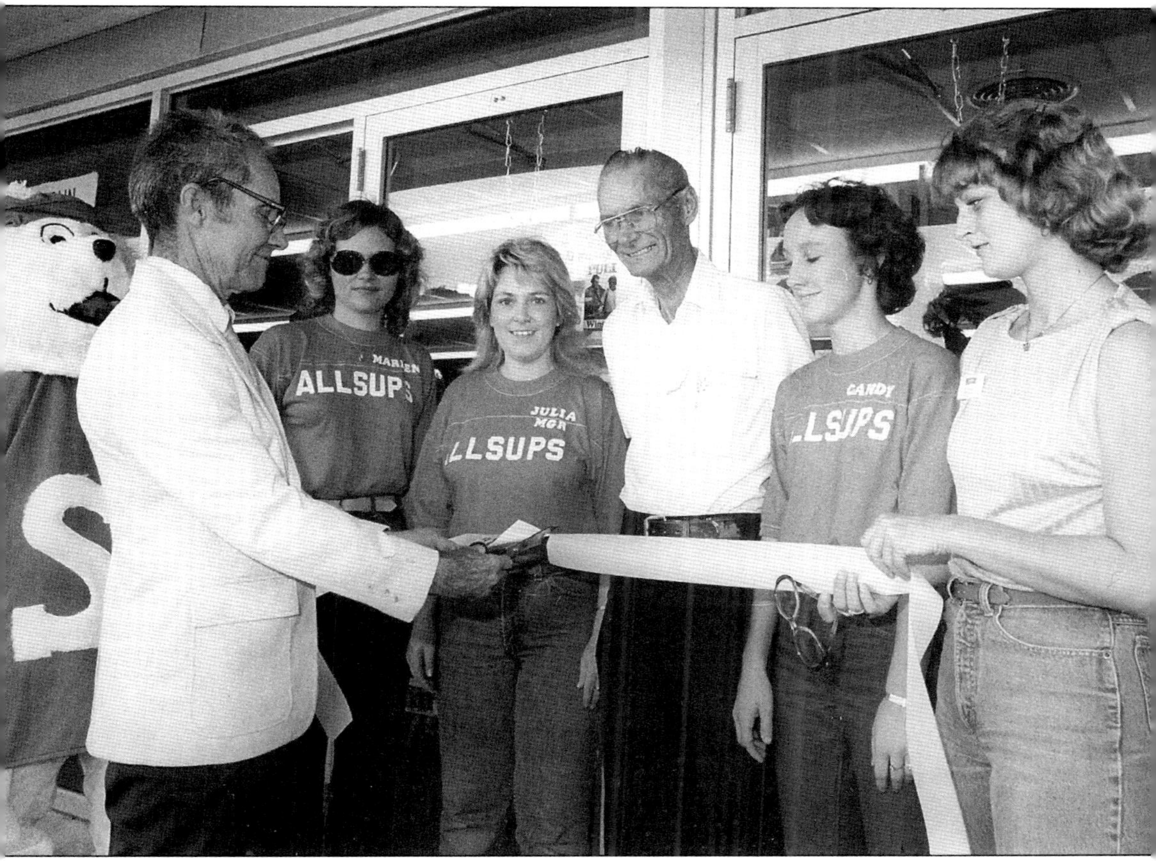

Allsup's was the only 24-hour convenient store in Crane County for decades. Truckers and late-night travelers in need of gas or fuel for their bellies continue to take advantage of Allsup's, as it is one of the last chances to stop for many miles. In this 1983 photograph, the store's staff performs a ribbon-cutting ceremony in celebration of its "world-famous burrito," which has been a hit in Crane for years. Allsup's is a franchise store with locations throughout Texas and New Mexico.

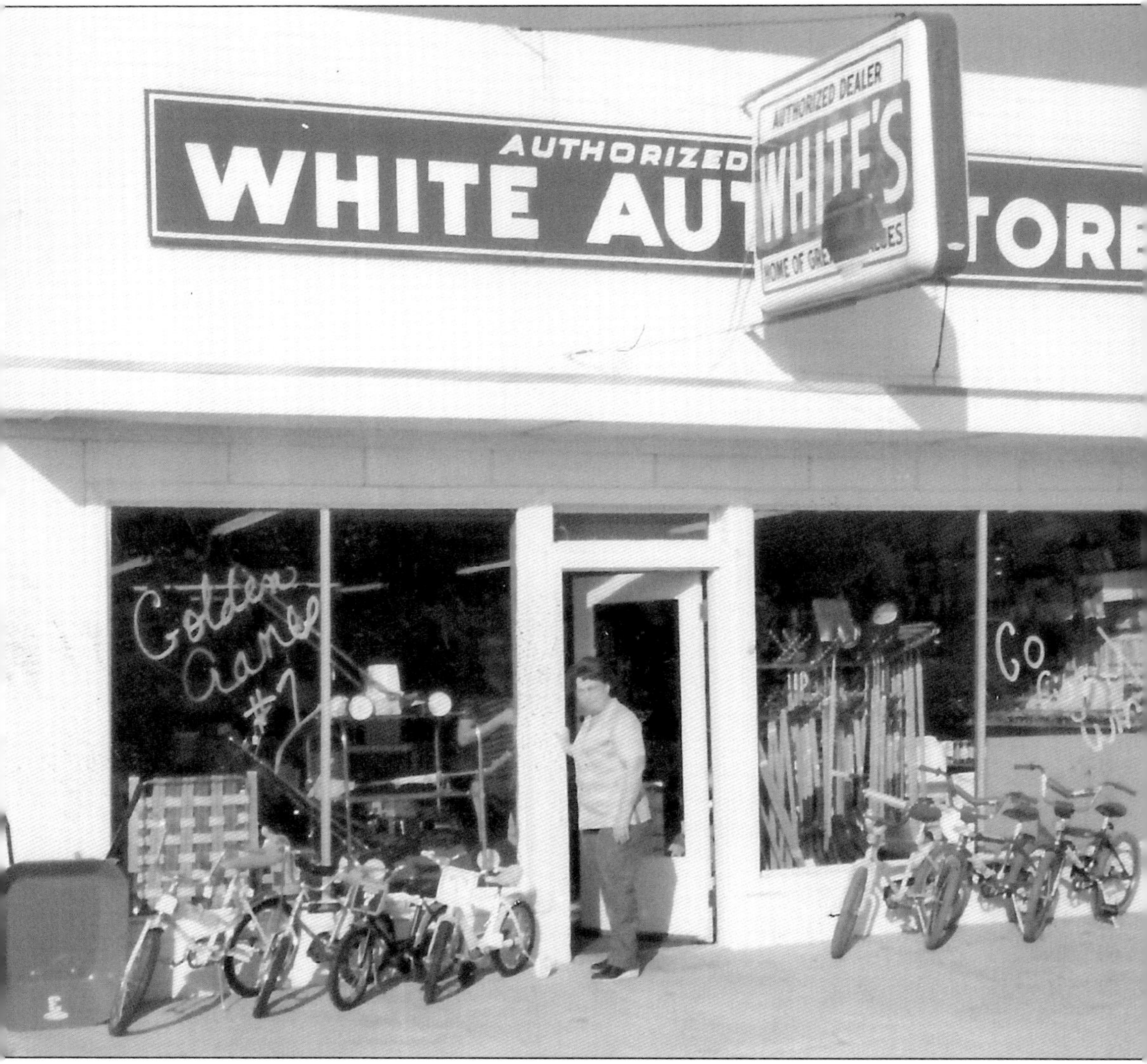

White's Auto Store provided a place for Crane's citizenry to pick up much-needed appliances. A vital business up through the 1980s, White's Auto Store was subsequently supplanted by Western Auto, which later became Stone's Home Center. Stone's Home Center is now the only auto parts store available to Crane County citizens.

Five

Hometown Happenings

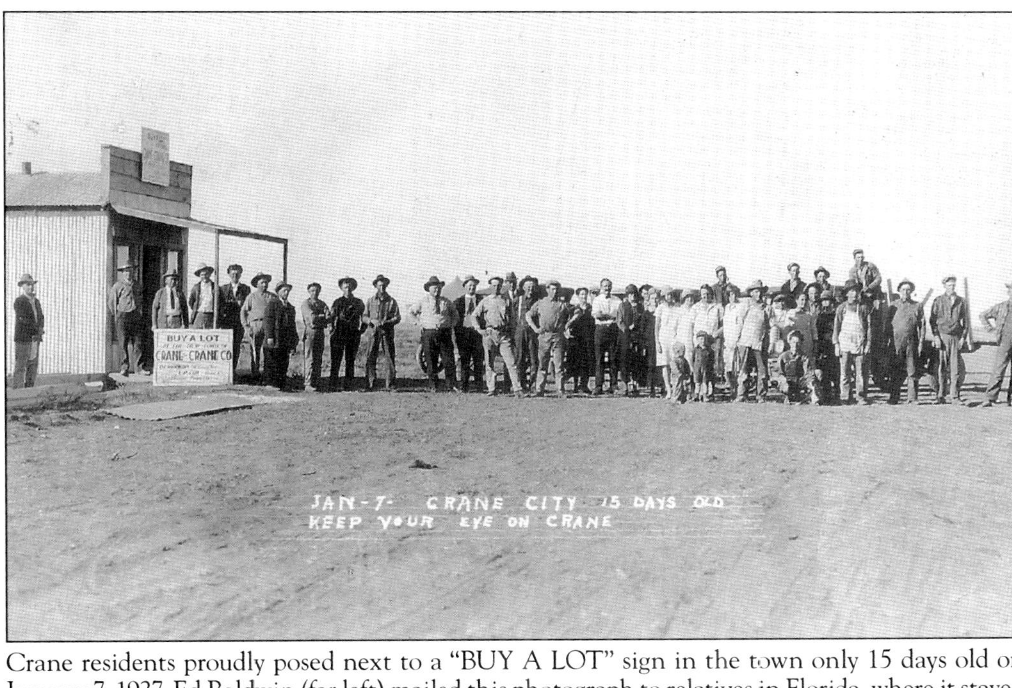

Crane residents proudly posed next to a "BUY A LOT" sign in the town only 15 days old on January 7, 1927. Ed Baldwin (far left) mailed this photograph to relatives in Florida, where it stayed until his niece mailed it back to the Crane Chamber of Commerce many years later.

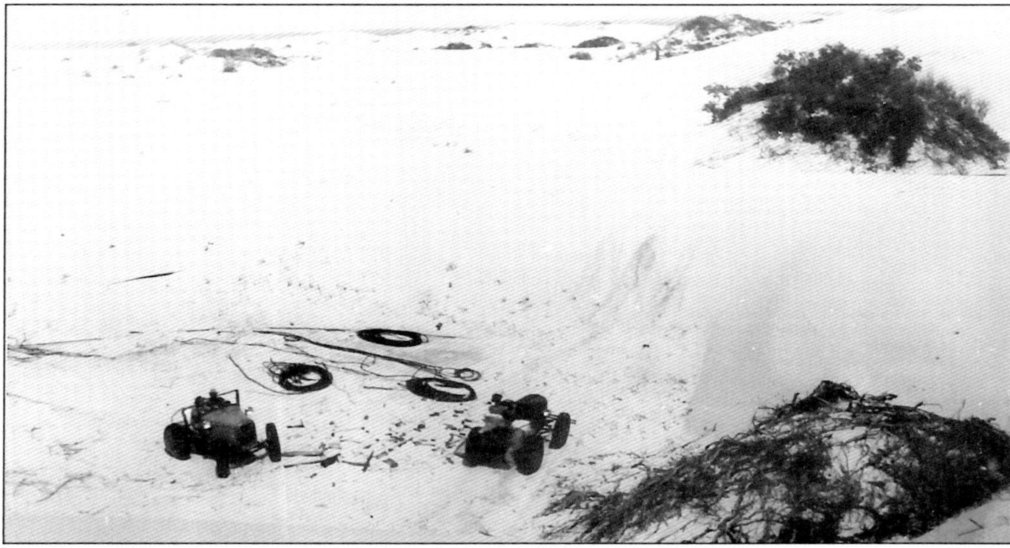

A favorite local landmark, the Crane sand hills have been the location of fun for many occasions throughout history. Homemade sand dune buggies were designed to operate over the loose terrain of the hills and served perfectly for those who went out to "run the dunes." Vehicles like these were also used for driving the road to Odessa, which used to be a sandy path. They checked the road for any deaths caused by hydrogen sulfide, because it flared from the oil wells at lethal levels during the early days of the industry. These photographs date back to the 1930s.

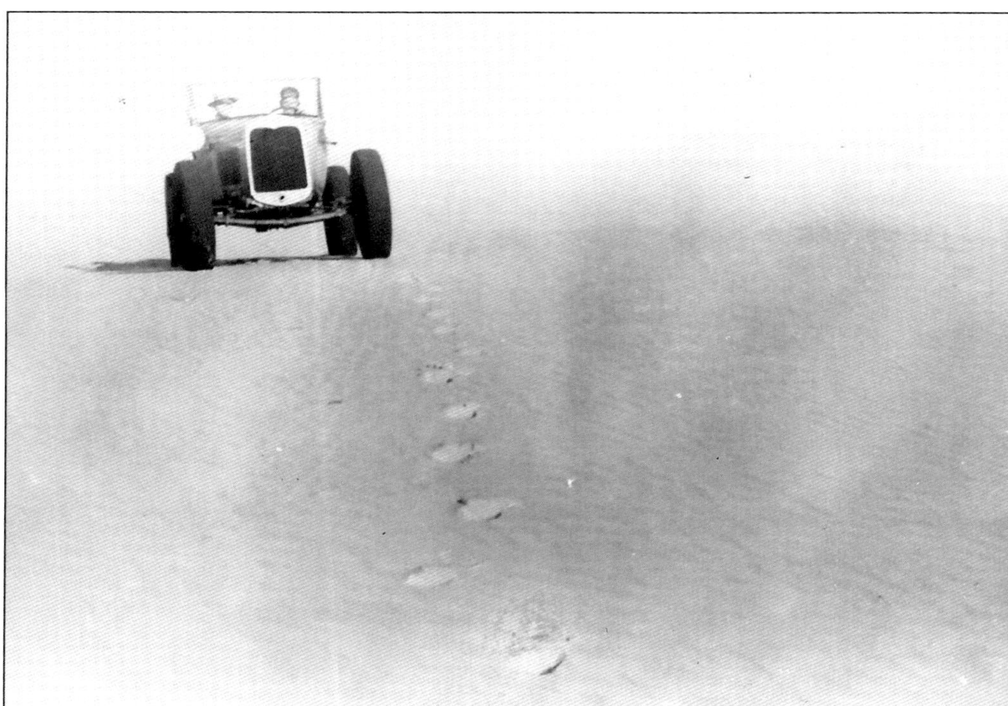

Slim Curfew and ? Ashburn bet on different candidates for the 1936 presidential election and agreed that the loser would have to pull the winner in a wagon 20 miles south to McCamey. Curfew boasted the victory and wore a sign that touted, "ROOSEVELT WON AND I RIDE," while Ashburn's sign lamented, "I KNOW NO BETTER I BET ON ALF LANDON." Curfew rounded up a little radio flyer along with a jug of whiskey and Ashburn hitched the wagon and began hauling the winner along the highway. A very tall and slender man, Slim started to feel cramped in the wagon and actually offered to pull Ashburn for a while. News about the deal spread so fast that spectators even started lining the road to watch the two comrades roll into town as they took turns pulling each other.

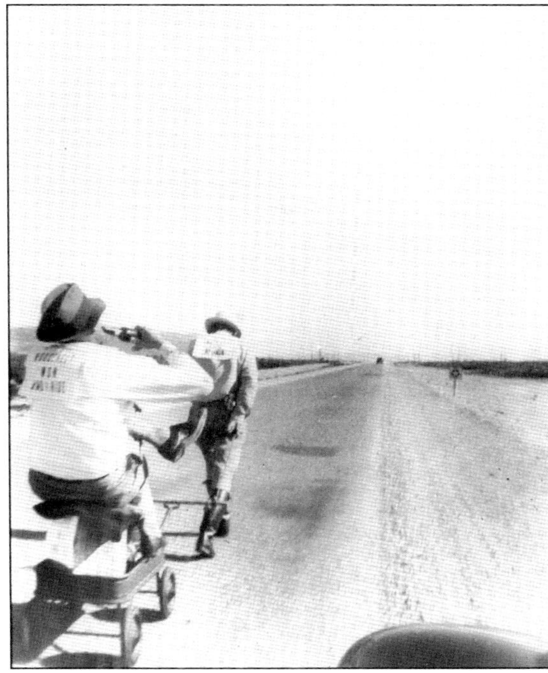

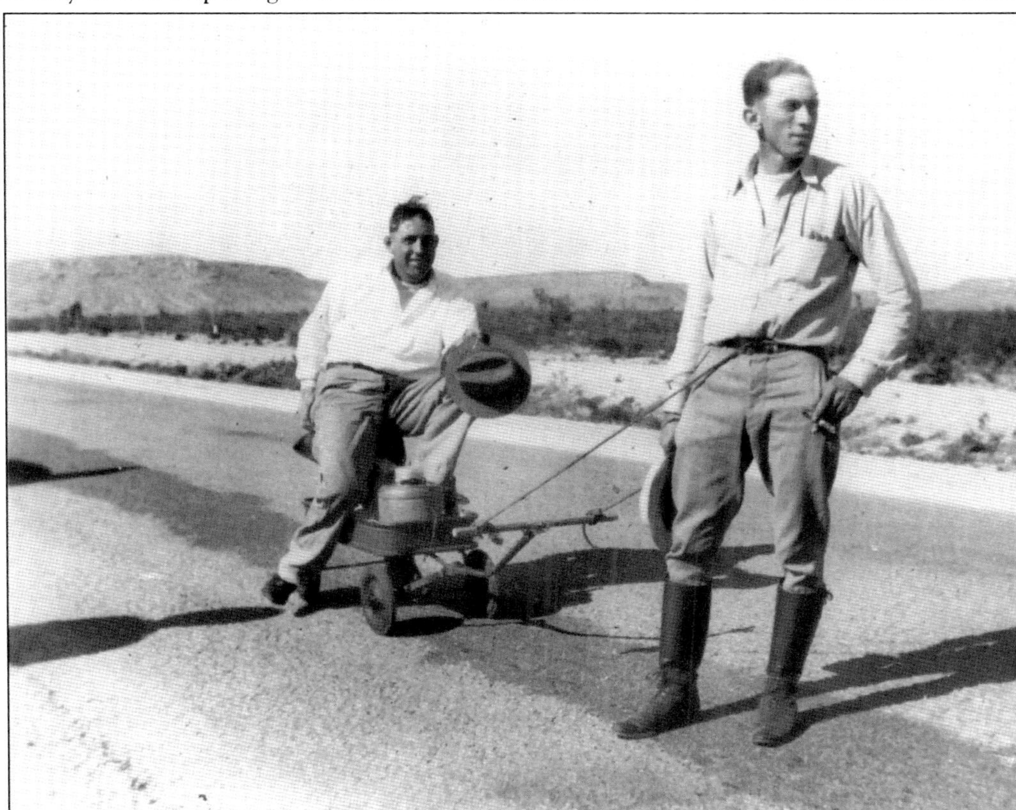

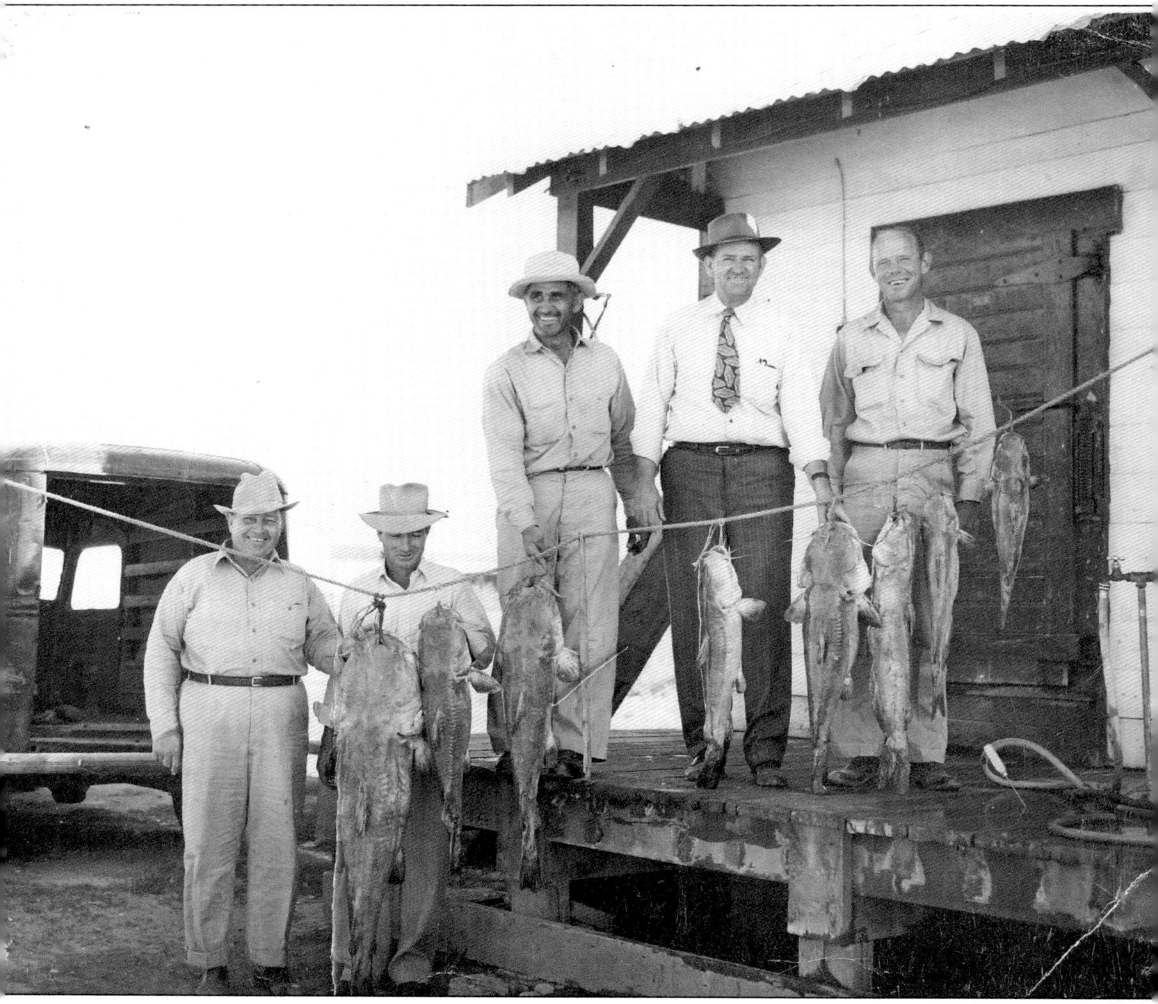

Area residents used to enjoy fishing trips to the Rio Grande, where impressive catches of catfish, like this one, made it well worth the drive. This 1940s photograph shows, from left to right, Oscar Reynolds, Ned West, Jimmy Zarafonetis, R.D. Shaffer, and John W. Willis, grinning happily in light of their successful day.

Devastation left by a tornado that passed through sent local residents rummaging amongst the rubble. Located on the edge of Tornado Alley, Crane has taken many hits throughout the years from the afternoon storms that whip up in the intense summer heat. Children (right) can be seen scouring the debris where a house once stood, and the remains of a bed frame show how uprooting the weather can be for a household. A Humble gas station (below) stood visibly intact beneath the passing storm clouds above it. Taken in 1939, these photographs capture the grief that Tornado Alley residents are often acquainted with and remind Crane today of the resilient character by which the community has thrived.

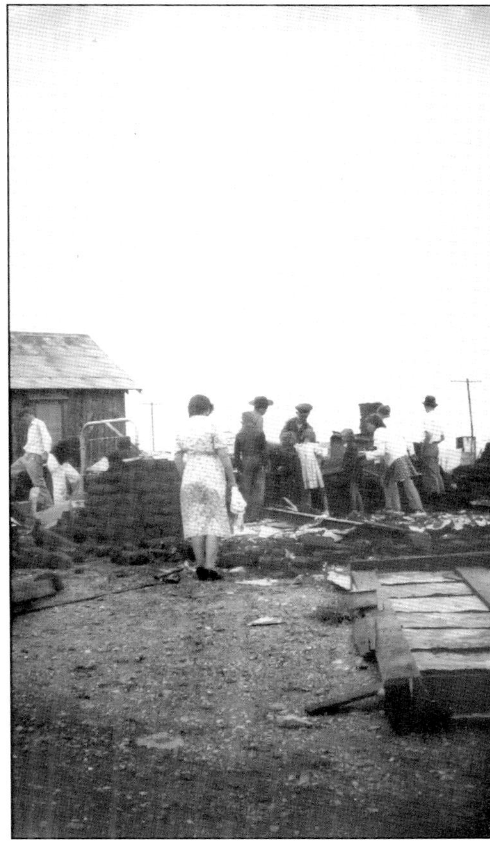

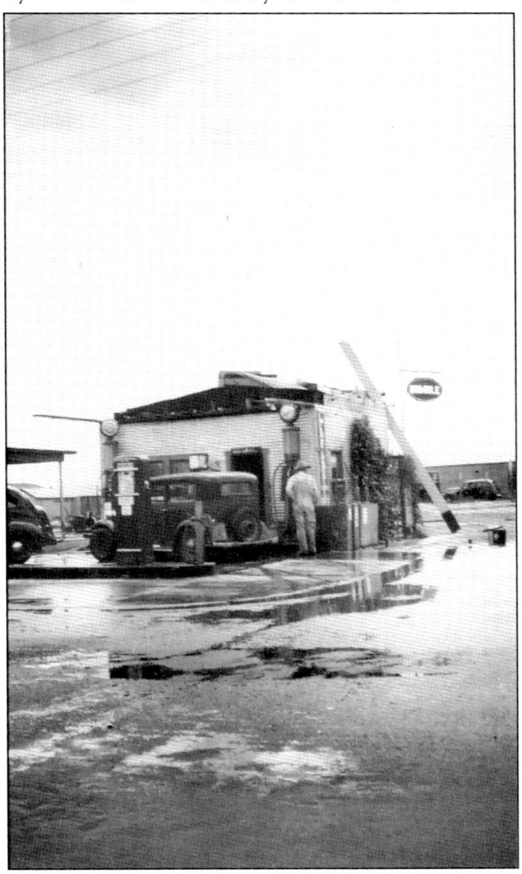

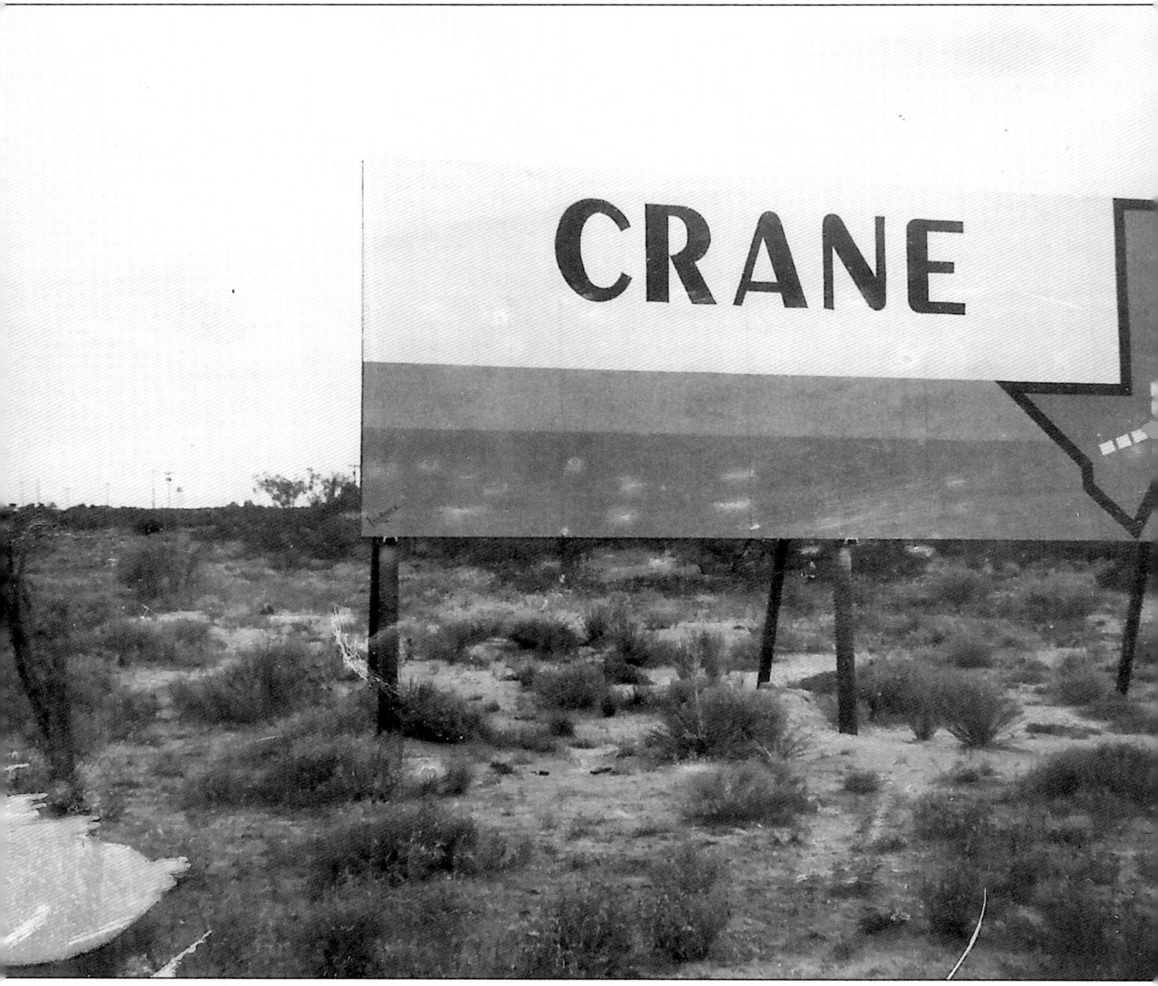

A sign on the side of the highway leading into town marked Crane's location on a Texas map. Dated from around the 1950s, this landmark is not there anymore, but it still stands in the memory of the town's older generations. The terrain remains much the same—brush, sand, and the big West Texas sky are all familiar sights.

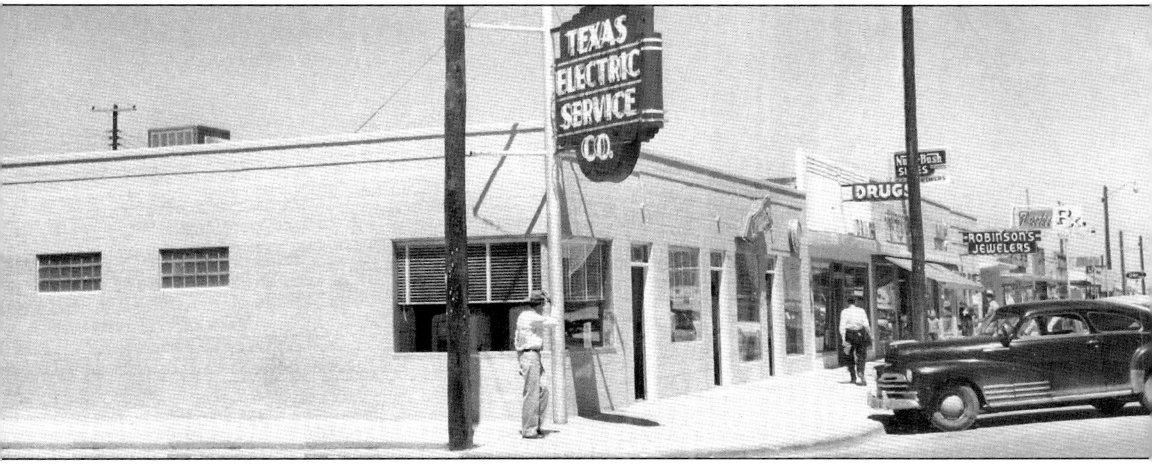

A photograph of one corner on Crane's "Main Street" shows the bustling community as it was in the late 1940s. Texas Electric Service Company, on the corner, stood next to Pat Passur's liquor store. T&P Clothiers housed their business by Robinson's Jewelers, which was next to the Keltner Drugstore, then owned by Darryl Keltner.

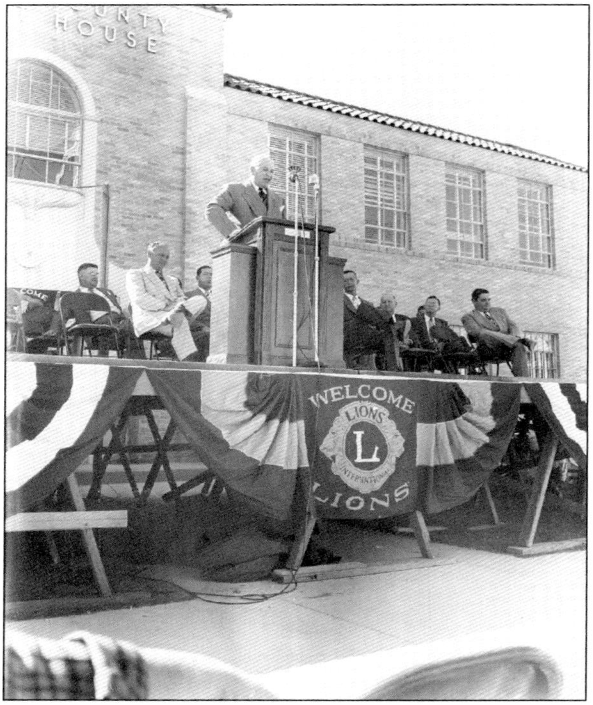

Crane County celebrated the dedication of the county courthouse on October 13, 1949. The county attorney at the time, Ken G. Spencer, was present for the big event along with H.D. Christian, preacher for the First Baptist Church, and speakers Associate Justice McGill and Congressman Ken Regan of Midland, Texas. The courthouse has undergone several remodels since the dedication day, but it still remains in the same location on Sixth Street. Local resident Ed Doshier remembers when he and his wife were making plans to move to Crane—they had never heard of the town before receiving a job offer there, but when they learned it was the county seat, they were pretty impressed. Expecting to move to a decently sized city, they soon learned that it is the only community in the entire county.

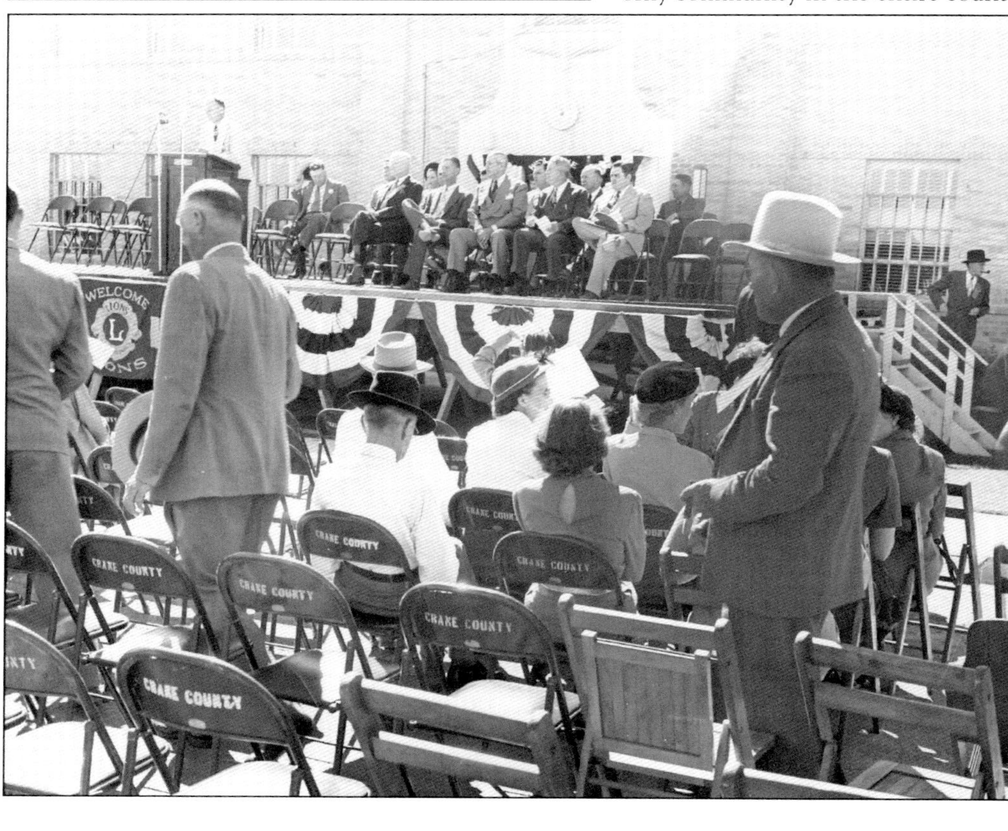

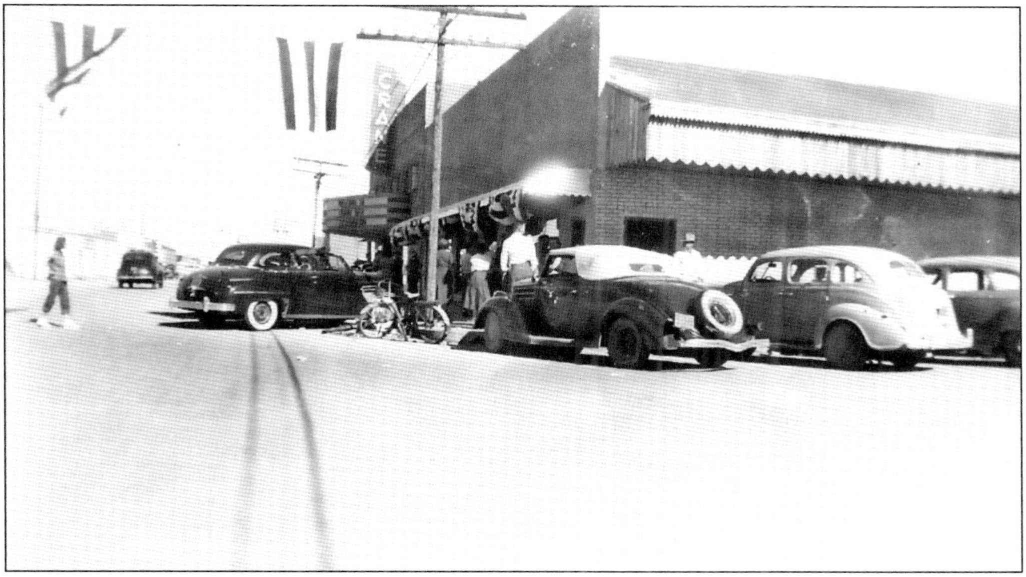

A photograph of the local theater around the 1940s shows what the cinema looked like during its prime. This particular day, the marquee read "WELCOME TO CRANE DAY CELEBRATION." Decorated with flags and banners, the street jittered along as spectators gathered around the entrance to the movie house. No longer in operation, the theater quietly stands today as another addition to the collection of nostalgic buildings throughout the town.

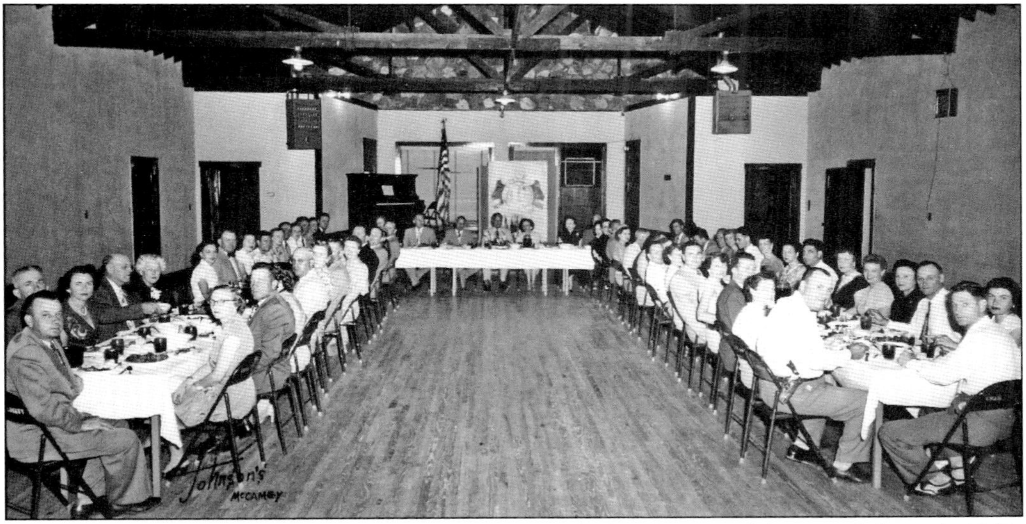

The only man identified in this image at a meeting of the local Lions Club around the early 1950s is Don Chaney—fifth from the front on the left side of the right-hand table. Hometown musician Spud Curfew has whimsical memories from playing at Lions Club meetings during this era of the men jovially chunking biscuits at him when the women were not present.

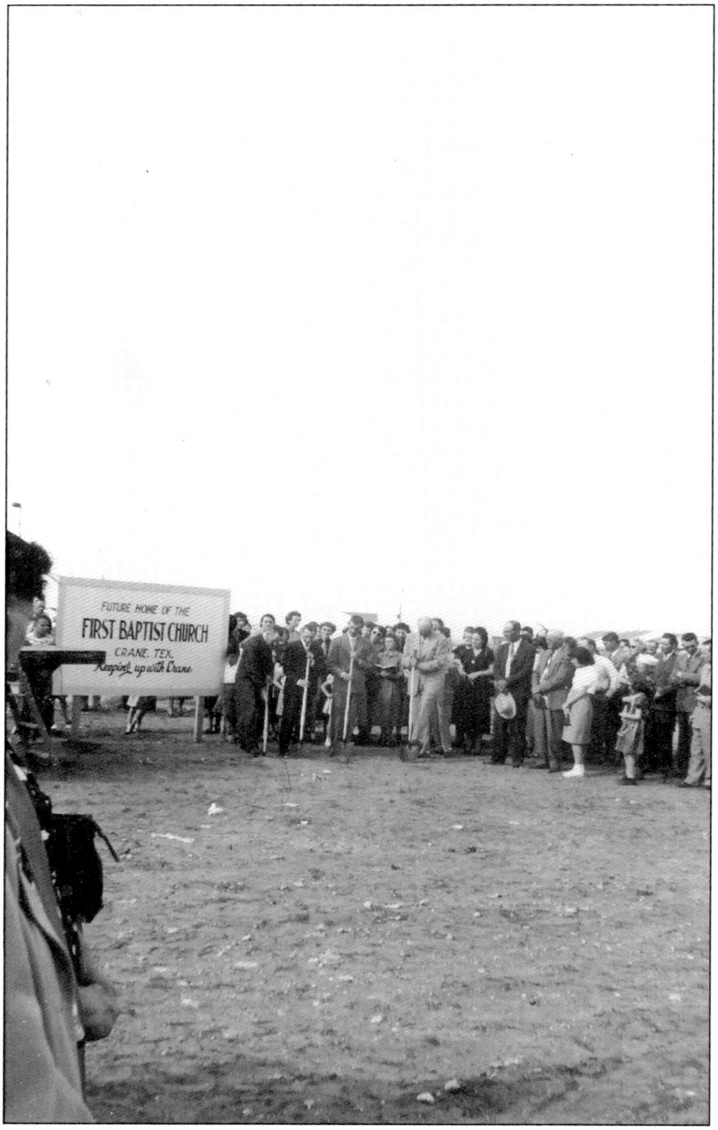

Crane's First Baptist Church held the groundbreaking for its new building in the early 1950s on the corner of Sue and Fourth Streets. The structure burned down in an arson fire in 2010. Crane's history with the Baptists is actually traced back to its origins; the town is named after Baptist preacher William Carey Crane, who served as president of Baylor University for 25 years. Despite this, he never even visited the town.

Crane Independent School District's football field is home to many Friday nights of a favorite Texas pastime. The two-story building behind the field pictured here was previously the county courthouse and was located on Sixth Street. When the remodel took place for the new courthouse, this older one was moved behind the field.

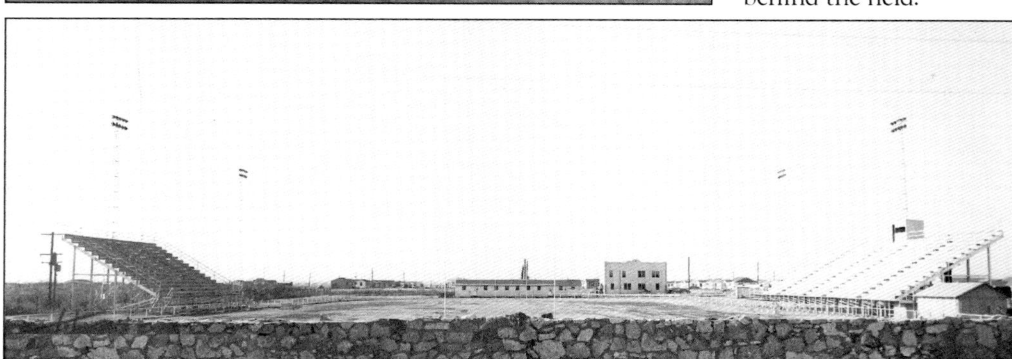

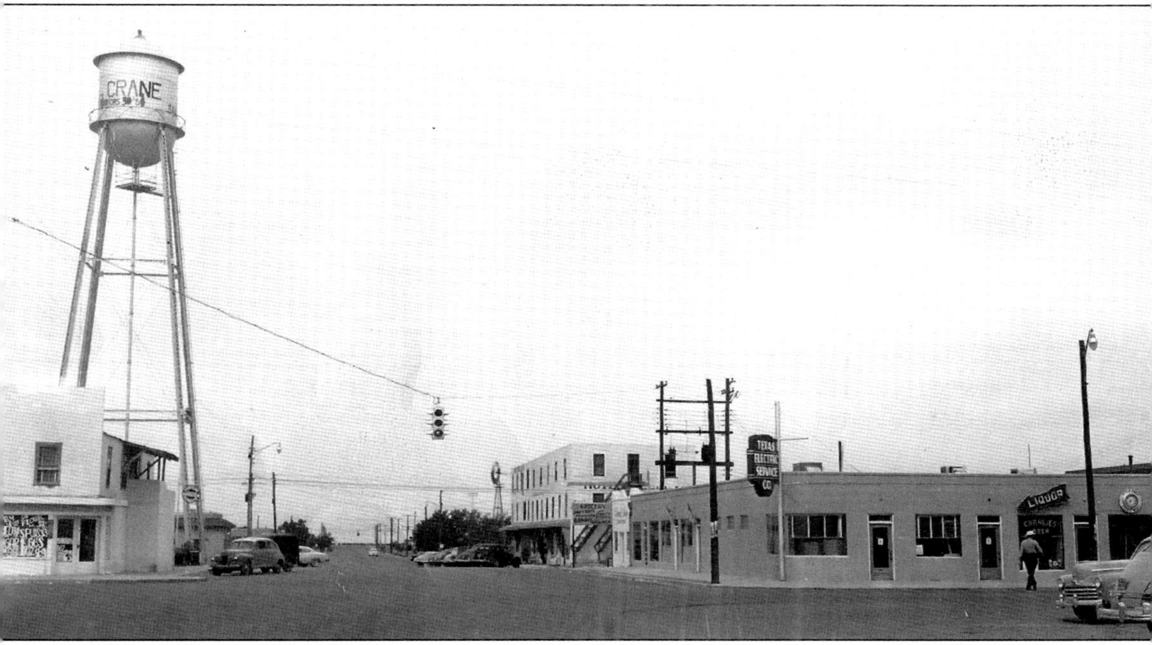

The Schaffer's grocery store (front left) stands where Crane Independent School District currently keeps its office. The old water tower is seen here with the high school class of 1950–1951's "signature" on it. The three-story building (back right) used to be the Neely Hotel, which now houses the Crane Pharmacy. Texas Electric Service Company (front right) had its office on the corner next to Pat Passur's liquor store.

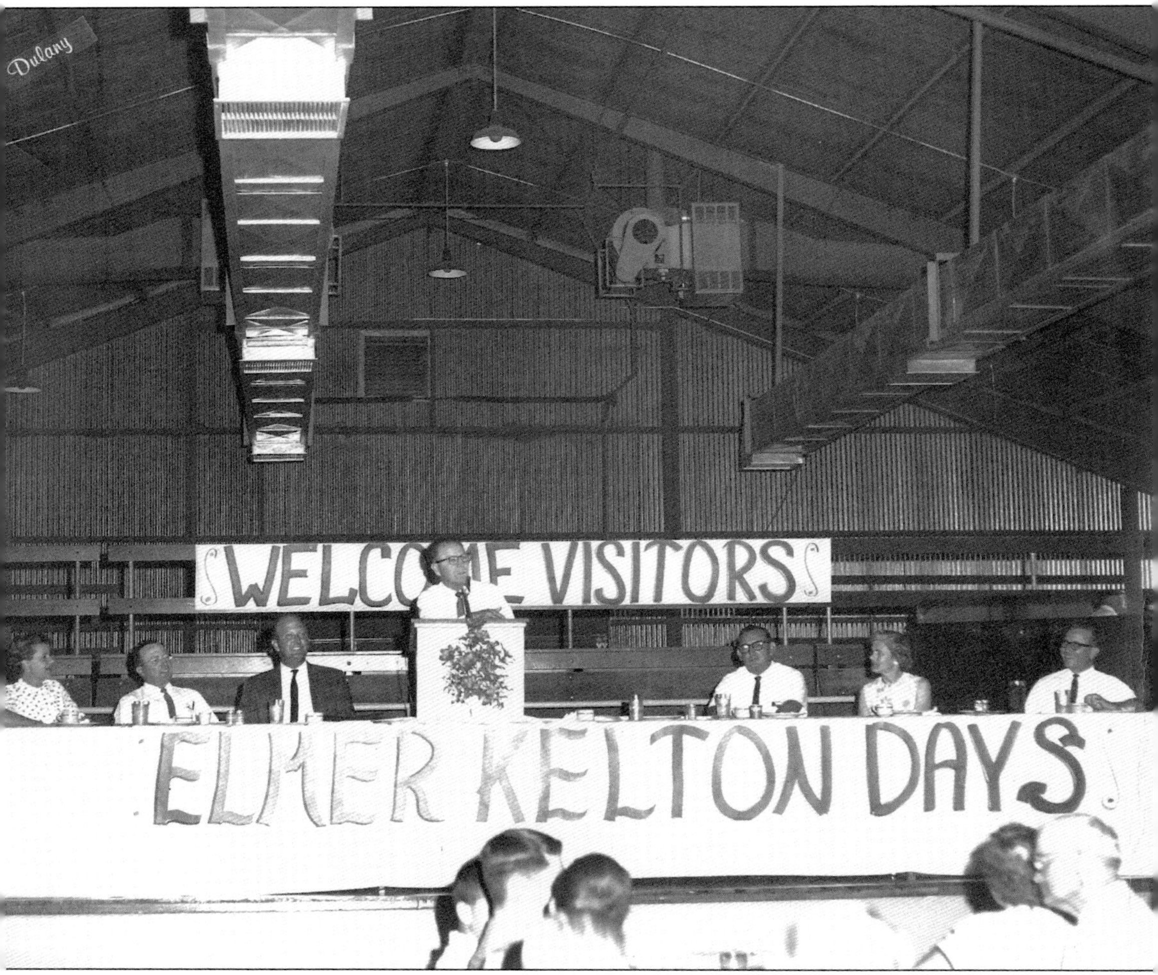

The chamber of commerce frequently held banquets for different events, and on one occasion, it held one in honor of hometown Western author Elmer Kelton. Pictured in this photograph at the Elmer Kelton Breakfast are, from left to right, Annie Kelton (Kelton's wife), Elmer Kelton, Ace Reed (also known as "The Cowpoke"), guest speaker Paul Patterson (Kelton's former teacher and master of ceremonies), Hugh McManus, Buella McManus, Melvin Prather, and Mrs. Prather.

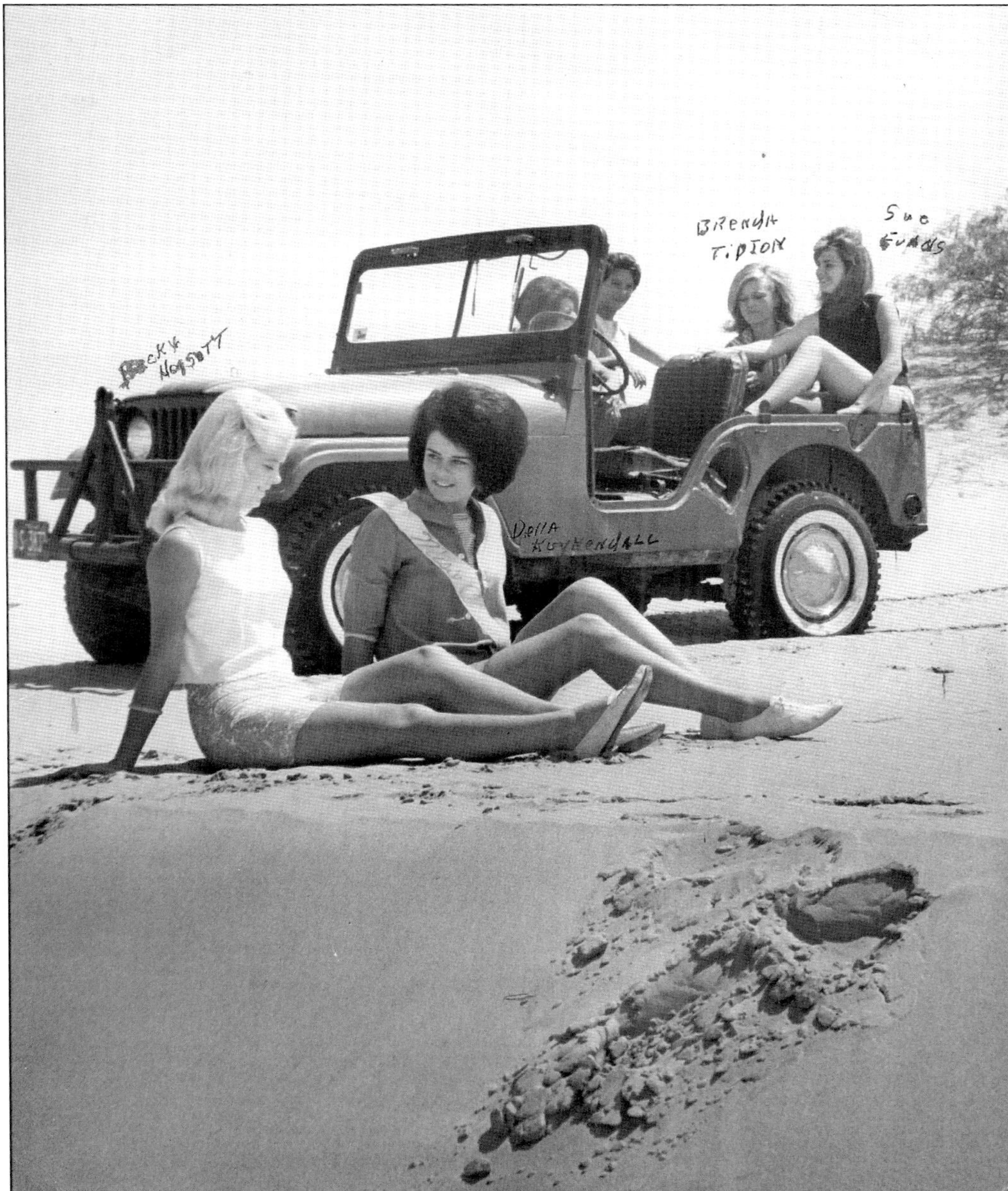

For the purpose of creating an article that was to announce the results of the Miss Crane contest, the Miss Crane court headed out to the sand hills one sunny day with a jeep and plenty of smiles for a photo shoot. Intended for the *Odessa Lifetime* magazine, this photograph shows, from left to right, Becky Hoggett, two unidentified, Della Kuykendall, Brenda Tipton, and Sue Funds.

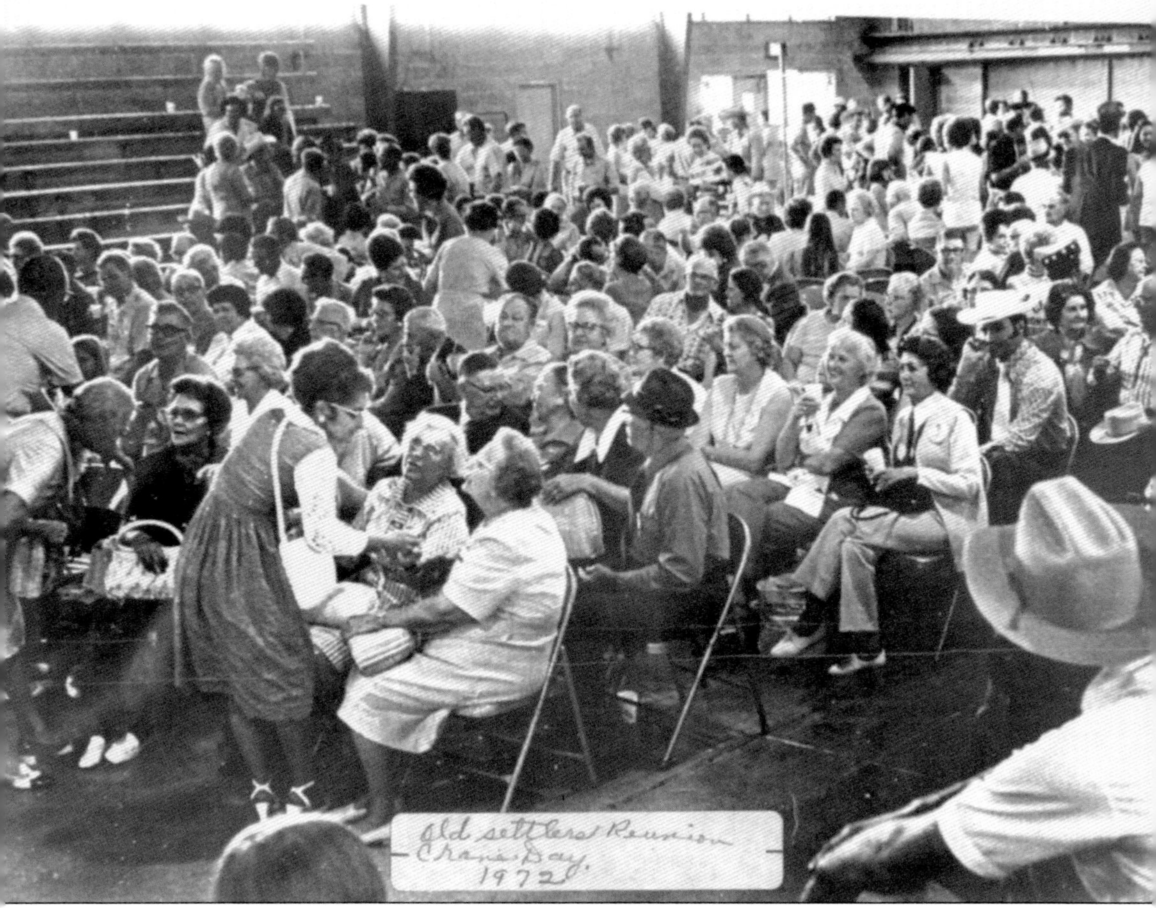

What began as a Gulf Corporation Sand Hills Reunion later developed into the Old Settlers' Reunion. Crane's heritage in the oilfield is a very proud part of its history and continues to live on in the work and way of life of successive generations. Pictured here are visitors at the reunion in 1972.

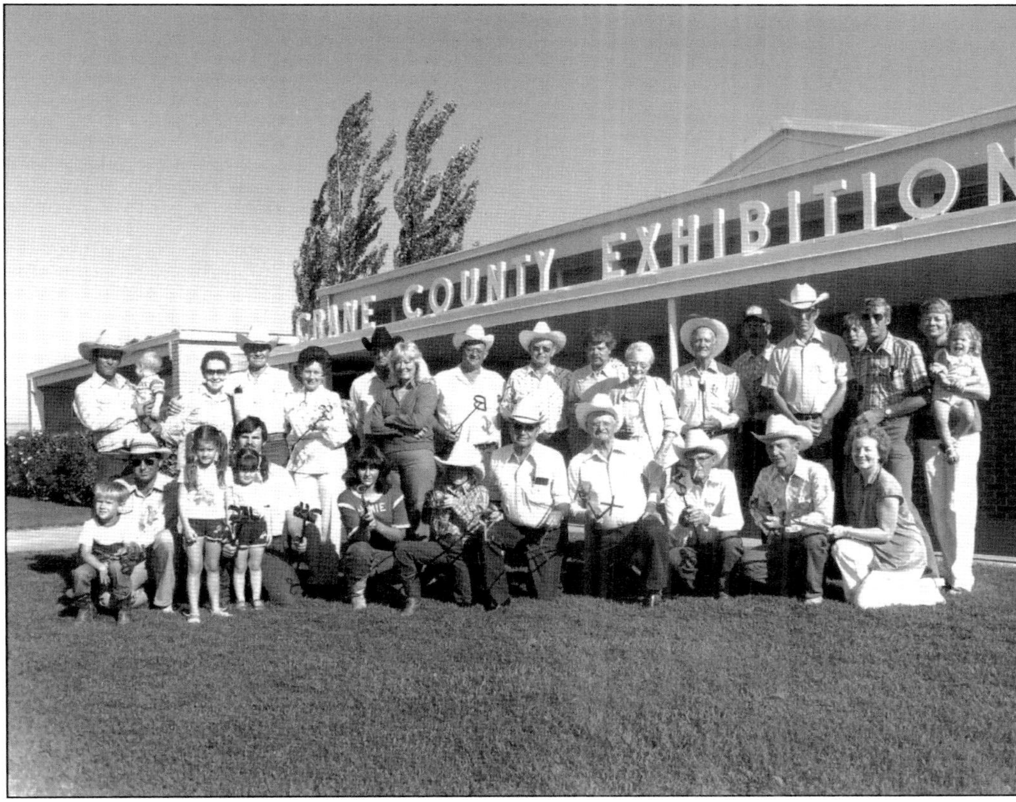

Rancher's Day welcomed, from left to right, (first row) Bill Boyd, Gene Cowden and daughters, Sunny and Shannon Cowden, Jamie and Jana Pierce, John Hargrove, Marven Hooper, M.F. Clark, and Bobby and ? Bowden; (second row) Gaylord Russell and ? Russell, Mary Ward, Tiny Earp, Mildred Earp, John Pierce, Carlton Pierce, Billy Url Butler, Jack Crider, Bobby Crider, Emma Hooper, Quay Clark, Rusty Earp, Fred Wilkerson, Trey Morgan, Gordon and Peggy Morgan, and ? Morgan.

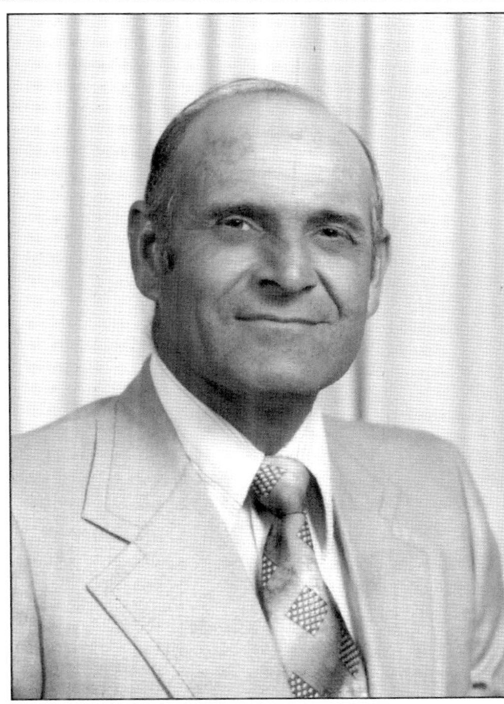

Douglas H. Damron was elected mayor in 1979 after four years on the chamber of commerce board (one year as president) and eight years as a city councilman. He and his family moved to Crane when he was only a few months old and lived in the Gulf Camp, where his father, Hayes Damron, worked in the oilfield. Doug also owned Damron Welding Service, Inc.

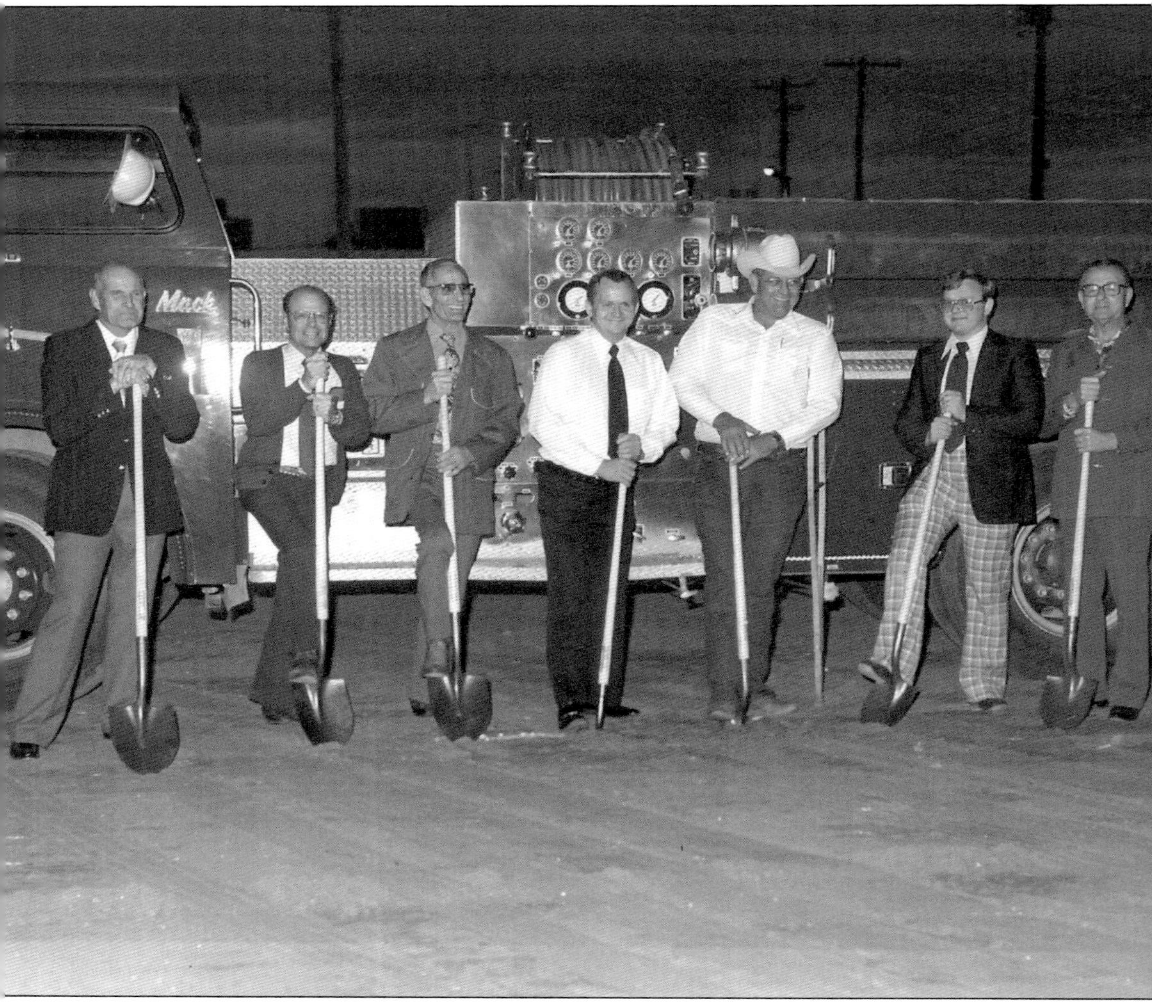

The ground-breaking for Crane's new fire station was celebrated with, from left to right, Doug Damron, Jack Atkinson, Glen Grishon, Fiddle Blue, Billy Earl Butler, Johnny Ainsworth, and T.N. White. The very first fire that prompted the town to develop a firefighting crew occurred when Smoky Swift's feed store burned down in 1948 without the means to put it out.

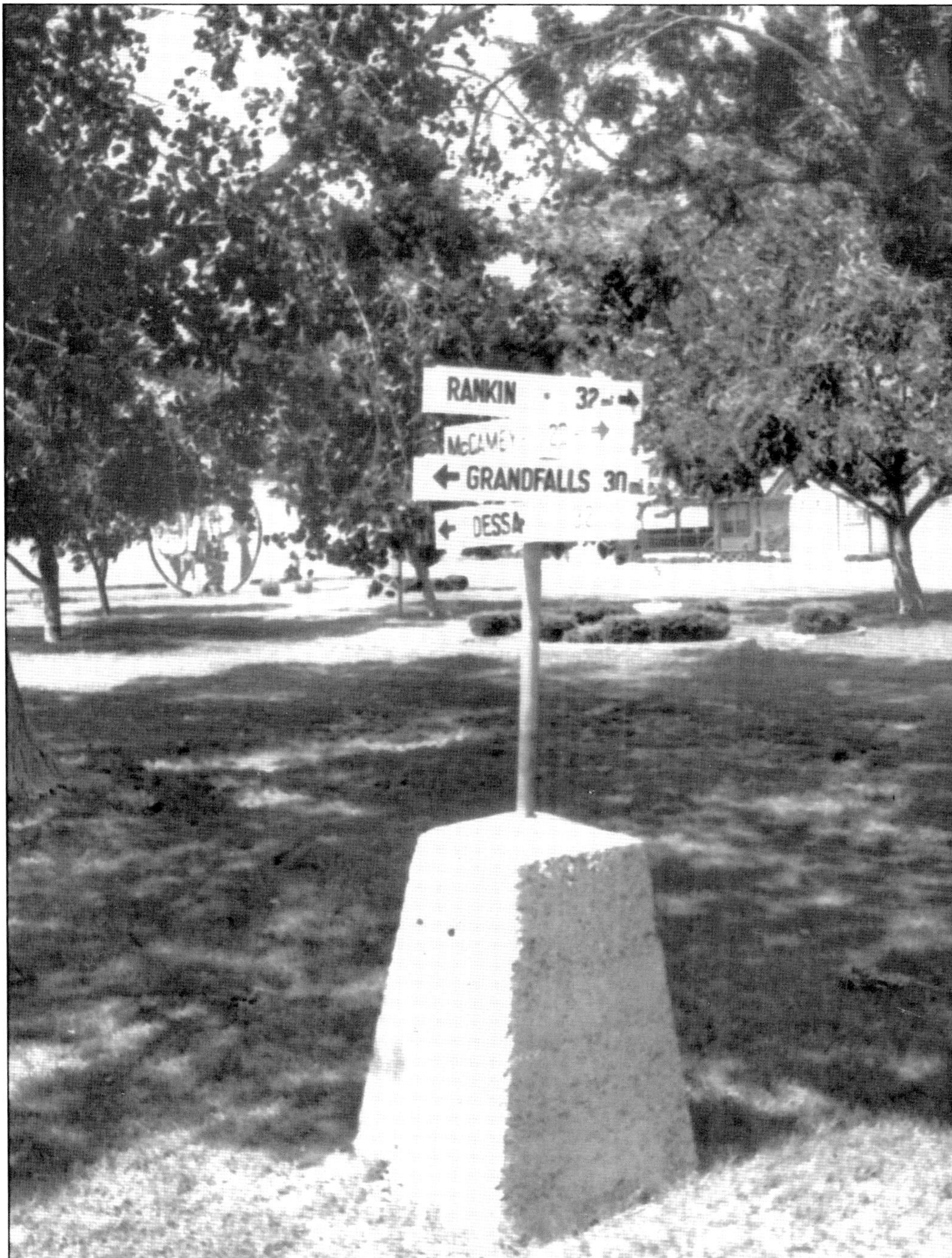

The well-known sign that points the ways to the towns of Rankin, McCamey, Grandfalls, and Odessa was originally in the middle of the main intersection of town, Highway 329 and Gaston Street, also known as Highway 385. It was later moved to the park on Sixth Street across from the courthouse. This sign has since been donated to the Museum of the Desert Southwest in Crane.

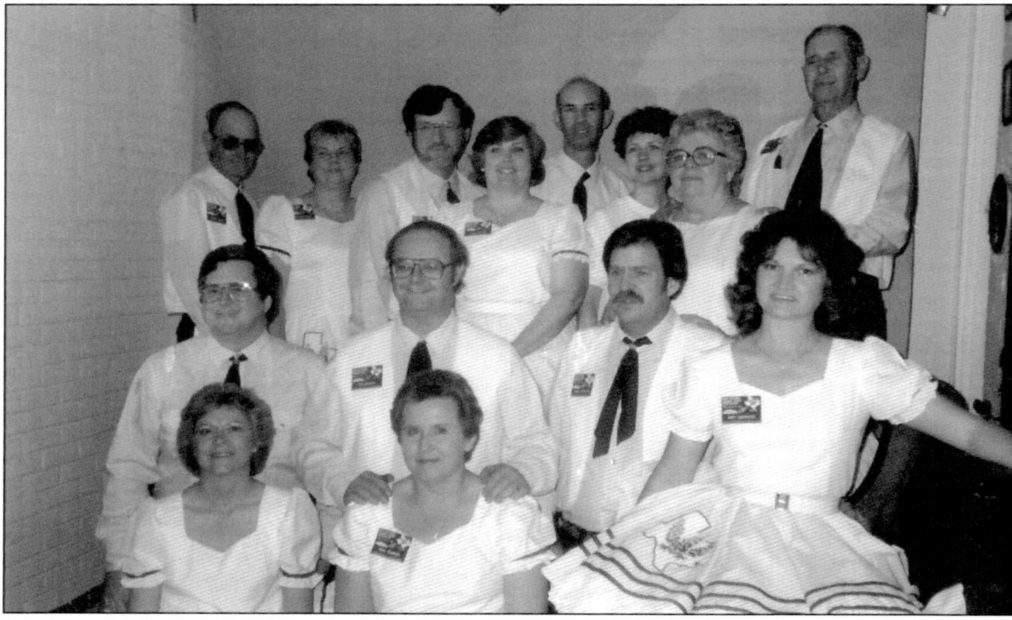

The Castle Gap Squares was a square dancing group that consisted of members from Crane, McCamey, Iraan, and Odessa. Formed in 1972, the group enjoyed 27 years together. The first two rows in this photograph (above) are unidentified, but pictured from left to right in the third row are Arnold Durham, Louise Durham, Charles Watson, Janet Watson, Tommy Carpenter, Mary Carpenter, Juanita Wittenberg, and Dar Wittenberg at the 1988 State Square Dance Festival in Houston, Texas. The Permian Basin Square Dance Association officers of 1988 (below) are, from left to right, (first row) Ray Brown, Don Boothe, Arnold Durham, Owen Tyler, and Jim Lietner; (second row) Shirley Brown, Johnnie Boothe, Louise Durham, Pat Tyler, and Julie Lietner. (Both, courtesy of Louise Durham.)

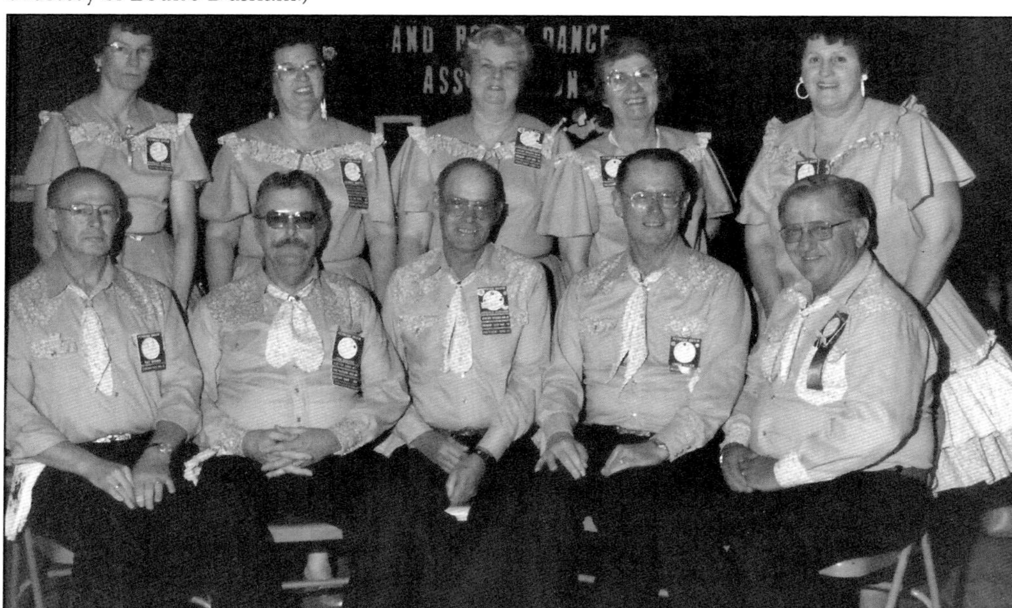

Six

COMMUNITY CHARACTERS

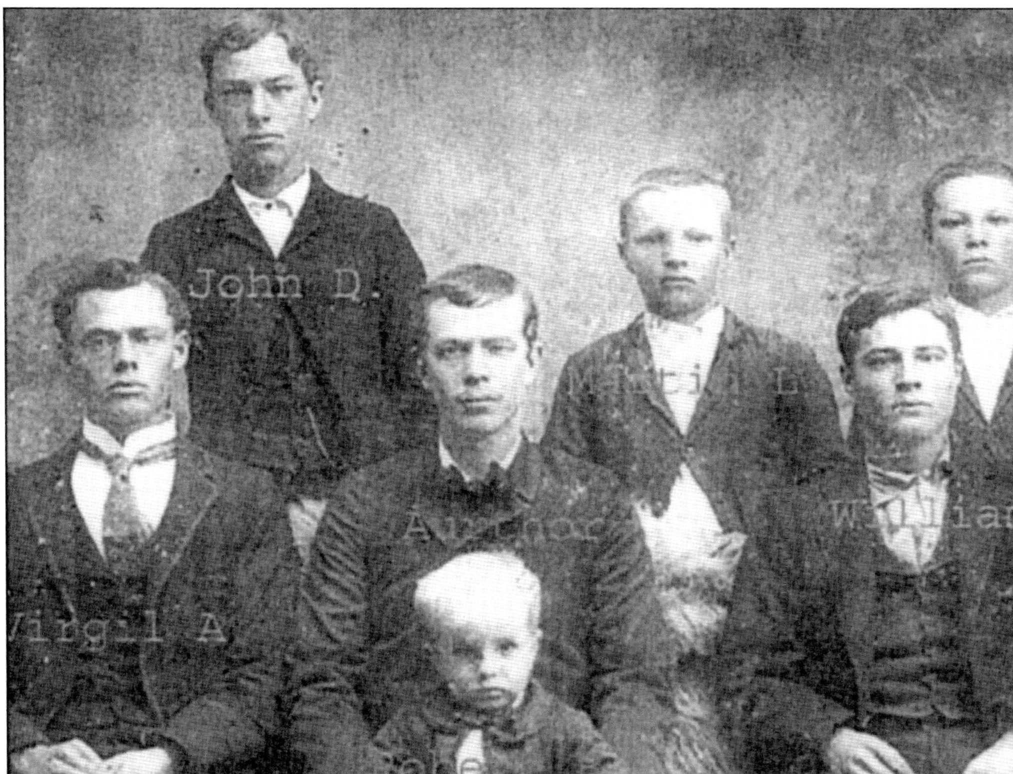

The Kinnison brothers pose for this photograph taken some time in the 1890s. Ollie Kinnison, who was better known as "O.C.," was the town realtor who drew up the Crane map, naming the city streets after his daughters. O.C. opened the first real estate office in Crane and even plotted the town site. The Kinnison brothers' first names are visible on the photograph, except for O.C., who is located at the top right. They are, from left to right, Virgil, John, Aurthor, Robert, Martin, William, and O.C. (Courtesy of Bill Kinnison.)

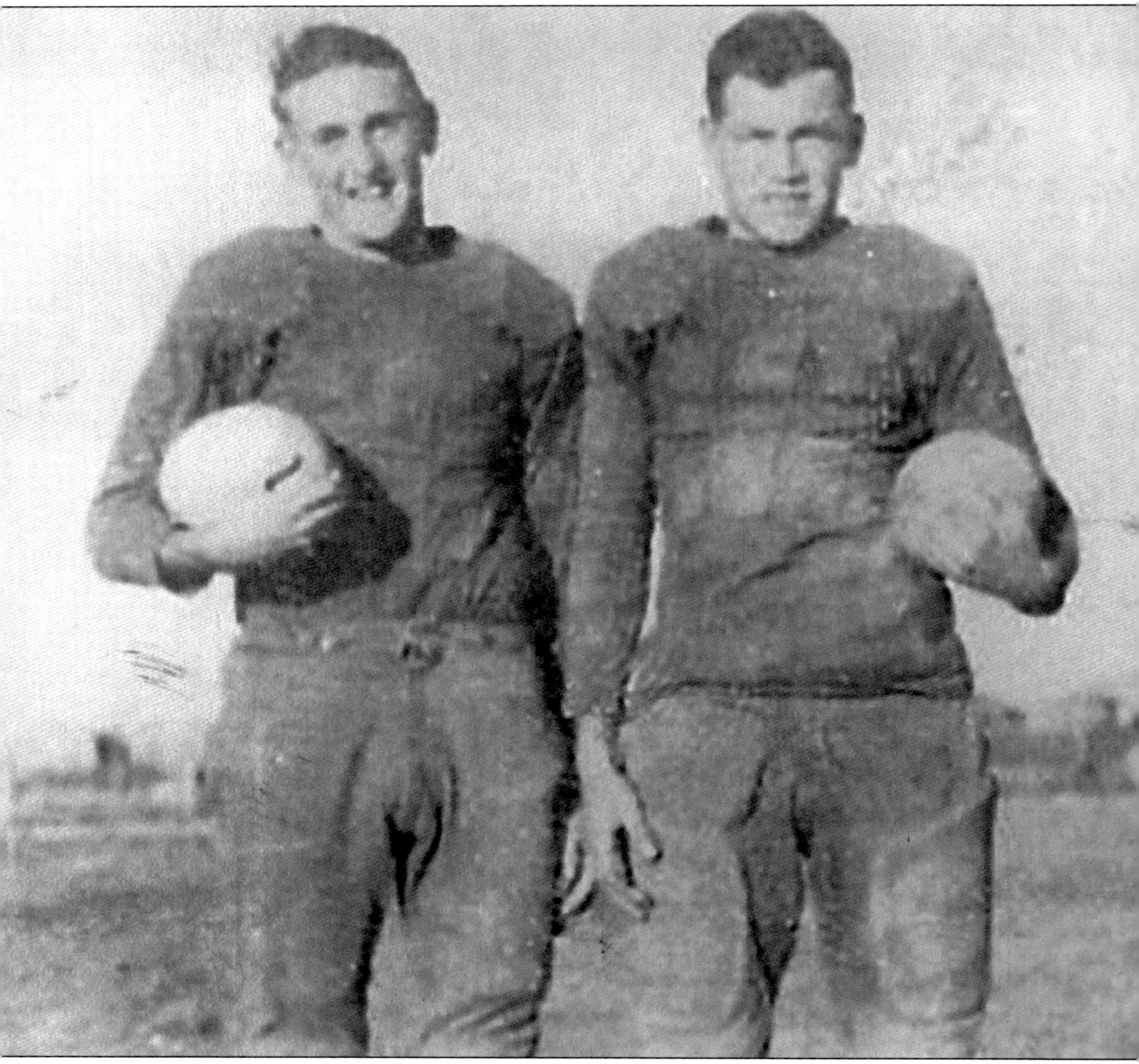

Two Crane High School football players from the class of 1935 are shown here. C.D. Ham is on the left, and A.M. "Aggie" Thorton is on the right.

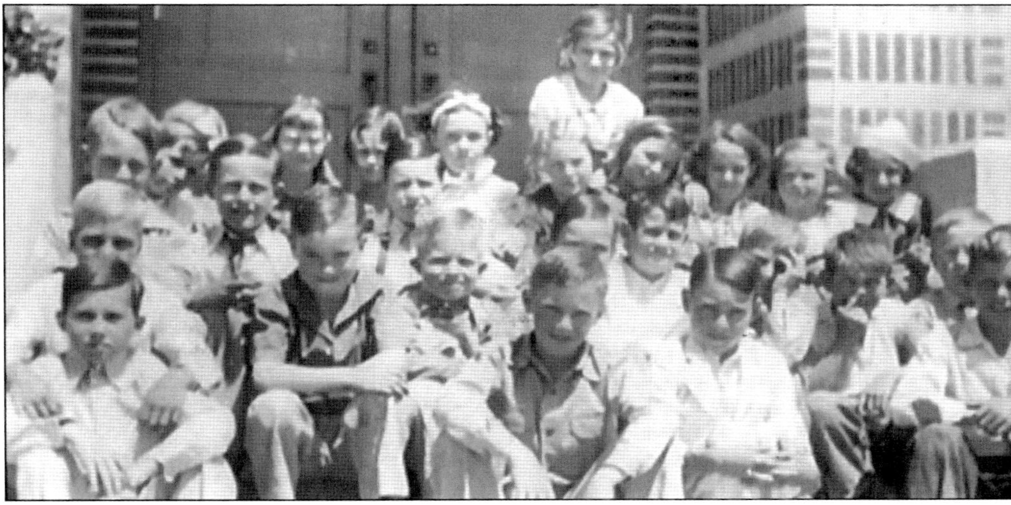

This photograph of Crane Elementary students was captured on May 9, 1937, as part of a class project. The image was subsequently copied and used as Mother's Day cards for the students to take home.

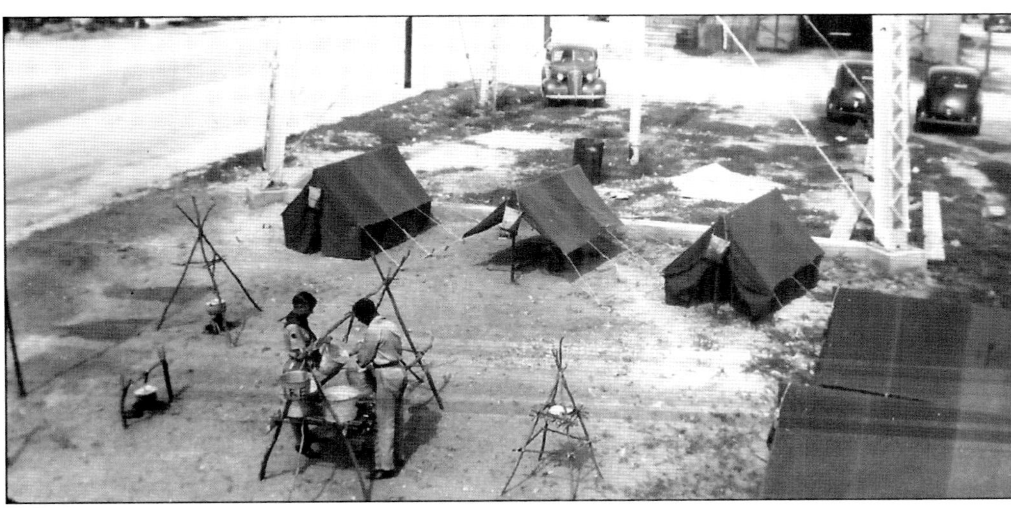

The Boy Scouts of America Troop 57 is shown here camping out beneath the city water tower in Crane. The Crane Booster Club provided tents for the campers, which the Boy Scouts erected slightly before this 1940 photograph.

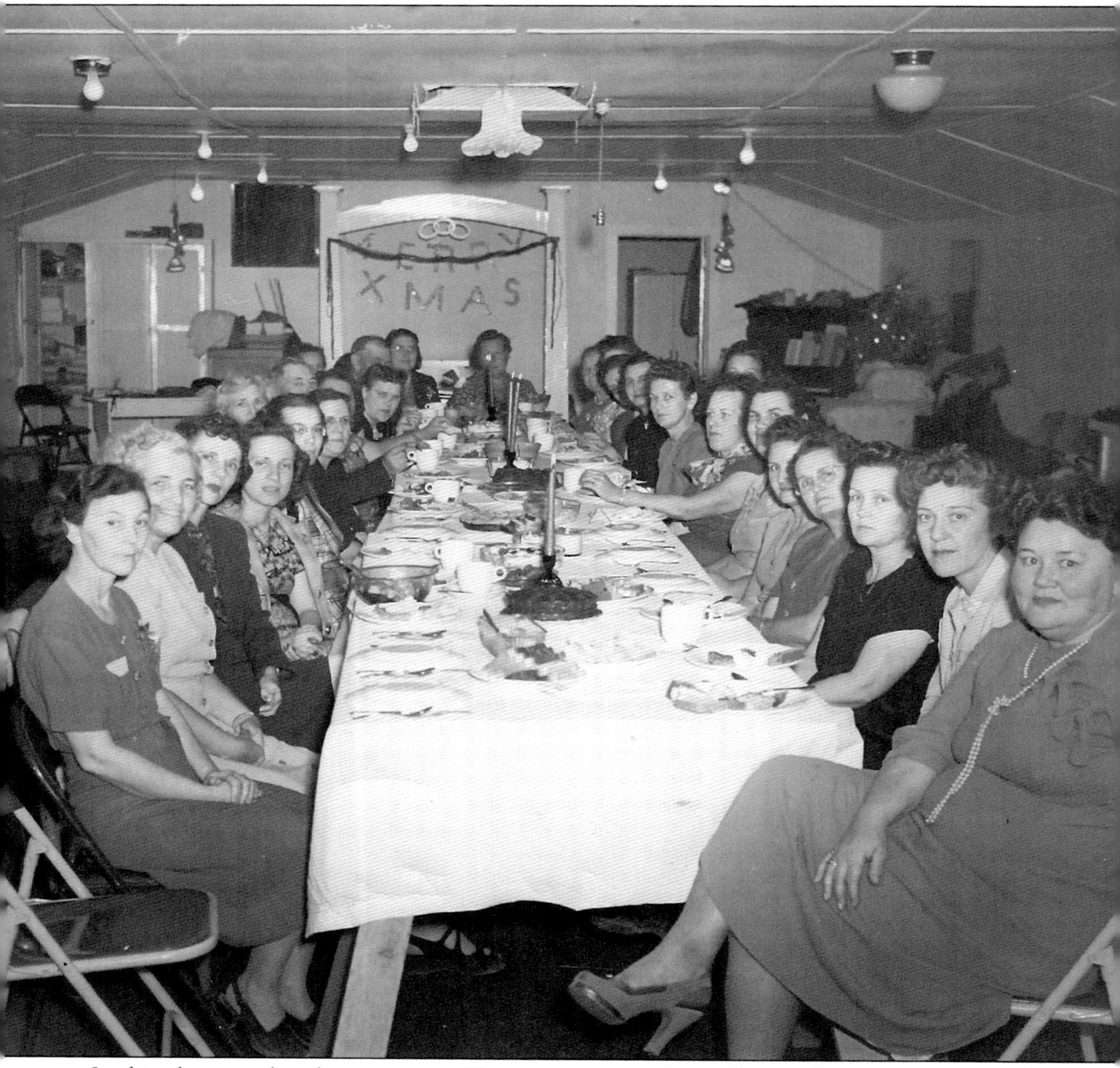

In this photograph, taken at a town Christmas party in the early to mid-1940s, a group of women pauses to reflect on the previous year and capture a special moment in time.

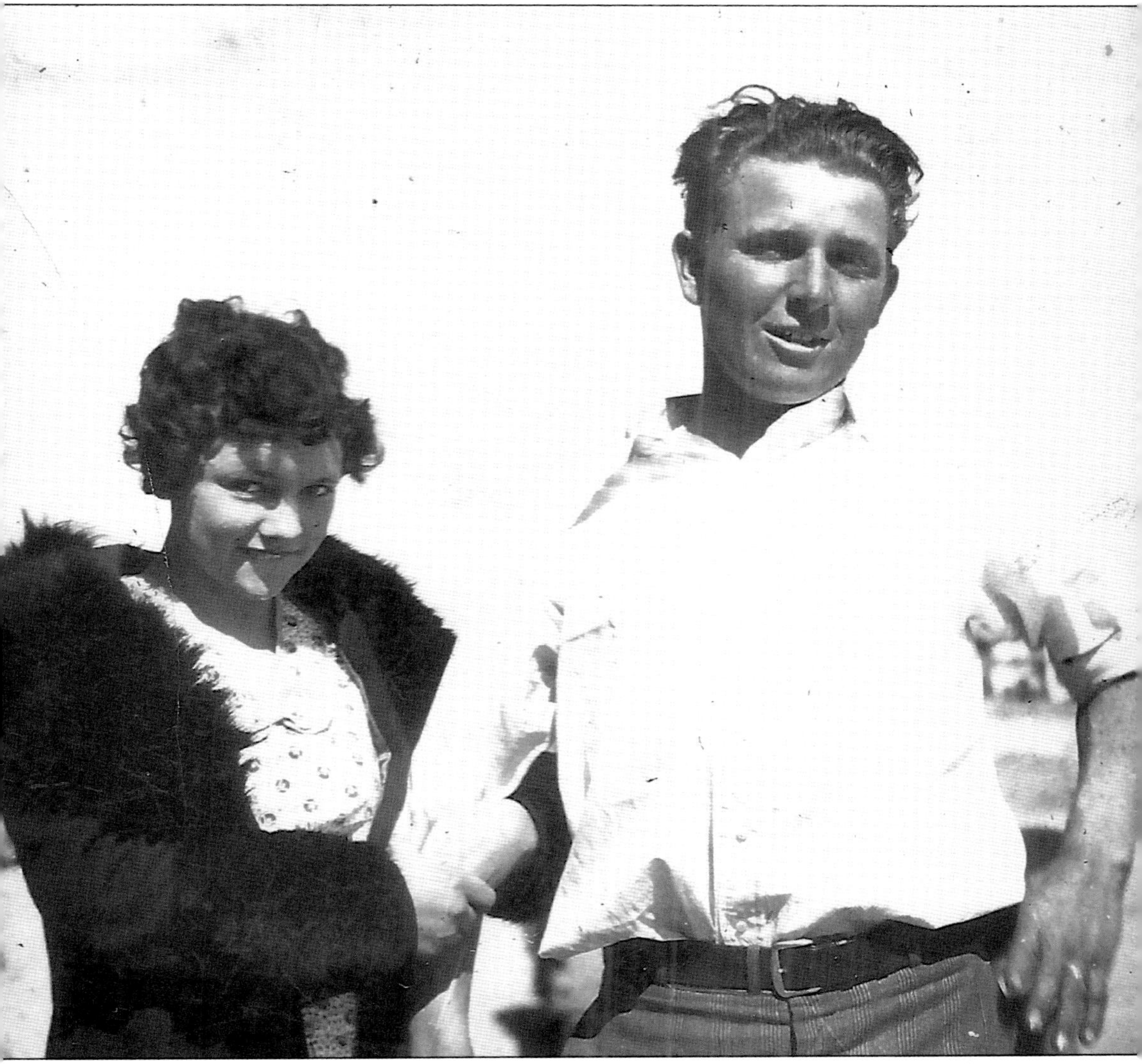

Paul Patterson, at 19, hams for the camera with a young lady in tow. Patterson was one of Crane's most prominent citizens. He taught for approximately 40 years, many of them while employed in Crane. Patterson was known for his novels, poetry, articles, and essays. Among his many achievements as an educator was being a strong influence on the bestselling writing career of Elmer Kelton. "Without Mr. Pat, I never would have gotten into writing," Kelton stated in an *American Cowboy* interview in 2008. Patterson passed away on March 14, 2008, and Kelton died one year later.

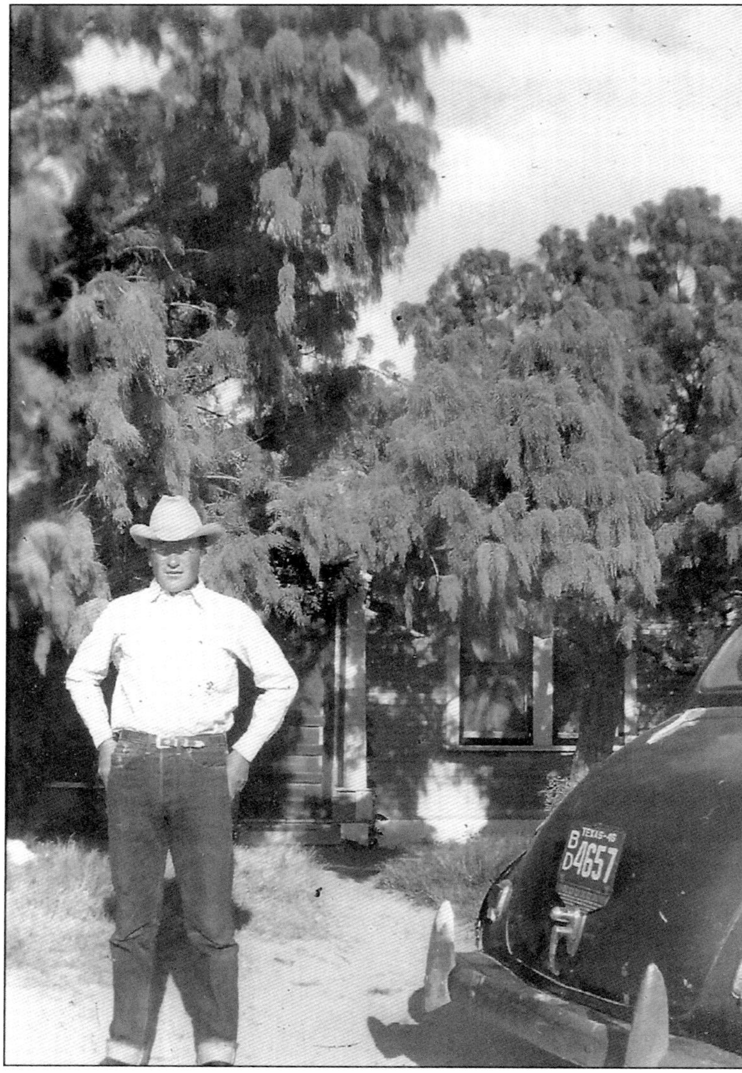

Elmer Stephen Kelton was born in Andrews, Texas, but he spent his formative years on the McElroy Ranch in Crane County. Kelton is pictured here in 1946, shortly after returning from his overseas tour with the US Army during World War II. This photograph was taken at the back of Kelton's parents' house, located on the McElroy Ranch headquarters. Kelton stated many times throughout the years that most of what he learned about the soul of the American cowboy he learned while living on the McElroy Ranch. After graduating from Crane High School, Kelton went on to earn a journalism degree at the University of Texas at Austin. Kelton met and married his wife, an Austrian woman named Ann, while serving in World War II. In his postwar career, Kelton became a very successful Western writer. In the 1990s, the Western Writers of America, a group of Kelton's Western-writing peers, named Kelton the "All-Time Best Western Author." Kelton's book *The Good Ol' Boys* was one of his most successful. In fact, famed actor and Permian Basin native Tommy Lee Jones directed and starred in a TNT television movie based on the book. Sissy Spacek costarred in the film, which aired in 1995. Another of Kelton's massively successful books is *The Time It Never Rained*, which Hollywood producers have discussed bringing to the silver screen as well. (Courtesy of Steve Kelton.)

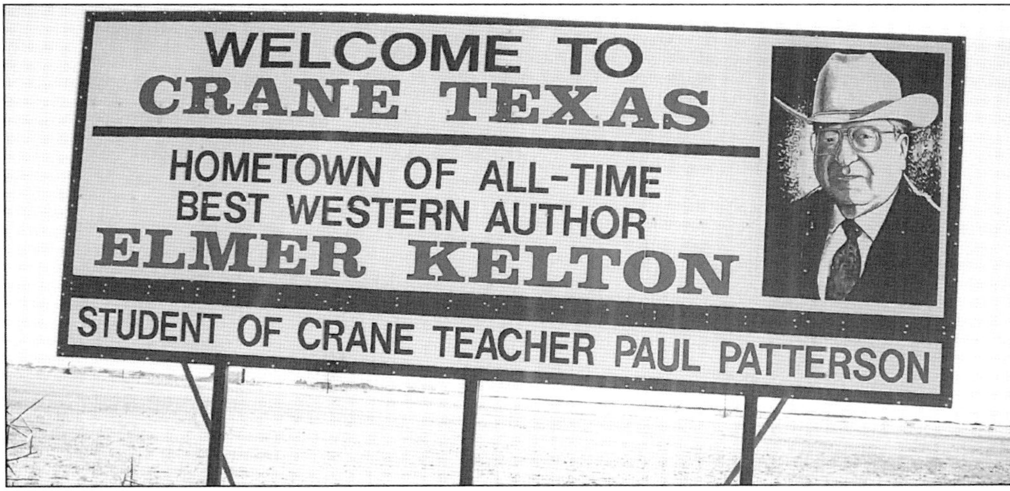

Prior to Kelton's death from multiple health problems on August 22, 2009, the Crane Historical Commission, with the assistance of a group of Crane citizens, erected a huge billboard sign on the outskirts of town that recognized Kelton's literary achievements. At Kelton's request, the billboard sign attributed much of his success as a writer to Paul Patterson, his journalism teacher in high school. Patterson, known by the locals as Mr. Pat, was also a writer and close personal friend of Kelton. Together and separately, Kelton and Patterson published countless Western stories and volumes of cowboy poetry throughout their lives.

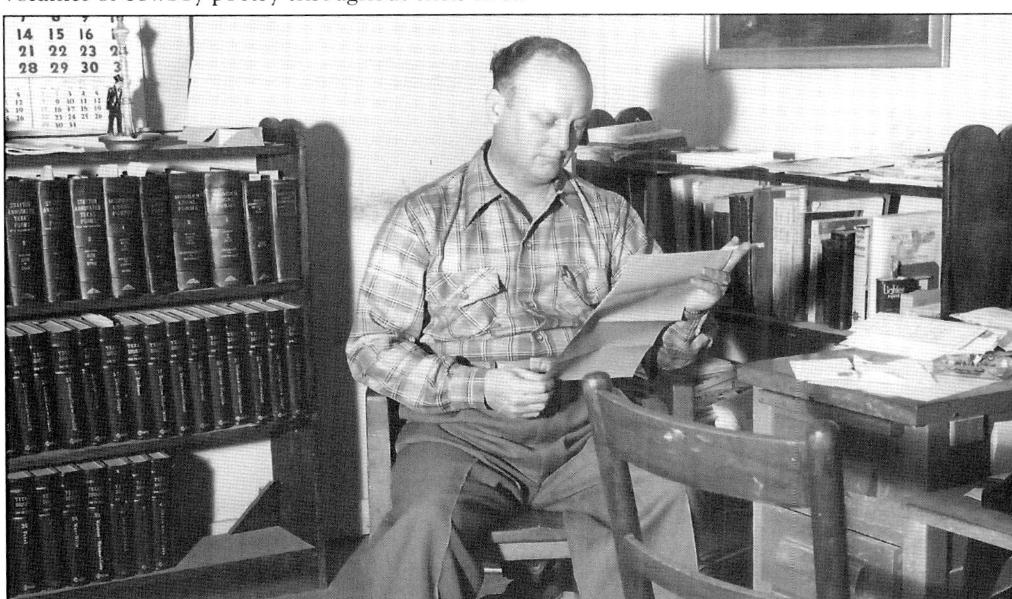

Ken G. Spencer, former district judge and 30-year Crane resident, reviews a document in his law offices in 1949. Spencer was a well-respected Crane citizen, so much so that in 1976, the Crane County Chamber of Commerce named him "Outstanding Citizen." Spencer was honored for his 30-year service to the Crane community. Spencer came to Crane in search of a place to practice law, and from 1948 to 1953, he held the post of city attorney. Subsequent to this term, he was elected Crane County attorney, a position he held until 1974, when he was elected 109th District judge, serving Crane, Winkler, and Andrews Counties.

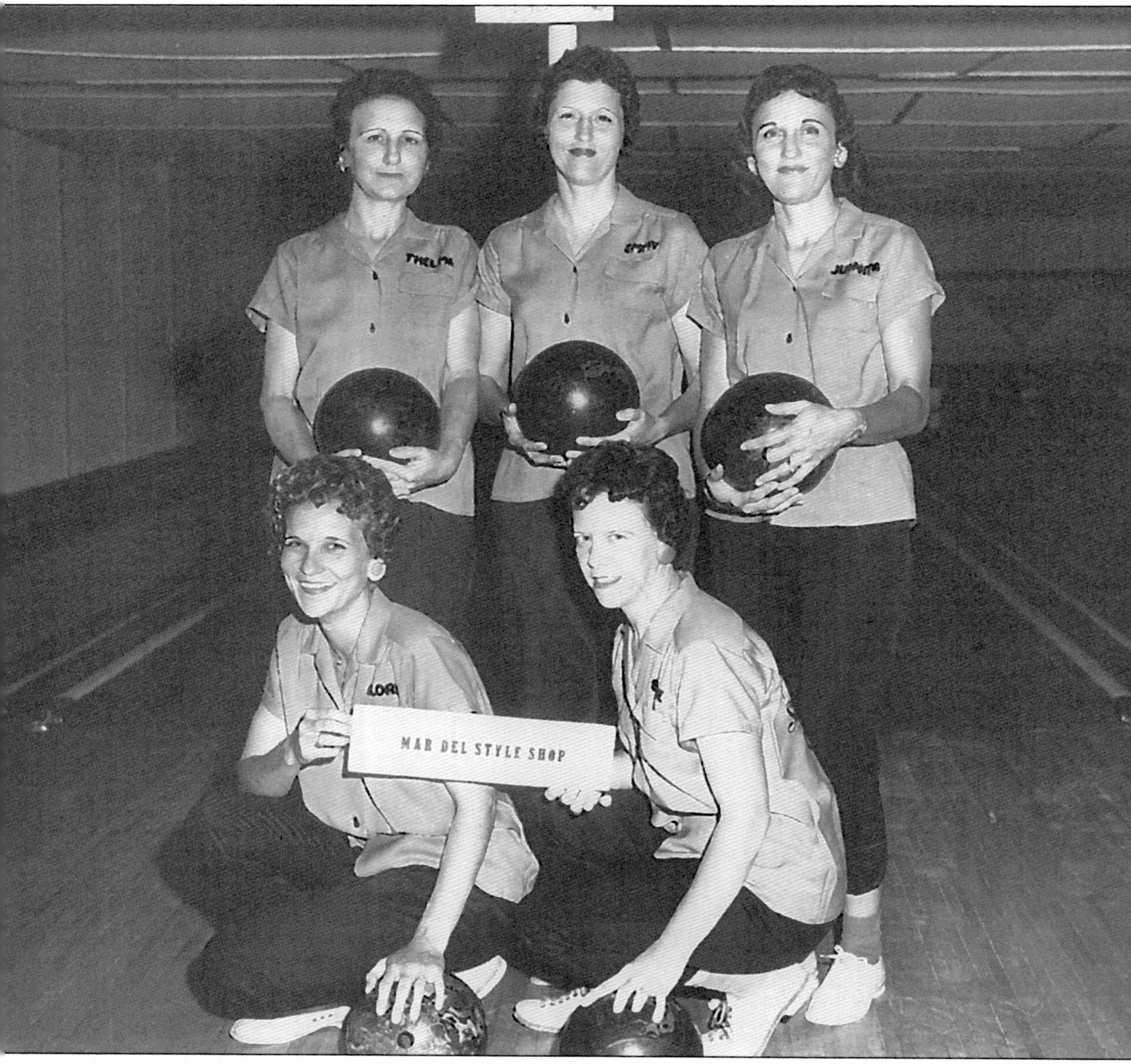

During the late 1950s, Crane could boast of having its very own bowling alley. This photograph showcases the Mar Del Style Shop bowling team. Mar Del Style Shop was a staple of Crane fashion for decades. From left to right are (first row) Gloria Milam and Billie Adkins; (second row) Thelma ?, Emma Lou Milam, and Juanita Ellison.

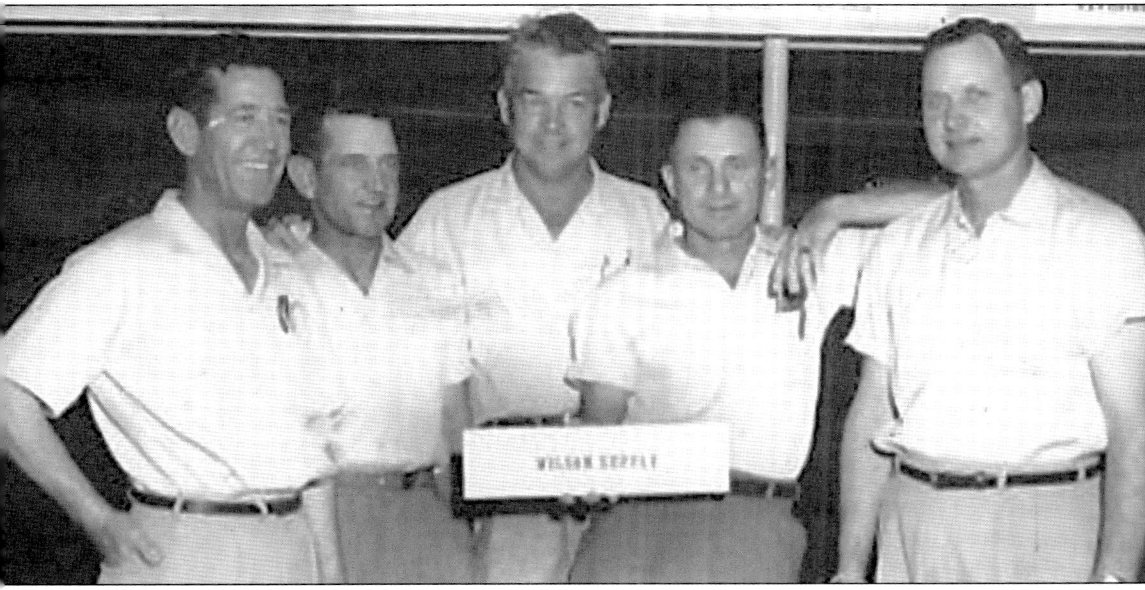

The Wilson Supply bowling team poses for the camera in this 1959 photograph. Pictured from left to right are Foster Plummer, M.J. "Mutt" Plummer, Cecil D. Griffin, John Loyless, and Curtis Stiger. (Courtesy of David Griffin.)

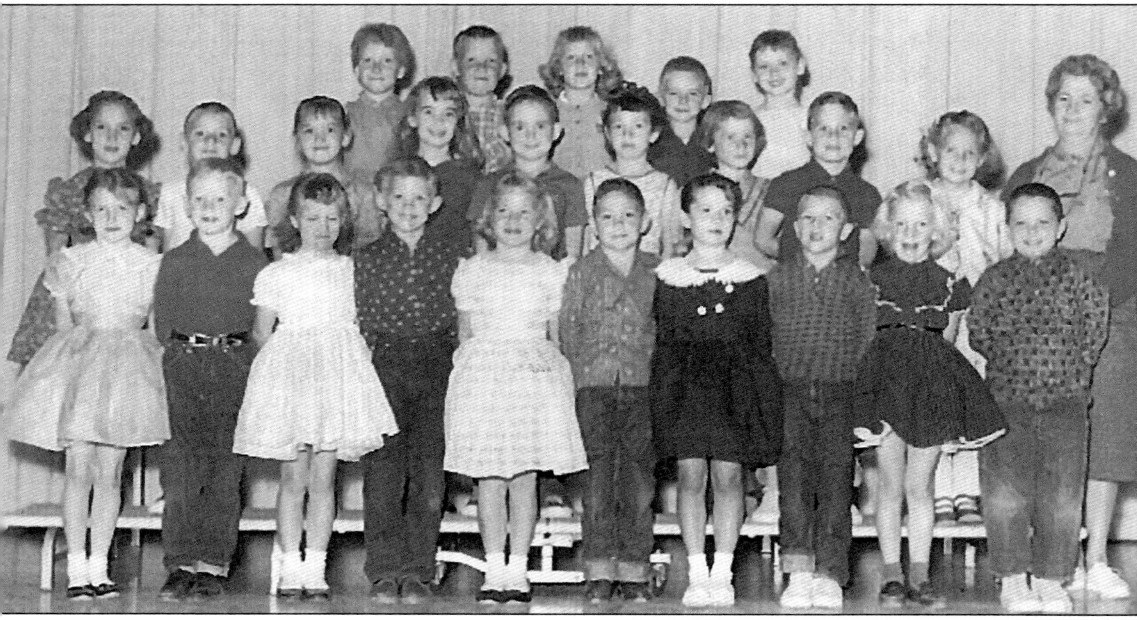

A Crane Elementary School first-grade class takes a break from a busy day of learning to pose for this group photograph during the 1960–1961 school year.

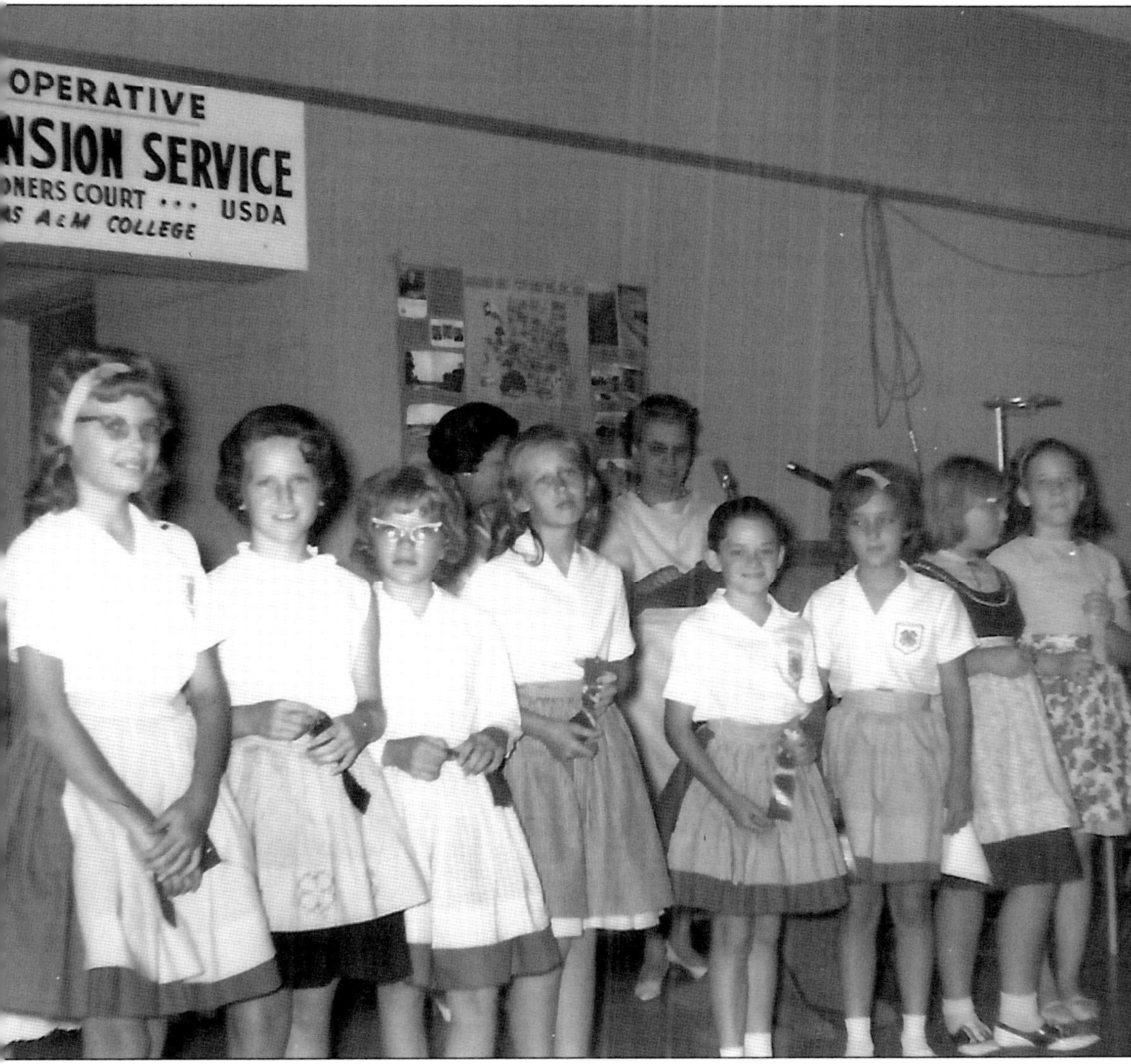

Young women involved in 4-H pose for a photograph following a baking and sewing competition held in Crane County in the early 1960s.

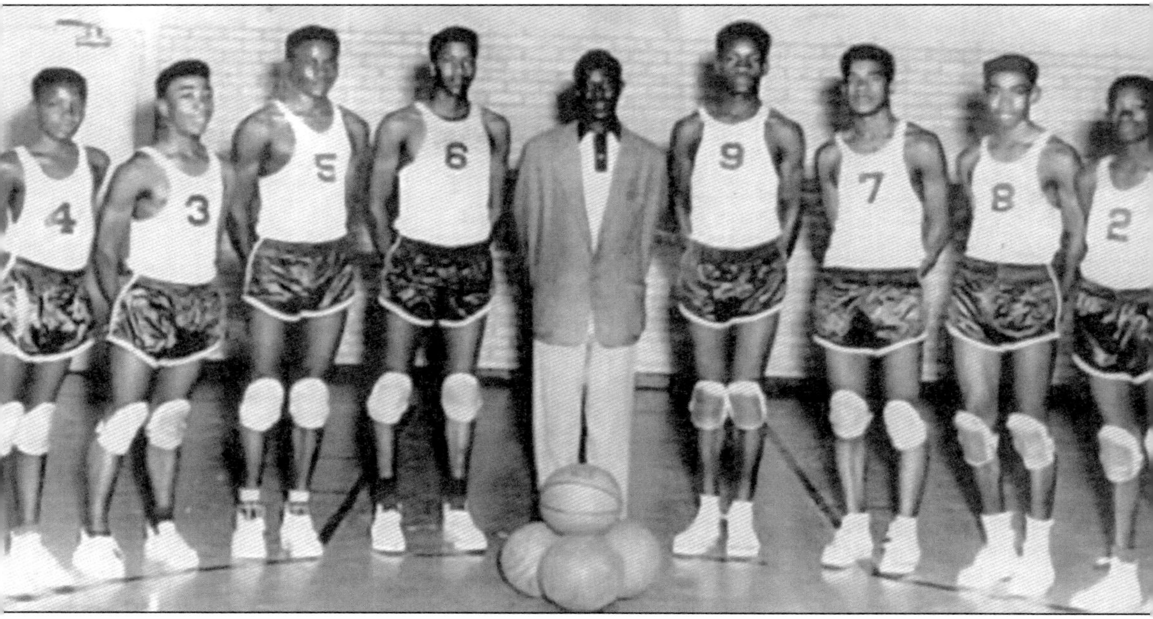

Shown here is the Bethune High School boys' basketball team in 1964. From left to right, they are Willie Dale Morris, Maurice Walker, Gene Harmon, Sherman Price, Coach Akins, Tommy Lee Hollins, James Hollins, Freddie Walker, and Roy Milton Jones. (Courtesy of Daisy Jeffery.)

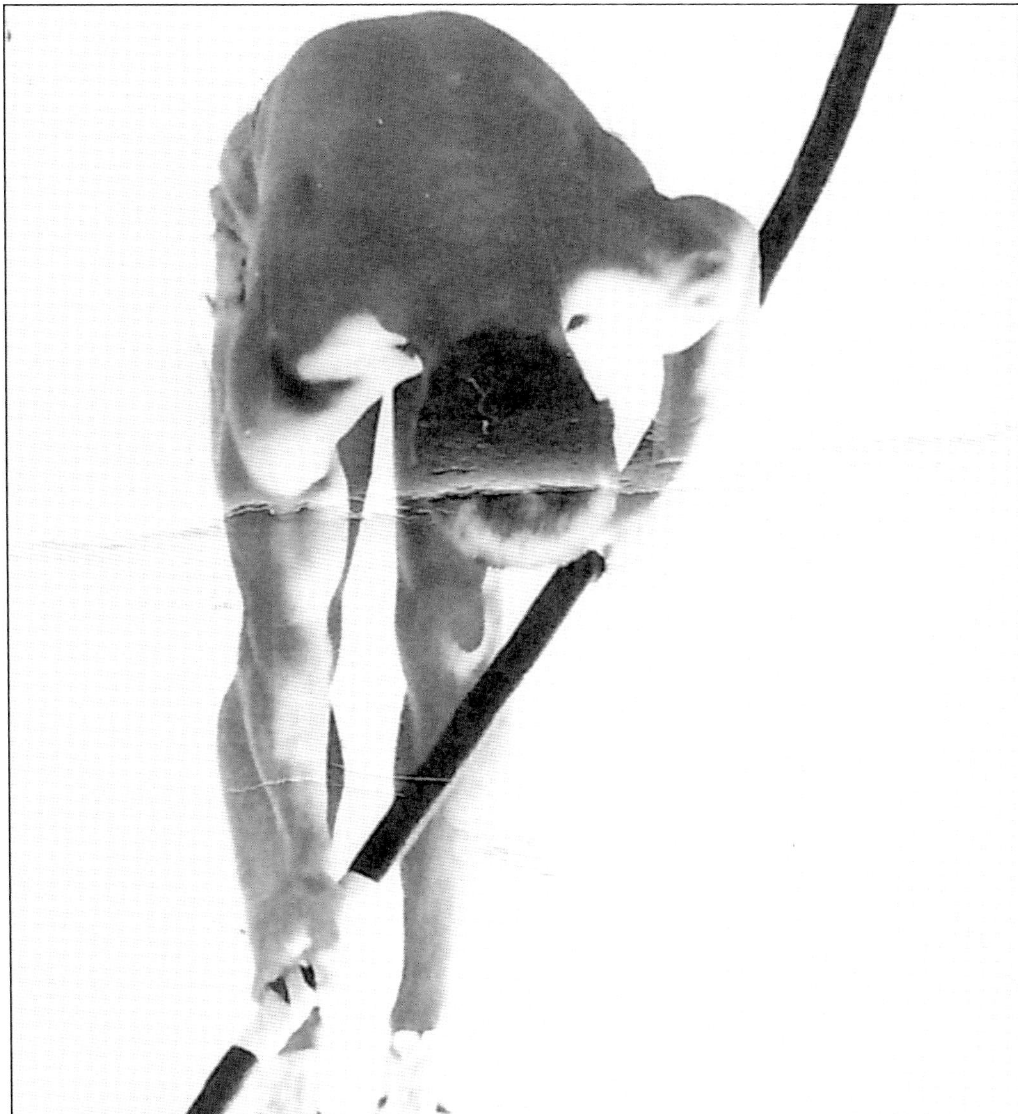

Steve Pettit set numerous records in the pole vault throughout his high school career from 1966–1969. In fact, he set a record at every track meet he attended his senior year except for the state meet. At one point, he was ranked in the top 10 pole-vaulters in the nation. Pettit achieved his highest vault while on athletic scholarship to Sul Ross State University, where he cleared 16 feet. In high school, Pettit soared over 14 feet 3 inches, which was quite a feat considering the quality of the pole-vault poles at the time. Many of Pettit's records from area high schools remained for several years after his vaulting career was over.

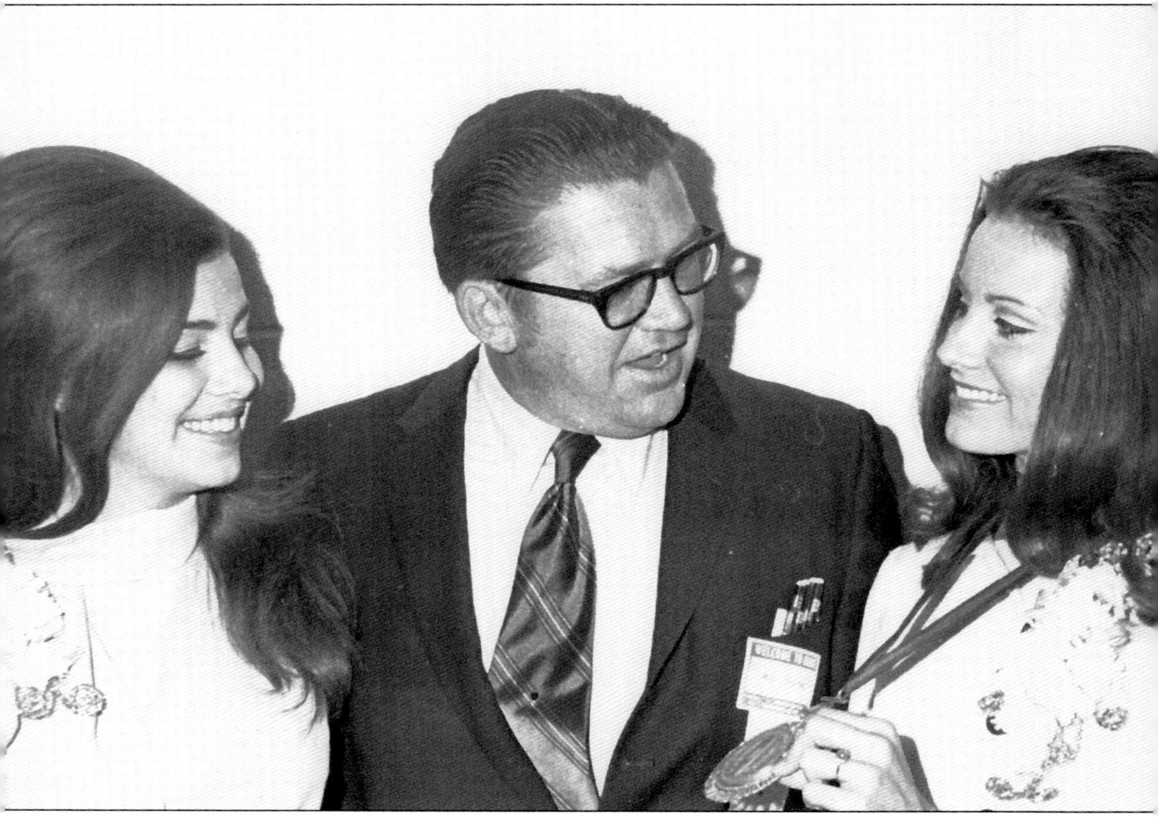

Sue Evans (right), a 1969 graduate of Crane High School, shows off one of her many awards to pageant attendee Bill Payne (middle) and Debbie Patton, 1970 Miss Teenage America (left). Evans finished second runner-up in the 1971 Miss Texas Pageant after previously being crowned Miss West Texas. Her Crane contemporaries knew Evans as a "natural beauty."

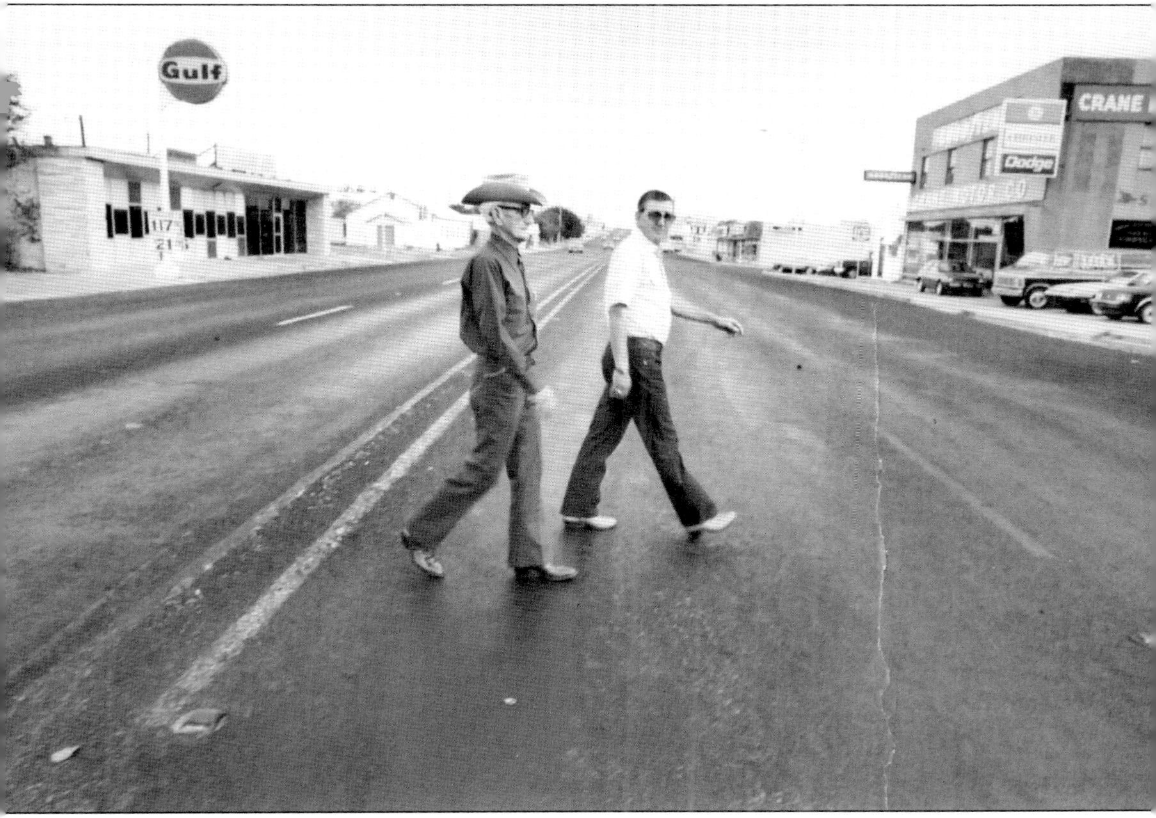

In 1980, things looked a lot different in downtown Crane. Shown here crossing Gaston Street are George Darden Sr. (in the cowboy hat) and his son George Darden. Notice the price of gas. You sure cannot beat $1.17 a gallon! (Courtesy of Justin Burks and Jincy Burks.)

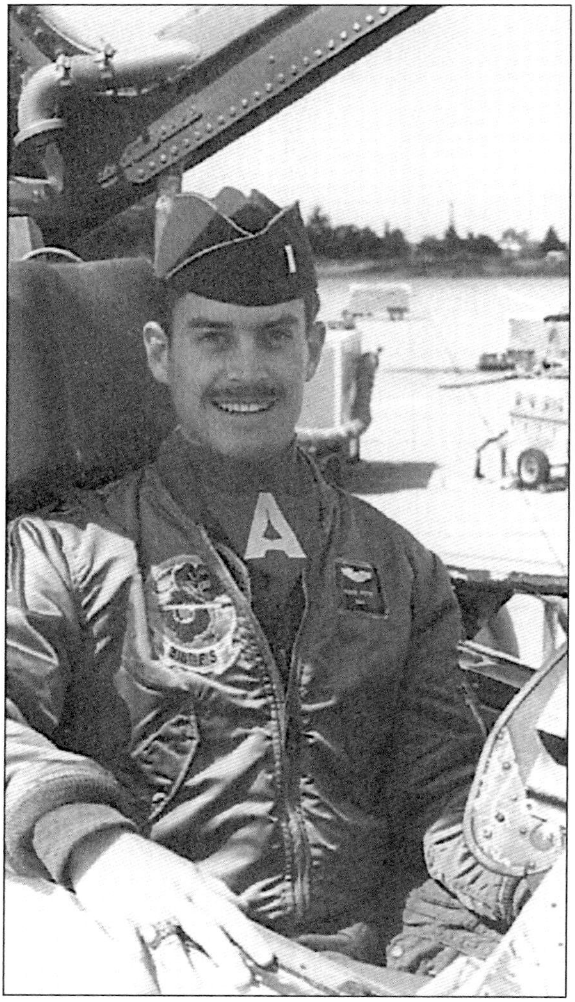

Roger Alan Pettit, shown here in his days as an Air Force fighter pilot, was raised in Crane and died doing what he loved. For eight years, he served honorably and admirably in the US Air Force, flying both the F-15 and the F-106. With his loving wife and two young children to consider, Pettit decided to leave the Air Force but not the business of flying. He was subsequently hired to fly for Air Florida, where he piloted the Boeing 737. He was a devoted family man and an excellent pilot. Tragically, Pettit succumbed to a fatal accident when Air Florida Flight 90, which he was copiloting, crashed into the Potomac River shortly after takeoff on January 13, 1982. His body was recovered on January 20, and he was returned home to Crane for burial. The accident was attributed to ice on the wings at the time of takeoff. A made-for-television movie chronicling the accident, entitled *Flight 90: Disaster on the Potomac*, was released in 1984.

Roger Pettit's love of flying was passed down to his two children, Cory and Jason, who are both pilots for Southwest Airlines. This is the last family photograph made prior to Pettit's death. Shown from left to right are Roger, Donna, Cory, and Jason Pettit.

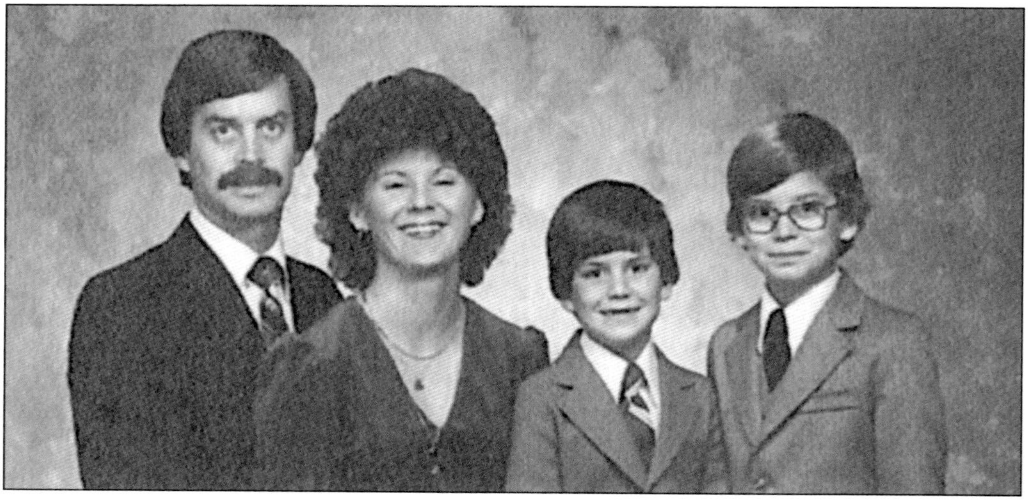

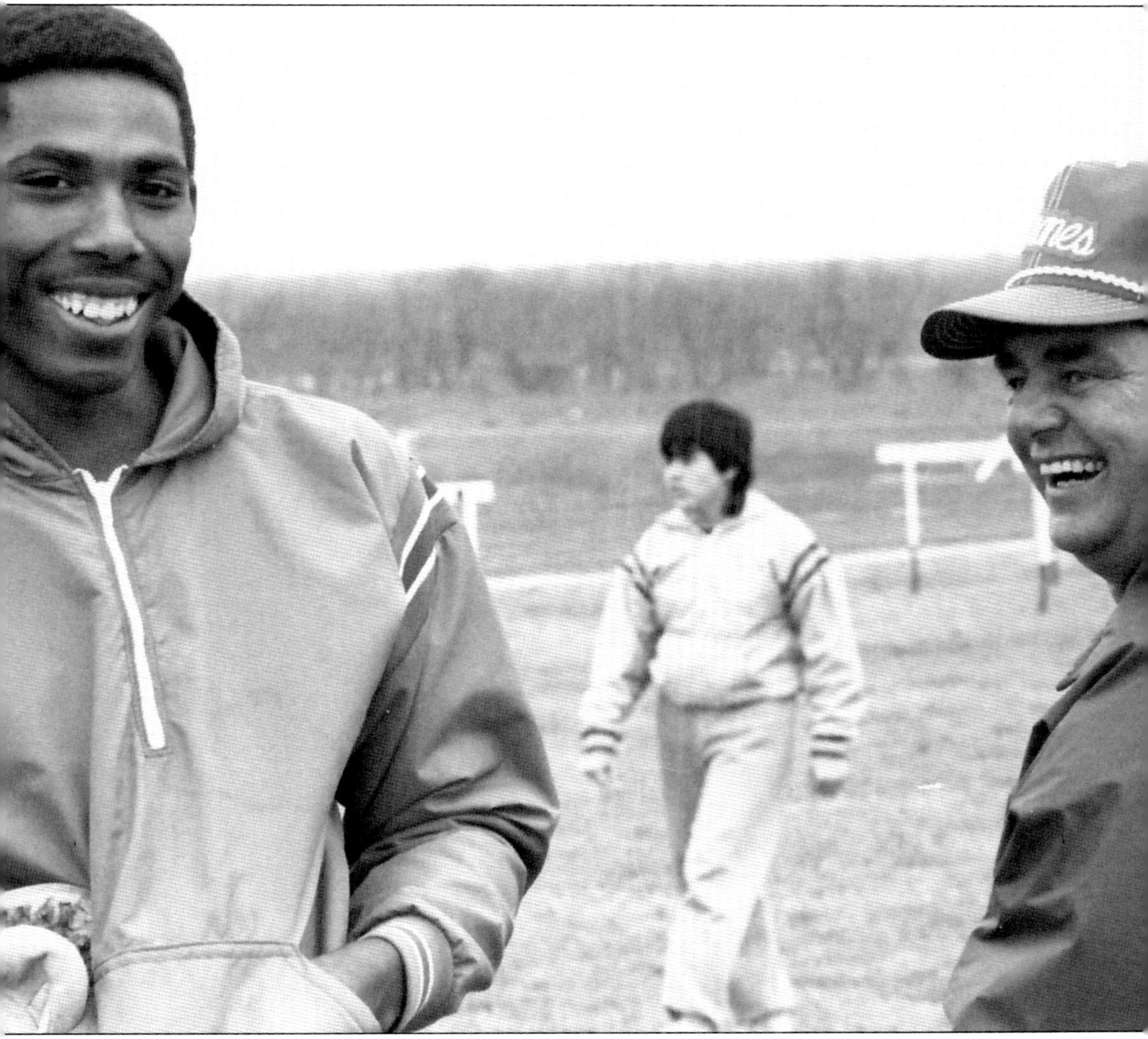

Kenny Wayne Walker (left) gets some last-minute advice from Crane High School coach Ricky White prior to winning yet another race at a regional track meet. Walker would go on to make history as a professional athlete, while White left an indelible mark on Crane High School athletics. Walker was a hometown hero when he wore purple and gold for the Crane Golden Cranes. Born in Crane in 1967, Walker lost his hearing at age two. Walker went on to overcome his handicap by becoming an All-American player for the University of Nebraska. When he trotted onto the field for his last game with the Cornhuskers, the capacity crowd stood and signed "applause" to signify its appreciation for Walker's dedication and abilities. In 1991, he was selected by the Denver Broncos in the eighth round of the NFL draft. He was the second player in the history of the NFL to be completely deaf. Walker later transferred to the Canadian Football League, where he played for the Calgary Stampeders. He made history in the CFL as well, becoming the first deaf player in the history of the league. While playing for the Stampeders, Walker shared a room with Dwayne Johnson, more famously known as "The Rock." Walker's playing career ended after his last season with the Stampeders in 1995. Walker wrote and published an autobiography in 1998 entitled *Roar of Silence: The Kenny Walker Story.* After his retirement from football, Walker became a coach, teaching young athletes the many skills he acquired throughout his impressive career.

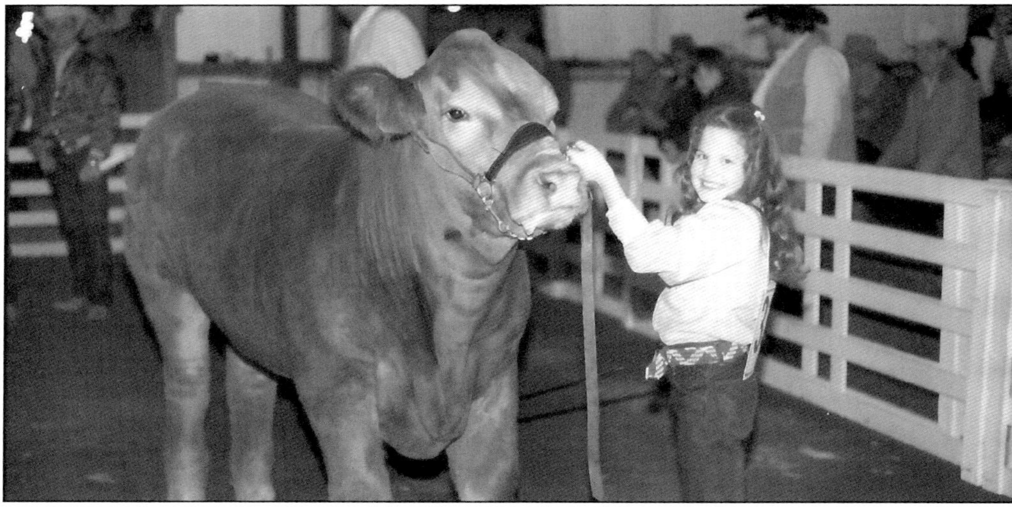

Shonnery Cowden participates in the Livestock Achievement Show in January 1984. She showed an impressive steer that earned her the Champion Steer Belt Buckle. She was also named Grand Champion of the event. The 4-H program aims to engage young people to reach their fullest potential and has always been very popular among Crane's youth. Cowden excelled in 4-H programs and activities throughout the 1980s.

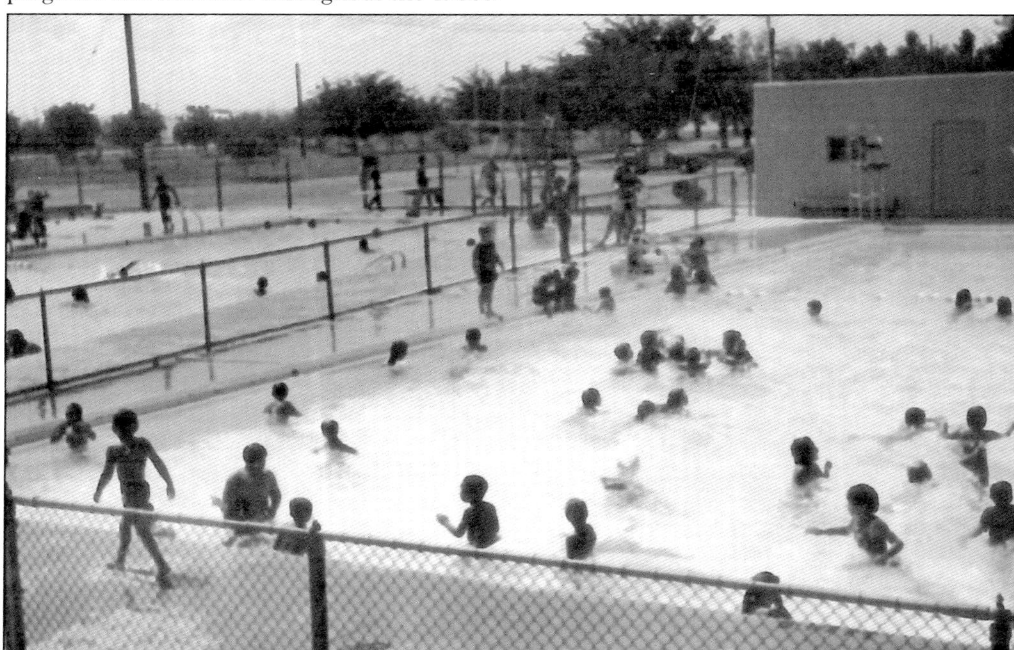

Crane County residents in need of cooling down during the sweltering days of summer often gather at the Crane County Swimming Pool. The swimming pool, shown here in July 1985, bubbles with children on a particularly hot summer day that reached the hellish temperature of 108 degrees Fahrenheit. During the days of segregation, African American residents were required to swim in a separate pool. However, as the days of segregation ended, the Crane County Swimming Pool became a common recreational spot for Crane citizens of all races.

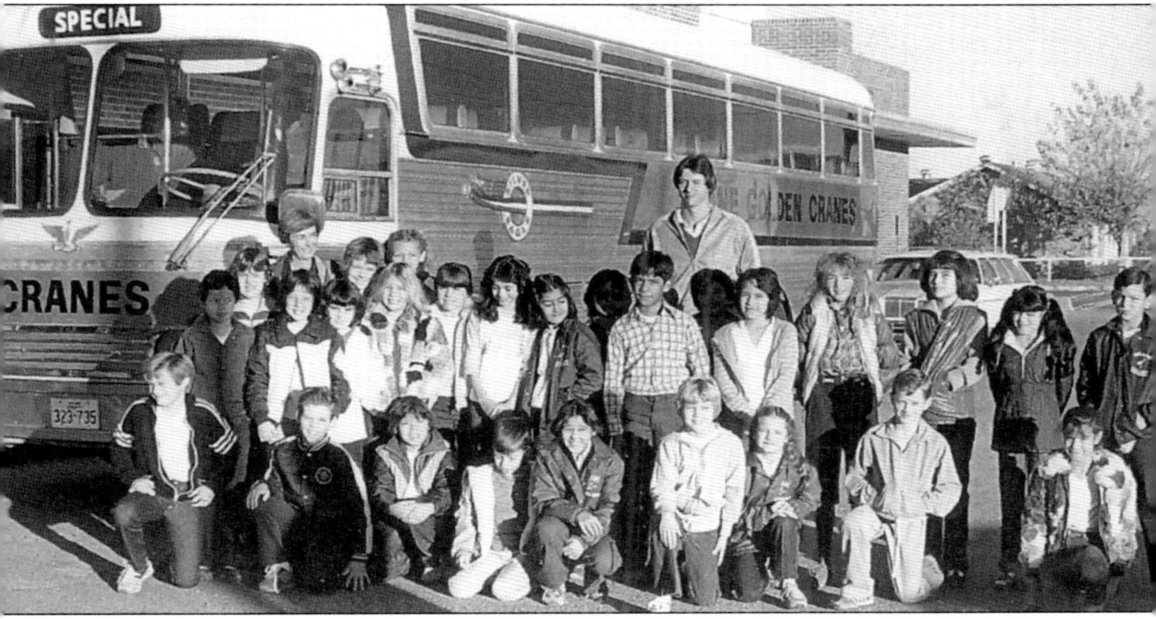

A group of Crane students poses for a photograph following a field trip to Sul Ross State University in Alpine, Texas.

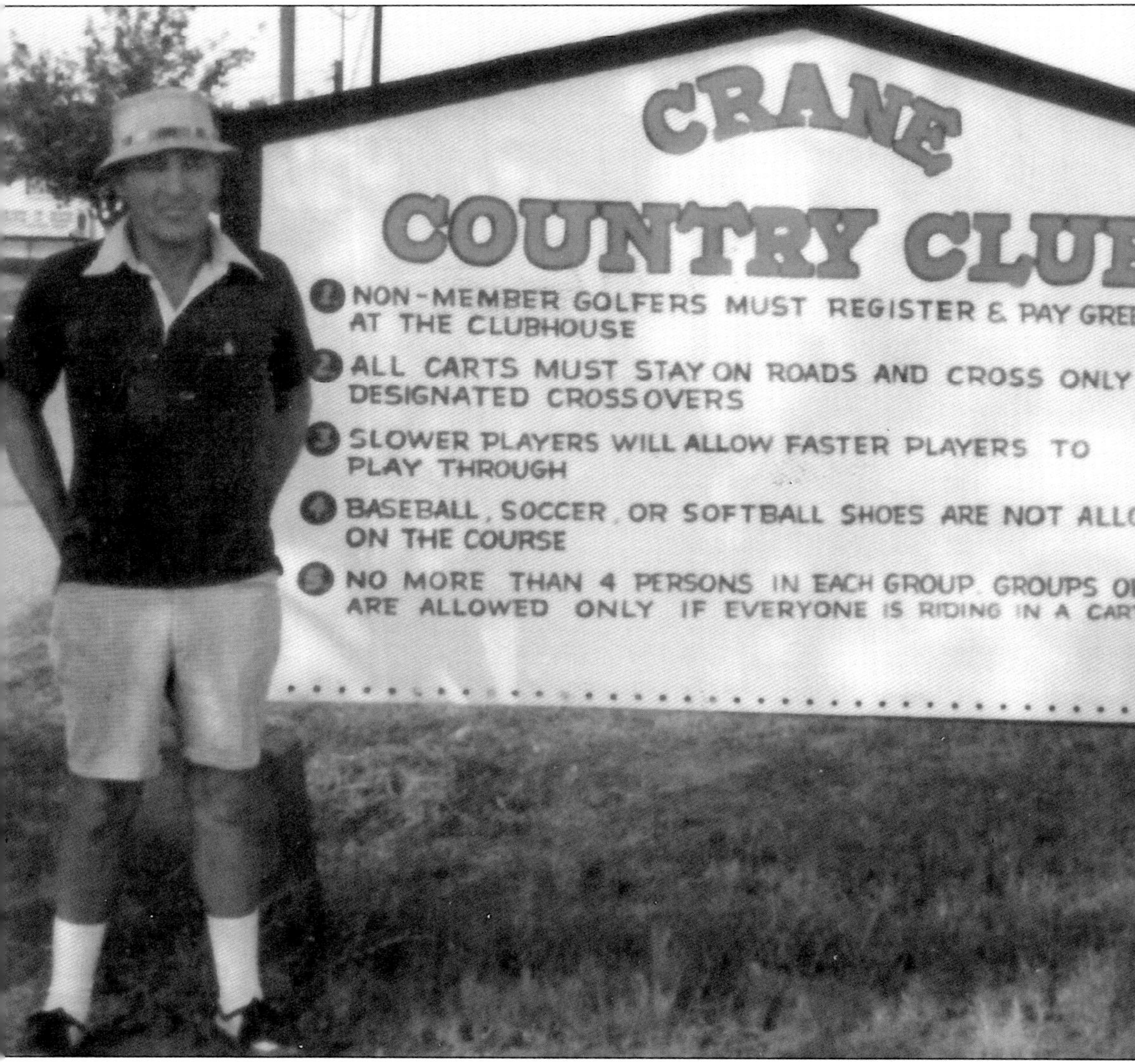

Murry Ford, former superintendent of Crane Independent School District, poses beside the Crane Country Club sign north of town. Following his retirement, Ford spent many days taking advantage of Crane's nine-hole golf course.

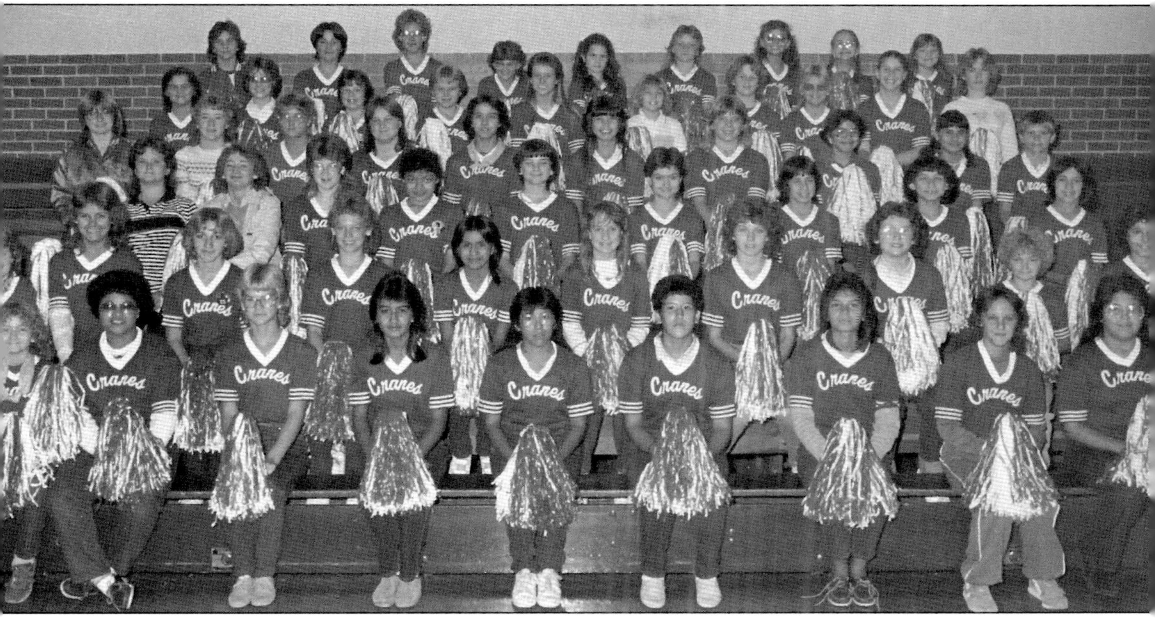

The Crane Middle School pep squad poses for this 1985 photograph. The pep squad supports the cheerleading teams at many Crane school athletic events.

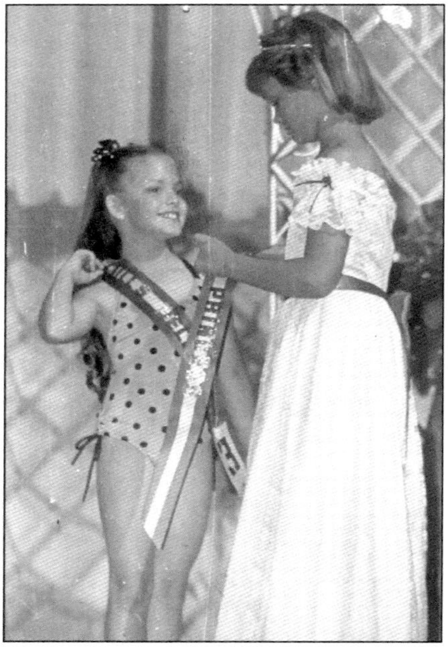

Charla Robnett participates in a beauty pageant held in Crane County in 1986. Ten years old at the time, Robnett won the Miss Princess crown. In this photograph, the reigning Miss Princess is crowning her.

Tiffany McWhorter participates in the "Roll-o-Roper" game, a booth that belonged to Gene, Debby, Shonnery, and Sunny Cowden at a Fourth of July celebration on Sixth Street. The Cowden family charged $5 for three throws of the lasso in this Independence Day celebration contest.

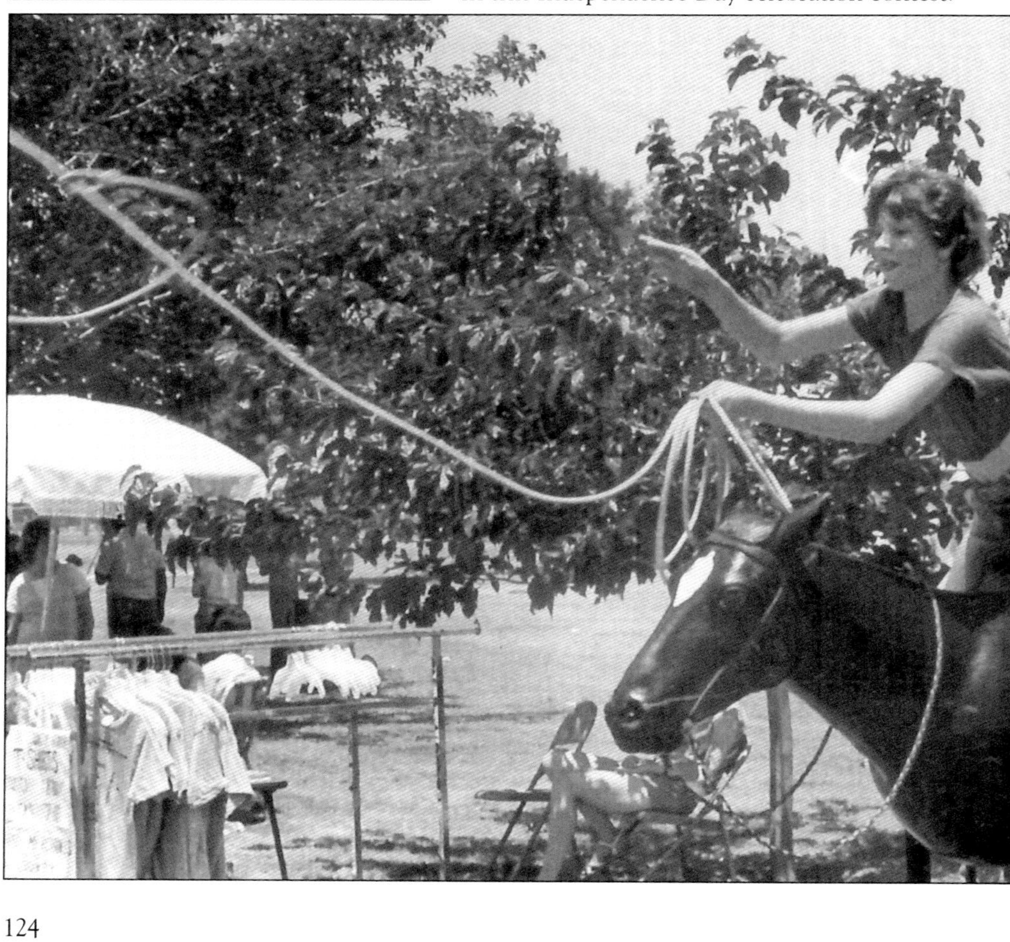

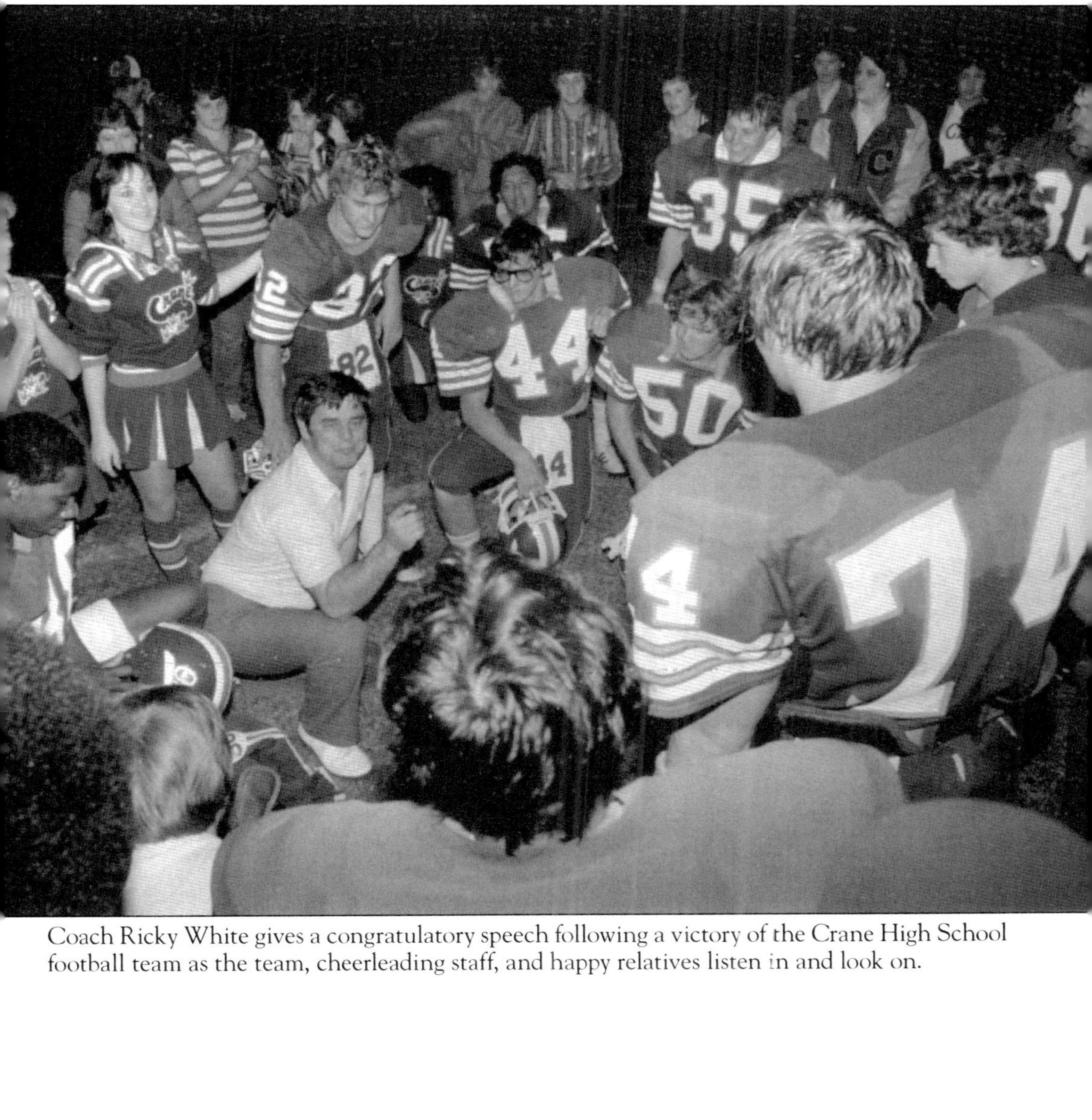

Coach Ricky White gives a congratulatory speech following a victory of the Crane High School football team as the team, cheerleading staff, and happy relatives listen in and look on.

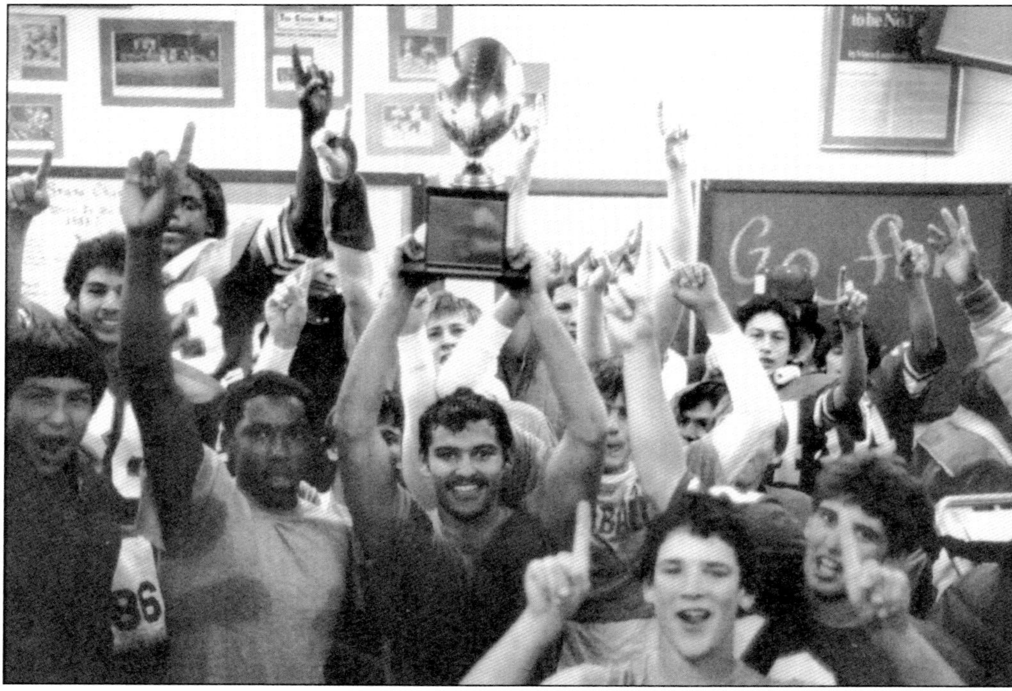

A proud Crane High School football team holds up the District Championship trophy they earned for excellent play during the regular football season.

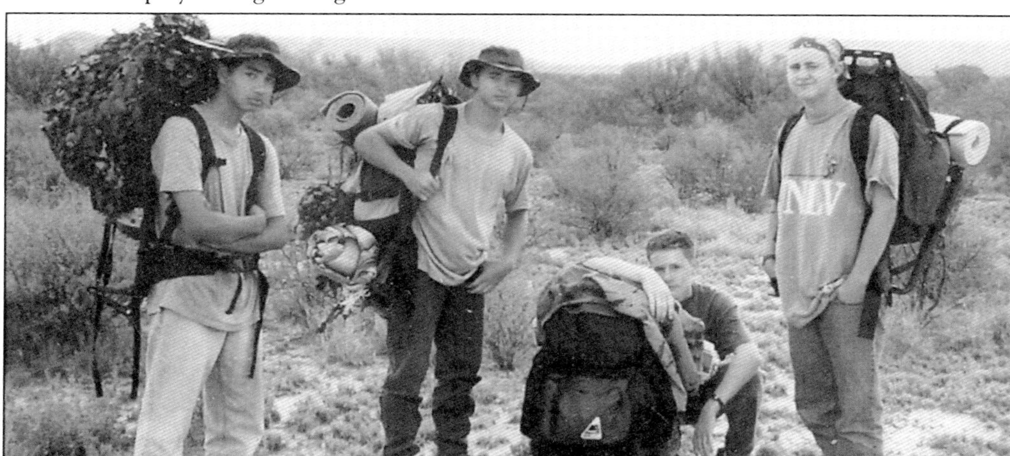

As legends of lost treasures in the area abound, many amateur treasure hunters have put together treks throughout Crane County in search of buried riches. Shown from left to right are amateur treasure hunters Roy Morales, Jarad Smith, Daniel Phillips, and Starr Feeler while on a 1993 scouting expedition to investigate various locations within Crane County believed to contain hidden treasures. Using maps collected from several Crane citizens, including Tiny Earp, the group additionally talked to everyone able to offer information regarding the treasure legends. The group ultimately took several treasure-hunting trips into Castle Gap, but they have remained close-mouthed about their discoveries, if any were in fact made. Interestingly, the group amassed an extensive collection of research, maps, and interviews that vanished shortly before they could be submitted for publication. (Courtesy of Daniel Phillips and Jarad Smith.)

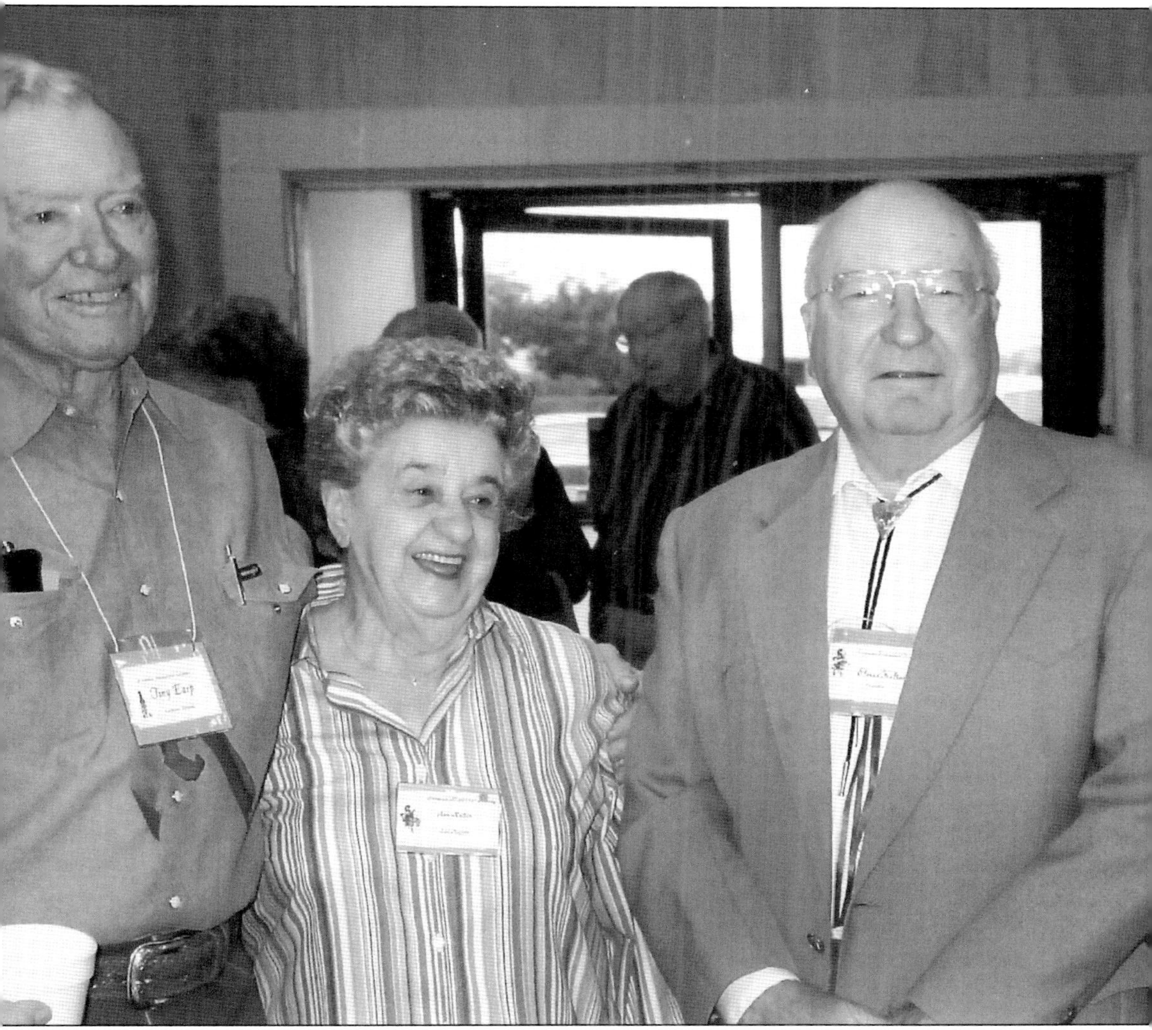

Tiny Earp (left), who as a young man rides the donkey on the cover of this book, is pictured along with Ann and Elmer Kelton as they visit with one another during a meeting of the Permian Historical Society held in Crane's Sixth Street Community Center in 2004. The Permian Historical Society is dedicated to preserving the history of the Permian Basin of West Texas. Earp and the Keltons, along with Crane luminary Joe Allen, were prominent members of the society during this time.